BASIC CONCEPTS OF
MEASUREMENT

BASIC CONCEPTS

OF

MEASUREMENT

BY

BRIAN ELLIS

*Senior Lecturer in History and Philosophy of
Science, University of Melbourne*

CAMBRIDGE

AT THE UNIVERSITY PRESS

1966

PUBLISHED BY
THE SYNDICS OF THE CAMBRIDGE UNIVERSITY PRESS

Bentley House, 200 Euston Road, London, N.W.1
American Branch: 32 East 57th Street, New York, N.Y. 10022
West African Office: P.M.B. 5181, Ibadan, Nigeria

©

CAMBRIDGE UNIVERSITY PRESS
1966

Printed in Great Britain at the University Printing House, Cambridge
(Brooke Crutchley, University Printer)

LIBRARY OF CONGRESS CATALOGUE
CARD NUMBER: 65–19150

To
JENNY, BRONWYN & DAVID

CONTENTS

ACKNOWLEDGEMENTS

My interest in the nature of measurement was first stimulated by my former teacher, Professor J. J. C. Smart, who introduced me to the writings of E. Mach and N. R. Campbell, and taught me most of what I know in philosophy. This interest has since been sustained by the valuable criticism and encouragement of my colleagues and students in the Departments of History and Philosophy of Science, and of Philosophy in the University of Melbourne. I am especially grateful to Mr F. J. Clendinnen, Dr G. Buchdahl, Professor D. A. T. Gasking, Miss D. Dyason, Mr G. O'Brien and Mr H. Lacey for the detailed and careful criticisms that they have made of various aspects of my work. Mr Lacey is responsible for the proof in Appendix II and Mr M. J. Scott-Taggart for the translation of Mach's 'Critique of the Concept of Temperature' which appears in Appendix I. I wish to thank Mr Scott-Taggart for the many hours of work that went into making this translation.

A first draft of the manuscript for this book was finished at the end of 1961. Mr R. Harré and Professors J. J. C. Smart, M. Scriven, and P. Edwards all read the draft and suggested improvements. I may not always have acted upon their advice, but I am sure that their suggestions have made it into a better book.

I wish to thank Mrs G. J. Reum and Mrs S. Tatlock for their secretarial assistance, and the editors of the *Australasian Journal of Philosophy* and *Philosophy of Science* for their permission to use material from articles of mine that have appeared in recent issues of these journals.

B. E.

University of Melbourne
March 1965

INTRODUCTION

Measurement is the link between mathematics and science. The nature of measurement should therefore be a central concern of the philosophy of science. Yet, strangely, it has attracted little attention. If it is discussed at all in works on the philosophy of science, it is usually dismissed in a fairly short and standard chapter. There are notable exceptions; but for the most part the logic of measurement has been treated as though it were neither interesting nor important. Why this should be so, I do not know. Its importance can hardly be questioned: to understand how mathematics is applied is to understand the most significant feature of modern science.

The pioneer work in the field was undoubtedly Campbell's *Physics; The Elements,** which appeared in 1920. This was followed by his *Account of the Principles of Measurement and Calculation* in 1928.† But apart from Bridgman's *Dimensional Analysis* (1931),‡ there have been no major works of a primarily philosophical nature dealing with measurement since that time—although there have been many individual papers in scientific and philosophical journals, and many technical books concerning measurement.

One reason for this neglect may be simply that there are no traditional philosophical problems of measurement to challenge us. Like Kant, we need to be awakened from our dogmatic slumber. Consequently, the logic of measurement lacks some of the glamour of other areas of philosophy. But if this is a reason for its neglect, it is also a result of it. When philosophers of radically different philosophical persuasions express similar views concerning the nature of measurement, this is not because their general philosophical positions are irrelevant; it is because they have failed to take their own positions really seriously.

There is thus a climate of philosophical agreement about measurement. It is felt that nothing much remains to be said about it, and that the only problems that remain are peripheral

---

* Campbell (1920). Full details of all references are given in the bibliography.
† Campbell (1928).   ‡ Bridgman (1931).

ones. It is recognized that there are some unanswered questions concerning microphysical measurement, and some difficult problems of formalization (for example in constructing axiom systems for fundamental measurement). But for the most part there is little dispute; and hence, it is felt, little room for dispute. Much of the fundamental work of Campbell, for example, has never been seriously challenged.

But why should there be this climate of agreement? One can only believe that the agreement is superficial, resulting not from analysis, but from the lack of it. Philosophers ranging in viewpoint from positivists to naïve realists all seem to agree about measurement; but only because they have failed to follow out the consequences of their various positions. In fact, I believe the positivists are largely to blame for this situation. For usually they have proceeded from a concealed realist standpoint. It is not surprising, therefore, that realists should find little to argue about.

Positivist criticisms concerning the Newtonian concepts of absolute space and time are now fairly generally admitted. Few philosophers nowadays would be prepared to defend these concepts against a positivist attack. But the attack has never been carried through to other quantitative concepts.

It is fairly generally agreed that we cannot speak of the velocity of an object without at least implicit reference to other objects. Velocity has come to be regarded as an essentially relative concept. It is also widely agreed that size is another essentially relative concept; although there are still some philosophers, for example, naïve realists, who maintain that it does make sense to speak of the size of an object without reference to anything else. But, generally speaking, quantities are thought to be 'properties' of objects— characteristics which things must possess to some *specific* degree or other, even if we have no way of measuring or determining this degree. If, for example, we are asked to imagine a universe consisting of a single spherical object 3 ft. in diameter and moving at 3 ft./sec., there are few who would consider this request legitimate. But if we are asked to imagine such a universe in which the single object is spherical, has a mass of 5 g., and is highly elastic, few would object to this description.

There are some philosophers, it is true, who would reject the idea of absolute magnitude, whatever quantities are concerned.

But even the most ardent positivists and operationists accept Bridgman's principle of 'the absolute significance of *relative* magnitude'. There is, as we shall see, a harmless non-metaphysical interpretation that can be given to this principle. But the usual interpretation is plainly metaphysical, and reflects a belief in absolute magnitude. Thus we find that a distinction is commonly drawn between 'linear' and 'non-linear' scales for the measurement of a given quantity. On a linear scale, our numerical assignments are supposed to be 'proportional to the quantities themselves'. A non-linear scale, on the other hand, is supposed to be a distorted scale—one on which the numerical assignments are disproportional to the pre-existing magnitudes.

My aim in this book is to give a consistent positivist account of the nature of measurement; although, when I say 'positivist', I mean only that it falls vaguely within the positivist tradition. I propose to examine what I consider to be the basic concepts of measurement, and to explicate these concepts wherever possible. My main thesis is that certain metaphysical presuppositions, made by positivists and non-positivists alike, have played havoc with our understanding of many of the basic concepts of measurement, and concealed the existence of certain more or less arbitrary conventions. My problem is to state these conventions, and to discuss what reasons we may have for choosing some rather than others.

Finally, to illustrate the conceptual advantages that come from thinking about scale and quantities in the way that I propose, I shall apply my analysis to consider two special quantitative concepts, number and probability. Concerning probability, I shall show that while we can distinguish two concepts of probability, one logical and the other empirical, it is totally at variance with general scientific practice to do so; for in precisely the same sense, we can distinguish two concepts of every other quantity, one logical and the other empirical.

CHAPTER I

THE APPLICATION OF ARITHMETIC

All measurement involves the application of arithmetic. The logic of measurement is concerned with the kinds of applications of arithmetic that can be made, and how it is possible to make them. It is important, therefore, that we should consider what is meant by 'an application of arithmetic', and examine the distinction between pure and applied arithmetic upon which this concept depends. We should aim to clarify the distinction, and state necessary and/or sufficient conditions for the application of arithmetic. In the discussion, we shall distinguish three fundamental kinds of applied arithmetical statements. One of these is the principal concern of the logic of measurement.

A

The distinction between pure and applied mathematics

The distinction between pure and applied arithmetic is at least as old as Plato, and it is one Platonic contribution to the philosophy of mathematics which has rarely been questioned. With the possible exception of J. S. Mill every important writer on the philosophy of mathematics has made such a distinction. Philosophers have differed only in their manner of conceiving it. Plato and later idealist philosophers conceived pure and applied arithmetical propositions to be about radically different kinds of entities. An applied arithmetical proposition might, for example, be a statement about groups of stones. But stones are destructible, impermanent objects, known only through sense experience, and our concept of them is imprecise (in the sense that there are borderline cases of stones and non-stones). For these reasons, it was argued, our knowledge of them is imperfect, and the stones of which we say we have knowledge are also imperfect. They have a kind of lower order of existence.

A pure arithmetical proposition, however, is quite different in character. According to Plato it is a proposition about perfect, indestructible or timeless entities called Forms or Ideals. They are not known through sense experience (though sense experience may prod our 'memory' of them) but are apprehended directly or by our intellects. Consequently, our knowledge of the Forms is not contingent upon sense experience, and does not suffer from the imperfections of such knowledge. Our concepts of the Forms are perfectly precise. We may be in doubt which Form a given physical object most closely resembles. But there can be no danger of our confusing the Forms themselves. There are no borderline cases in the world of the Forms. For these reasons, it was supposed, the Forms must possess a higher order of reality than ordinary physical objects, and our knowledge of them must be of a higher order than our knowledge of such objects.

The relationship between pure and applied arithmetical propositions was supposed by Plato to depend upon resemblances between the Forms and other lower-order existences. Where a certain Ideal relationship exists between Forms, we may suppose that a similar relationship exists between physical, empirically given entities which resemble these Forms—the physical relationship being nearer or further from the Ideal one according as the empirically given entities more or less closely resemble the Forms. According to Plato, then, pure arithmetic becomes applied by noticing resemblances between physical and Ideal objects, and the accuracy of the applied arithmetical proposition, or of any consequences which may be drawn from it, is a function of the closeness of the initial resemblances.

Plato's theory of the relationship between pure and applied arithmetic is no doubt aesthetically appealing. But if truth and descriptive accuracy is our aim, such considerations must be put aside. The distinction between pure and applied arithmetic was based upon the following claims:

(a) That pure arithmetical propositions are known a priori and with absolute certainty to be true or false. No changes in the structure of the physical world are relevant to their truth or falsity. They are timeless propositions.

(b) That the concepts of pure arithmetic are perfectly precise. The number 4 has certain definite properties: for example, it stands in certain definite relationships to other numbers, and it is inconceivable that the number 4 should not have these precise properties, or that it should change its properties in any way.

(c) That applied arithmetical propositions are not known a priori to be true or false, and the structure of the physical world *is* relevant to their truth or falsity.

(d) That empirical concepts are not perfectly precise, in the sense that it is not inconceivable that things which fall under these concepts may have a variety of different properties, or that they should change their properties.

Thus stated, Plato's claims seem less fantastic, and I am sure that there are many philosophers today who would assent to all four of them. We shall discuss the merits of claims (a) and (c) presently. We should note in passing, however, that Plato's theory seems to fit the case of geometry much better than arithmetic. It is not difficult to understand what is meant by saying that a physical object resembles more or less closely a Euclidean circle, but what could be meant by saying that a group of stones resembles the number 4? It seems that if Plato had had to present his theory of Forms, using only arithmetical examples to illustrate his thesis, he would have found his task much more difficult. And this leads us to the suspicion that geometry and arithmetic do not share precisely the same logical status. At least, it seems that if we are interested in describing the logical status of arithmetical propositions, we should be very wary of illustrative arguments from geometry. What is true of geometry may not be true of arithmetic. If a clear distinction between pure and applied arithmetic can be made out, it should be possible to make it out in arithmetical terms alone.

A second, and at the present time, very influential way of conceiving the distinction between pure and applied arithmetic is that of such formalists as Hilbert and Curry.* For them, as for Plato, pure arithmetical propositions are radically different in character from applied arithmetical statements. But, unlike Plato, the formalists consider that pure arithmetical propositions are not *about* anything at all. They are merely the well-formed formulae of a particular formal system. Indeed, strictly speaking, they are not even propositions—for they do not assert anything. We can, of course, make assertions *about* any given formal system. We may say

* Curry (1951).

6

of a given well-formed formula that it is or is not a *theorem* of the system. And then, this metamathematical statement is a legitimate proposition. It is a statement about what can (or cannot) be done within the system. But the formulae themselves are not assertions, and the only considerations relevant to whether they or their contradictories are theorems are the formal considerations which constitute their proof or disproof.

The propositions of pure arithmetic, then, cannot be shown to be true or false by such operations as counting or measuring, and the results of such operations are, of course, quite irrelevant. The propositions of applied arithmetic, by contrast, are empirical propositions, and their truth *is* dependent upon the results of counting and measuring operations. Consequently, the dichotomy between pure and applied arithmetic, according to the formalist manner of conceiving the distinction, is a radical one. Pure arithmetical propositions are not even analytic, since their truth cannot be demonstrated by conceptual analysis. They are mere configurations of signs satisfying certain formal requirements. Applied arithmetical statements, on the other hand, are fully fledged empirical propositions.

The formalists, in fact, recognize three different classes of arithmetical propositions. There are, first of all, the pure arithmetical formulae of which we have already spoken, there are the applied arithmetical formulae, and there are the meta-arithmetical statements to the effect that such and such formulae are or are not theorems in the formal system of arithmetic. The contrast between the second and third of these classes of statements is somewhat less spectacular than that between the first and second. For it may be argued that both are classes of empirical propositions. Nevertheless, an important contrast exists. For the kinds of considerations relevant to the truth or falsity of applied arithmetical propositions are very different from those relevant to the truth or falsity of the meta-arithmetical statements. The first are usually experimental and involve the use of counting and measuring operations. But the second involve the procedures of proof—of constructing a proof within the formal system of arithmetic.

Like the idealists, the formalists consider that the application of arithmetic depends upon the recognition of similarities. But the similarities are not resemblances between Forms and physical objects. Rather they are formal similarities between, on the one hand, the operations and relations of pure arithmetic, and on the other, certain physical operations and relationships. For, given such formal similarities, there is no logical barrier to using arithmetical operators and relation signs to designate these physical operations and relationships. Thus, the numerals of arithmetic may be taken to stand for the measures of certain quantities, the arithmetical operators $+$, $-$, $\times$, $\div$, and so on, for certain physical operations on the objects possessing these quantities, and the symbols $>$, $=$ and $<$ for certain physical relationships connecting these objects. And, being thus interpreted, pure arithmetical formulae become empirical propositions—propositions that inform us of the results of performing certain physical operations.

A third, and equally influential way of conceiving the distinction between pure and applied arithmetic is that of the logicists, following Frege and Russell.* To these philosophers, pure arithmetic is conceived to be a part of logic, and according to this conception, pure arithmetical formulae are analytic statements in the calculus of classes. Thus, according to Russell, two classes are *similar* if and only if their members can be set in one-one correspondence. Let E be any class such that:

$$\text{(i)} \qquad (\exists x)(x \in E)$$

and $\qquad$ (ii) $\quad (x)(y)[\{(x \in E)(y \in E)\} \supset (x = y)]$.

Then E is a unit class, and the number 1 is defined as the class of classes similar to E. Let F be any class such that:

$\qquad$ (i) $(\exists x)(\exists y)[(x \in F)(y \in F)(x \neq y)]$

and $\quad$ (ii) $(x)(y)(z)[\{(x \in F)(y \in F)(z \in F)$
$$\supset \{(x = y) \vee (x = z) \vee (y = z)\}].$$

Then F is a binary class, and the number 2 is defined as the class of classes similar to F. The pure arithmetical formula: $1 + 1 = 2$ is then translated by the following analytic formula:

$$(x)(y)[\{(x \in 1)(y \in 1)(x \neq y)\} \supset \{(x \cup y) \in 2\}]. \qquad (1)$$

It would be quite beside the point of this essay to consider the general difficulties which the logicists must face. For our interest here is only in the account which they give of the distinction between pure and applied arithmetic. Evidently, the logicist must

* Russell (1903).

distinguish two different kinds of applications of arithmetic. There are, first of all, what we may term *primary* applications of arithmetic. Such an application would be, for example, the proposition that one apple and one other apple make two apples. This is simply an instantiation of the general formula (1) above, and it would be represented symbolically by the following scheme:

$$\{(a \in 1)(b \in 1)(a \neq b)\} \supset \{(a \cup b) \in 2\}. \qquad (2)$$

And if (1) is analytic, so also is (2). There is then, as far as primary applications of arithmetic are concerned, no radical distinction between pure and applied arithmetic—such as is found in the formalist and idealist accounts. The distinction is simply one of generality—both propositions (1) and (2) being analytic statements.

The second kind of application of arithmetic which, apparently, the logicist must recognize, is what we may term a *secondary* application. This is an applied arithmetical statement correlating the results of measurements made on a particular scale under certain specified conditions. Here are some examples:

(*a*) If a rod of length 1 ft. is joined end to end with another rod of length 1 ft. then the composite rod is of length 2 ft.

(*b*) If a wire of electrical resistance 1 ohm is perfectly joined in series with another wire of resistance 1 ohm, then the resistance of the resultant system is 2 ohms.

Clearly, these two applications of the arithmetical formula: $1 + 1 = 2$ cannot be regarded as instantiations of the general formula (1). For, whatever formal similarities there may be between the physical operation of placing rods end to end, and the logical operation of forming the logical sum of two classes, these two operations cannot be identified. Hence, it appears that the logicists must give a separate account of these kinds of applications of arithmetic.

This point is seldom discussed by logicists, and it is not clear what account they would give of the distinction between pure arithmetic and secondary applications of arithmetic—or even, indeed, whether they would recognize such a distinction. It seems to me, however, that if the logicist view of the distinction between pure and applied arithmetic is to have any semblance of plausibility, this additional distinction must be made, and a separate account of the process of making secondary applications of arithmetic provided. The task of filling this gap will concern us in later chapters.

Meanwhile, it is important to be clear just what elements are in common between the various views we have outlined. First, it is agreed by philosophers of all ages that there is a distinction to be drawn between pure and applied arithmetic. The reason for this is simply that men have always been impressed by the necessity, the incorrigibility or the apodeictic certainty of pure mathematics. They have become convinced that this field of learning is distinct from all others (except, perhaps, pure mechanics), for it appears that in this field alone it is possible to show that certain relationships *must* hold no matter what the world is like, not merely that they *do in fact* hold. And it has been argued that while experience can show us that something is so, it can never show us that it must be so. This has always been the basis for the distinction. Formalists, it is true, may not agree that in mathematics it is possible to show that certain relationships must hold, or that the propositions of mathematics have apodeictic certainty. For this is to suggest that the propositions of mathematics are genuine propositions asserting the existence of certain relationships. But even they would agree that mathematical propositions are incorrigible, that is, that no empirical considerations, extraneous to a given formal system, can ever prove a given mathematical proposition to be or not to be a theorem in that system. They would admit that observations or experiments external to the system may suggest or make it extremely probable that a given proposition is a theorem. But they would argue that the only thing strictly relevant to the truth of a mathematical proposition is its mathematical proof or disproof.

Some philosophers, it is true, have challenged the distinction. J. S. Mill, for example, considered the supposed apodeictic certainty of elementary geometrical and arithmetical propositions to be a myth. He argued that the only reason why such propositions have ever been taken to have a special a priori status is that it is impossible for us to conceive of a state of affairs which would make us wish to say that they were false. But against this he argues that there is no need to postulate the existence of any special status knowledge together with all the paraphernalia of special faculties of knowledge, which this involves. For he thinks that it is possible to explain this inconceivability otherwise. For this he has two arguments.

First, he points out that what we are able to conceive or imagine depends upon our knowledge and upbringing.* To the Greeks it was inconceivable that the earth should be anywhere but at the centre of the universe. To them the heliocentric universe was inconceivable. Again to seventeenth-century philosophers, it was 'inconceivable that inanimate brute matter should operate on and affect other matter without mutual contact'. But today this is not only conceivable, it is almost universally accepted as true. So, he argues, the inconceivability of a thing must not be taken as proving that it is impossible or even that it is false.

Secondly, he argues that if all our experience tends to confirm a certain thesis, and we have no experience tending to disconfirm it, then since we can only imagine events like those which we have experienced, the contrary of such a thesis may well be inconceivable to us. And this, he suggests, is the situation with the propositions of elementary arithmetic and geometry. There is no need, therefore, to make any logical distinctions at all between the mathematical and other sciences. The propositions of mathematics are simply better confirmed (confirmed by the whole of our experience) and more universal.

The first of these arguments is not difficult to counter. Mill fails to distinguish between different senses of 'inconceivable'. The propositions which he cites were inconceivable in the sense of being unbelievable at the time. It was not that the Greeks did not know what they were expected to believe. They just couldn't believe it. They understood Aristarchus but they could not believe that what he said was true. Archimedes, for example, argued that if Aristarchus' view were correct, then we ought to be able to observe parallax of the fixed stars. But no such parallax was observable. So there can be no doubt that Archimedes understood the empirical consequences of Aristarchus' suggestion. Likewise, Newton understood action at a distance. He just could not bring himself to believe that the space separating the planets was absolutely empty. Now, contrast this with the sense in which $2+2 = 5$ is inconceivable. I might, for example, try to imagine myself having two apples in one hand and two in the other, and

* Mill (1875).

five apples altogether (in my two hands). But I find that I just cannot do it. And I express this by saying that the instruction to imagine this state of affairs is self-contradictory. In other words, the kind of state of affairs which this proposition (according to Mill) purports to describe is inconceivable in a much stronger sense.

Mill's second argument is more ingenious, and it cannot be similarly dispensed with. Nevertheless, it does not lead to his conclusion. For by this argument, the assertion: $2+2 = 4$ is no more intelligible than the assertion: $2+2 = 5$. If one is unintelligible in view of the consistency of our experience, so is the other. For in order to understand what would tend to confirm a certain thesis we must also understand what would tend to disconfirm it. We must know what possibilities it rules out. There can be no sense therefore in supposing that all of our actual and conceivable experience tends to confirm a certain thesis. We can't have it both ways. Either the propositions of elementary arithmetic are not empirical generalizations and their contradictories are inconceivable, or they are empirical generalizations and their contradictories are conceivable.

But, Mill aside, philosophers have generally agreed that the propositions of pure mathematics, and of pure arithmetic in particular, are radically different in character from the propositions of applied mathematics. It is true that some modern logicians (for example Quine) have wished to blur the distinction, and maintain that so-called logical truths are not to be sharply distinguished from empirical truths. The former are, to his way of thinking, propositions to which we are more firmly committed, and which, therefore, we are less willing to abandon in the face of apparent counter evidence. And since commitment admits of many degrees, so too does the spectrum from logical to empirical truth. Nevertheless, it is true to say that, historically, most philosophers have recognized a sharp distinction in logical character between the propositions of pure and applied arithmetic.

A second view that is shared by most writers on the relationship between pure and applied arithmetic is that arithmetic becomes applied by the recognition of similarities, and involves the substitution or use of arithmetical terms in place of terms designating physical objects or relationships. That something like this is involved in the application of arithmetic is certainly true. Our task is only to describe the process more exactly, and, if possible, to set out necessary and/or sufficient conditions for saying that an application of arithmetic has been made.

In the following sections we must attempt to elucidate further the distinction between pure and applied arithmetic and to set out general conditions for the application of arithmetic. For this purpose, it will be convenient to centre our discussion around a pure formalist viewpoint.

B

A pure formalist view of the relationship between pure and applied arithmetic

Formalists consider that arithmetic is a formal system. A formal system is usually supposed to have the following characteristics:

(*a*) There is an initial set of undefined terms. These terms are supposed to be meaningful only in the sense that they have a role in the formal system. Apart from the system they are supposed to be nothing but squiggles on paper.

(*b*) There are rules for combining or arranging the undefined terms into configurations which are described as the *propositions* or *well-formed formulae* of the system.

(*c*) There are initial propositions which are described as the *axioms* or *postulates* of the system.

(*d*) There are rules for manipulating the terms of these propositions so that new propositions can be derived from the initial ones. These rules are usually described as the *rules of inference* of the system, and the new configurations thus derived, the *theorems* of the system.

And, in addition to these, we must add:

(*e*) There are rules of contradiction, that is rules for saying that one proposition contradicts another.

Rules of contradiction are necessary for the simple reason that one configuration of marks on paper can never contradict another. Since by hypothesis they assert nothing, then also they contradict nothing.

Of course, one is at liberty to call systems without rules of contradiction 'formal systems'. But certainly most systems of interest to mathematicians have rules of contradiction. With almost every mathematical system we can at least ask whether the axioms are self-consistent. Hence, it would seem to be closer to ordinary usage to include rules of contradiction as an essential ingredient of formal systems. In ordinary usage, chess is not a formal system but a game, although it has the characteristics (*a*) to (*d*). Nor are the configurations of chess men on a chess board that can be reached by playing the game according to the rules, theorems. They are simply configurations of chess men on a chess board.

This point is not always understood, and it may be worthwhile to illustrate it further. Let us compare chess with, say, Russell's Propositional Calculus. Suppose that on a piece of paper *A*, I derive a proposition *P*, and that on another piece of paper *B*, I derive the proposition ∼ *P*—the two derivations being valid in Russell's system. Then I must say that Russell's system is inconsistent, and make some adjustment to the axioms. But there is nothing comparable in chess. If on chess board *A* I reach the configuration *P*, and on chess board *B* I reach the configuration *Q*, then I have simply reached two different configurations by playing the game according to the rules. There are no rules for saying that *P* is consistent or inconsistent with *Q*.

Now, as some view the matter, arithmetic is a fully fledged formal system. And like all formal systems, it must be applied before it can be used to tell us anything about the world. A formal system, it is said, becomes applied by its terms being interpreted. For example, any well-formed formula of pure arithmetic of the form $a+b = c$ may be interpreted in the following way:

(i) Let $a/b/c$ mean 'a piece of wire of electrical resistance $a/b/c$ ohms'.

(ii) Let + mean 'is perfectly joined in series with'.

(iii) Let = mean 'If..., then we obtain...'.

The pure arithmetical theorem $4+3 = 7$ is thus interpreted:

'If a piece of wire of electrical resistance 4 ohms is perfectly joined in series with a piece of wire of electrical resistance 3 ohms, then we obtain a piece of wire of electrical resistance 7 ohms.'

Similarly, it is supposed that any well-formed formula of pure arithmetic of the form: $a+b = c$, where *a*, *b* and *c* are integers, may be interpreted in the following way:

(i) Let $a/b/c$ mean 'a group of $a/b/c$ objects'.

14

(ii) Let + mean 'is added to' or 'is considered together with'.

(iii) Let = mean 'If... then we have...'.

Then the pure arithmetical theorem $4+3 = 7$ is interpreted:

'If a group of 4 objects is considered together with a group of 3 objects (as forming a single group), then we have a group of 7 objects.'

This, crudely, is how formalists consider that arithmetic is applied.

However, it is not the case that any interpretation of an arithmetical schema counts as an application of arithmetic. There are and must be certain rules of interpretation. For obviously if there are no rules, any set of signs can be interpreted to mean anything, for example $4+3 = 7$ could be interpreted to mean 'I like cheese very much' (as in a code). But this would hardly be said to be an application of arithmetic or of the theorem $4+3 = 7$.

The examples given suggest:

(*a*) that an application of arithmetic must be an interpretation of one or more formally defined classes of arithmetical propositions, for example propositions of the form $a+b = c$ where a, b and c are integers,

(*b*) that it must be a term by term interpretation rather than a formula by formula interpretation. That is, the individual terms of a formula in the given class of formulae must have a fixed interpretation, so that the interpretation of a new formula within that class can be predicted from a knowledge of the interpretations of the terms it contains,

(*c*) that within the given class of propositions, different terms are always interpreted differently, the same terms the same, wherever they may occur,

(*d*) that the numeral terms are always interpreted in the same kind of way, for example, if 4 is interpreted as 'a piece of wire of electrical resistance 4 ohms', 7 must be interpreted as 'a piece of wire of electrical resistance 7 ohms',

(*e*) that the numeral terms are always interpreted as the *number* of things in a group or as the *measure* of something in some respect,

(*f*) that the interpreted formulae are true statements if and only if the corresponding pure formulae are arithmetical theorems.

The adequacy of these rules will be considered in a later chapter.

It can be seen that this formalist view of arithmetic has much to recommend it. For the most serious philosophical problem about the nature of arithmetic is to explain the apparent incorrigibility of arithmetical propositions, and at the same time to account for their great usefulness in describing the world. And the formalists seem to be able to do both. For, on the one hand, they argue that since arithmetical propositions, uninterpreted, are merely the formulae of a formal system, saying nothing whatever about anything, the results of experiments involving counting or measuring must be irrelevant to their truth. Indeed, the theorems of the system can only be said to be true in the sense that they may be arrived at from the initial propositions by following the rules correctly. Hence, empirically, they are utterly incorrigible. If the results of our counting or measuring procedures were such that arithmetical theorems could not be interpreted in the usual ways to give true statements concerning them, then, it is argued, this would only show that the usual interpretations were inappropriate.

For example, if we were to find by measurement that the electrical resistance of a compound piece of wire, consisting of two pieces of wire joined serially, was not given by what we calculated to be the sum of the electrical resistances of the wires measured separately, then this would not have the slightest tendency to show that our methods of calculation were wrong, or that arithmetical propositions which we have long accepted are false. It would merely show that our application of arithmetic was inappropriate.

But, on the other hand, the formalists argue that arithmetic is extremely useful, because arithmetical propositions can be interpreted in so many ways to produce true generalizations. The arithmetical proposition $7 + 5 = 12$ can be interpreted as any of a dozen different true statements about the world without violating any of the rules for the application of arithmetic.

C

An examination of the formalist account

In spite of the evident power of the formalist view of arithmetic to cope with some important philosophical problems, it often strikes philosophically untutored students as an incorrect view. The basic reason for this, I suppose, is that it seems to misrepresent grossly the historical course of the development of arithmetic. Its formalization is a comparatively recent achievement. Of course, formalists point out that it is not meant to be an historical account. They admit that many basic arithmetical propositions were discovered as a result of counting or measuring operations. But they argue that this is irrelevant, for they are concerned with the logical status of arithmetical propositions as we know them today, not with how they came to acquire that status. By the logical status of a proposition we usually mean to refer to the kind of role that it has in ordinary discourse or argument, whether, for example, it is a description of some observed state of affairs, whether it is a hypothesis about the way things would be if certain conditions were fulfilled, or whether it serves merely to indicate the use of certain terms or phrases. It appears, then, that the formalist is suggesting that arithmetical propositions function in ordinary discourse as the propositions of a formal system or calculus and not, for example, as empirical generalizations about the results of counting or measuring procedures, or even as hypothetical propositions about the results that would be obtained by these procedures if they were perfectly carried out. They may admit that given that the calculus may be applied in a certain way, we may deduce certain hypothetical propositions about the results of perfectly executed counting or measuring operations from certain theorems of the calculus. But they would say that it is always an empirical question whether the calculus can be so applied, and hence, that the arithmetical propositions themselves do not entail these hypothetical propositions.

Unfortunately, however, the situation is not as simple as all this. For in the first place, the numeral terms have a meaning or use which is independent of their role in a formal system.* And, in the second place, pure arithmetical propositions entail and are entailed by certain propositions which are usually conceived as being applied arithmetical propositions. That is, they are logically equivalent to such propositions.

The first of these points depends upon an analysis of the concept of number, and it will be easier to make this point after we have

---

* Peano himself was aware of this; for he observed that if the words 'number other than o' and '1' are substituted for 'number' and 'o' respectively throughout his axioms, the axioms would still be seen to hold for ordinary arithmetic (see Russell, ch. XIV, p. 125).

discussed the nature of quantity. But roughly we may say that a group contains a specific number n of objects if and only if it has certain numerical relationships with other possible groups, and is equal in number to the numeral sequence 1, 2, 3, ..., n.* Now, since no axioms or rules of inference need to be stated or understood before we can use this criterion, it follows that the numeral sequence is not a sequence of meaningless terms, or terms whose only meaning is given by the part they play in a formal system. We can be taught to use correctly such sentences as: 'Here are 7 apples' without knowing any formal arithmetic.

It is true that a child can be taught something of the meaning of numeral terms by teaching him to handle a certain formal system in which the numeral terms appear as undefined elements. He can, I have no doubt, be taught to manipulate these arithmetical symbols according to certain prescribed rules and thus arrive at certain arithmetical propositions. In a word, he can be taught to do elementary sums formally. But it does not follow that when he has acquired this ability he knows all there is to know about the meaning of the numeral terms. If he still doesn't know how to use such sentences as 'Here are 7 apples', then he still does not understand them.

It is instructive to compare the numeral sequence with the sequences of terms used to designate family relationships, for example, 'father', 'paternal grandfather', 'paternal paternal great-grandfather', and so on. Both are non-terminating sequences of terms generated from an initial set of basic terms according to rules. And the terms of both sequences are meaningful quite apart from logical relationships connecting statements in which these terms appear. Further, I imagine it would be possible to devise a calculus of family relationships, in which these and other terms appeared as undefined elements, and to teach a child to handle this calculus without teaching him the meanings of the terms it employs. Thus he might be taught to solve the problem: 'if A is the brother of B, B is the daughter of C, C and is the grandfather of D, what is the relationship between A and D?' But although he could learn to solve such problems by manipulating the various terms according to the rules, he would not thereby learn the meanings of the terms he is handling. He would not thereby learn to be able to use such

* This point is discussed in detail in ch. x.

sentences as 'He is my grandfather' or 'She is my sister'. For, to put it bluntly, this involves knowing something about sex.

Now it is my belief that the numeral sequence is like this. It is a sequence of terms used to designate certain kinds of (actual or possible) relationships between things, not merely a sequence of terms, the only meaning of which is given by their role in a formal system.

The second point that arithmetical formulae are logically equivalent to certain statements usually regarded as applied arithmetical propositions may be illustrated by the following example:

(S. 1) If a group A contains a things of a certain type, and a group B contains b things of the same type, then the composite group consisting of A and B contains c things of this type, provided only that the groups A and B have no things of this type in common.

Now, if $a+b = c$ is an arithmetical theorem, then proposition (S. 1) is analytic, and if $a+b \neq c$ is a theorem, then proposition (S. 1) is self-contradictory. Hence we cannot assert that $a+b = c$, and at the same time deny (S. 1) without self-contradiction. Nor can we assert (S. 1) and deny that $a+b = c$. The relationship between these two propositions is, therefore, one of mutual entailment or logical equivalence. Hence, whatever the grounds for asserting (S. 1) may be, these are also the grounds for asserting that $a+b = c$, and, conversely, if by any means we can establish that $a+b = c$, then by this means we also establish proposition (S. 1).

Now it may be objected that this logical equivalence is contingent upon the conditions for enumeration being satisfied. If the world were such that men could never be taught or otherwise come to understand elementary statements like 'Here are seven apples', then the statement (S. 1) could not be understood. And hence it may be argued that our *discernment* of the logical equivalence of (S. 1) to $a+b = c$ is contingent upon the world being more or less as we know it. In other words, our having the concepts requisite for the understanding of (S. 1) is to some extent dependent upon the kind of world we live in, and this being the case, it is a contingent fact that pure arithmetical formulae of the form: $a+b = c$ can be applied in this way to yield analytic (or self-contradictory) propositions.

2-2

The formalist might then bolster his argument by saying that if $a+b = c$ is logically equivalent to (S. 1), it is also logically equivalent to:

(S. 2) If a perfectly rigid rod of length a cm. is placed end to end with a perfectly rigid rod of length b cm., then the length of the composite rod is c cm.,

since (S.2) is analytic if and only if $a+b=c$ is a theorem of arithmetic.

But no one would wish to say that the conventions of length measurement in centimetres which guarantee the analyticity of (S. 2), (provided that $a+b = c$ is a theorem of arithmetic), also guarantee the truth of the corresponding arithmetical theorem. On the contrary, it would be universally agreed that the existence of these conventions is irrelevant to the truth of the corresponding theorem. Moreover, the possibility of arithmetic in no way depends upon the facts which make the adoption of these conventions possible. Consequently, it might be argued, the logical equivalence of (S. 1) and the corresponding arithmetical proposition, no less than that between (S. 2) and this same proposition, does nothing whatever to destroy the formalist way of making the distinction between pure and applied arithmetic. It only shows that logical equivalence is not to be confused with semantic equivalence.

However, it is doubtful whether this argument really extricates the formalist from his difficulties. For, although we may imagine a world in which the conditions for the possibility of making length measurements (in centimetres) are not satisfied, but in which we may construct the formal system of arithmetic (and demonstrate that some proposition of the form $a+b = c$ is a theorem of the system), nevertheless, it does not seem possible to imagine a world in which the conditions for *enumeration* are not satisfied, but in which the formal system is yet constructible. For the possibility of enumeration simply depends upon the possibility of identification and re-identification. And the possibility of constructing a formal system is no less dependent upon this same condition.

Consequently, it seems that the logist is right in maintaining that there is a very special relationship between, for example, $1+1 = 2$, and 'one apple and one other apple make two apples'. For if this is to be called an application of arithmetic, it must be singled out as a unique kind of application of arithmetic. Later, we shall attempt to characterize this kind of application of arithmetic more fully.* For the moment, it will be sufficient if I merely give it a name and call it a primary application of arithmetic. The logic of measurement, as it is here conceived, is the study not of primary, but of secondary applications of arithmetic.

But in case the term 'secondary application of arithmetic' be misunderstood, let me make it clear that a secondary application of arithmetic does not necessarily yield synthetic propositions. This depends upon whether the arithmetical formulae of a given class are applied in determining or defining a scale for the measurement of a given quantity, or whether the scale is defined independently, and the arithmetical formulae of the given class are applied, as it were ex post facto, to yield further information concerning the physical relationships between those things which possess the given quantity.

The following is an example of a secondary application of arithmetic yielding synthetic propositions. Suppose that three bodies A, B and C are moving from left to right along a given straight line so that the velocity of B with respect to A is v_1 cm./sec., and the velocity of C with respect to B is v_2 cm./sec. Suppose also that $v_1 + v_2 = v_3$ is an arithmetical formula. Now it is clearly an empirical question whether v_3 cm./sec. will be the velocity of C with respect to A for all values of v_1 and v_2, since our scales for the measurement of velocity are not so defined that this is a logically necessary proposition. Hence the interpreted arithmetical formulae of the form $v_1 + v_2 = v_3$ are synthetic propositions, and these interpreted formulae neither entail, nor are entailed by the arithmetical formulae themselves.

However, not all secondary applications of arithmetic are like this. In the cases of length and mass measurement, for example, the applications of such arithmetical formulae are made in defining our scales. And consequently, the proposition (S. 2) is an analytic proposition. Nevertheless, I call it a secondary application of arithmetic for the reason that it is an empirical fact that we can set up our length scales in the way that we do, and introduce the concept of a centimetre by which the analyticity of (S. 2) is guaranteed.

Finally, there are certain secondary applications of arithmetic of

* See ch. x.

a rather indeterminate logical status. Consider, for example, the proposition that if a piece of wire of electrical resistance a ohms is perfectly joined in series with a piece of wire of electrical resistance b ohms, then the electrical resistance of the compound piece of wire will be c ohms. It is not clear whether, if $a+b = c$ is an arithmetical theorem, this proposition is analytic or synthetic. The reason for this is that there are alternative procedures for measuring electrical resistance in ohms. We may measure it fundamentally, in much the same way as we measure length, or we may measure it derivatively in much the way that we measure velocity. But, as far as we know, the two procedures always yield identical results when they are perfectly executed. Consequently, we have never been forced to choose between these procedures and say which we regard as definitive of the Ohm scale of electrical resistance. If we were to choose the fundamental procedure then the proposition would become analytic, but if we were to choose the derivative one it would become synthetic. As things are, we cannot say that it is either.

D

Secondary applications of arithmetic

Returning now to the original dichotomy between pure and applied arithmetic as drawn by Plato, I agree, of course, that there is such a distinction to be drawn. But, unlike Plato, I recognize a number of different kinds of applications of arithmetic. There are, first, what I have called primary applications. These are of such a fundamental nature that the very possibility of constructing a formal system of arithmetic logically ensures that the conditions for the possibility of such applications of arithmetic are satisfied. Secondly, there are what I have called secondary applications of arithmetic. These are less fundamental for the reason that the possibility of these applications is not logically ensured by the possibility of arithmetic itself. Nevertheless, these secondary applications are of prime importance in the logic of measurement.

Among the secondary applications of arithmetic, I distinguish two general classes, (although the distinction is not a sharp one). The first of these is the class of analytic applications, that is applications of arithmetic which yield analytic propositions. Roughly speaking, these are the applications of arithmetic which are involved in setting up scales of measurement. It is the meaning of the unit names which guarantees the analyticity of such applied arithmetical propositions. The second class is that of synthetic applications. Such applications yield synthetic propositions—propositions whose truth is not guaranteed by the conventions we have adopted in setting up our scales of measurement. They are, characteristically, applications of arithmetic which are made only after our scales have been adopted.

In the following chapters we shall have a great deal to say about analytic applications of arithmetic. We must attempt to describe, in general terms, some of the various procedures for making such applications, describe and classify the scales which they serve to define, and examine some of their properties. Synthetic applications of arithmetic are inherently less interesting. For as we shall see the most interesting problems of the logic of measurement are concerned with the adoption and classification of scales.

CHAPTER II

THE CONCEPT OF A QUANTITY

A quantity is usually conceived to be a kind of property. It is thought to be a kind of property that admits of degrees, and which is therefore to be contrasted with those properties that have an all-or-none character (for example being pregnant, or being crimson). According to this conception, objects possess quantities in much the same way as they possess other properties, usually called 'qualities'. Quantities, like qualities, are thought to be somehow inherent in the objects which possess them. Just how this should be understood is not clear, but at least it is supposed to make sense to imagine a universe consisting of a single object possessing a variety of different quantities and qualities. It may, for example, be imagined to be round, three feet in diameter, made of steel, coloured yellow, and be five grams in mass. All of this exists, so to speak, before measurement begins. The process of measurement is then conceived to be that of assigning numbers to represent the magnitudes of these pre-existing quantities; and ideally it is thought that the numbers thus assigned should be proportional to these magnitudes.

It is true that some quantities are not so conceived. Velocity, for example, is not thought to be a property which objects can have in isolation from other objects. Indeed, it is not thought to be a property at all; and it is supposed to make no sense to speak of the velocity of an object without reference to other objects. But this is an exception. For the most part, quantities are accorded a kind of primary ontological status.

But this account is extremely unclear, and to some it is totally unacceptable. H. Dingle, for example, rejects the whole account as being 'completely incompatible with the view of physical science which the Theory of Relativity forces us to take', and recommends that 'instead of supposing a pre-existing "property" which our operation measures, we should begin with the operation and its result, and then if we wish to speak of a property (which I do not think we shall do) define it in terms of that'.* According to

* Dingle (1950).

Dingle, there are no quantities in nature, only various kinds of measuring operations, yielding more or less coherent results. He thinks it metaphysical and obscure to speak of pre-existing quantities, or to suppose that these quantities have magnitudes.

It will be argued here that neither account will do. The first misses the essentially *relational* character of quantities. Objects do possess quantities; but when we say that a given object possesses a certain quantity to a certain degree, we are not making a statement about that object considered in isolation. Rather, we are talking about the relationships which exist between it and other objects. Moreover, the account presupposes certain naïve realist dogmas which must be rejected.

Dingle's account is also unacceptable. First, it is possible to give operational criteria for the existence and identity of quantities, without describing any measuring operations or defining any scales of measurement. It is not metaphysical, therefore, to speak of pre-existing quantities which our operations are designed to measure. Dingle rightly rejects the received account, but for the wrong reason. Secondly, if the programme of speaking only of well-specified measuring operations and their results (that is the programme which Dingle advocates) were seriously followed through, then we should be faced with such a diversity of quantitative concepts that science, as we know it, would be impossible.

A

The existence of quantities

Under what conditions should we say that something possesses a quantity? It can be said at once that if certain things have a quantity in common (whether it be mass, area, length, electric charge, or temperature) then these things must be *comparable* in some way. In particular, they must be comparable in respect of the given quantity. But two things A and B are comparable in respect of a given quantity q if and only if one of the following relationships connect them:

(i) A is greater in q than B (that is $A >_q B$);
(ii) A is equal in q to B (that is $A =_q B$);
(iii) A is less in q than B (that is $A <_q B$).

Let us call such a set of relationships a set of quantitative relationships. Then we may say that a quantity exists if and only if a set of quantitative relationships exists, and that a given object possesses a quantity if and only if it enters into such relationships.

But this does not get us very far. For how do we recognize a set of quantitative relationships? These purely verbal criteria for the existence of quantities do no more than transform the problem. Let R_+, R_0 and R_- designate any three binary relationships. Our problem is now to describe the properties which these relationships must have in order that they should qualify as a set of quantitative relationships. In other words, we must now try to state necessary and sufficient conditions for saying that one thing is greater than, equal to, or less than another in some respect.

It should first be noted that there are different kinds of equality. Sometimes it makes sense to say that two things are equal to one another in some respect when it makes no sense to say that one is greater or less than the other in this respect. For example, we can say that two things are equal or the same in colour or shape, but we cannot say that one thing is greater or less than another in colour or shape. An equality of this type may be described as a *qualitative* equality. However, if two things can be said to be equal in respect of some *quantity*, it must also make sense to say that one is greater or less than the other in this respect. It is with this kind of equality, namely *quantitative* equality, that we are concerned.

Every relationship of quantitative equality must in fact be symmetrical and transitive, although not every symmetrical and transitive relationship is a quantitative equality; for relationships of qualitative equality are also symmetrical and transitive. Every relationship of quantitative inequality must in fact be asymmetrical and transitive. But not every asymmetrical and transitive relationship is a quantitative inequality; the relationship of causality is asymmetrical and transitive, but it is not a 'greater than' or a 'less than' relationship. For any given quantity p, there must be three possible relationships of quantitative equality or inequality— a 'greater in p than', an 'equal in p to' and a 'less in p than' relationship, the last two being converse relationships. Together these three relationships must form a group of mutually exclusive alternatives. That is, if one in fact holds, neither of the others can in fact hold. But if one holds, it must be logically possible for either of the others to hold.

The following, then, are conditions which must be satisfied before we can say that one thing is greater than, equal to or less than another in some respect. The things concerned must in fact be connected by one or other of a group of relationships R_+, R_0 and R_-

(*a*) R_0 being in fact a symmetrical and transitive relationship;

(*b*) R_+ and R_- being in fact asymmetrical and transitive converse relationships;

(*c*) R_0, R_+ and R_- being mutually exclusive alternatives (in the sense explained).

The existence of such relationships is thus a necessary condition for saying that the things concerned have a quantity in common.

In view of the difficulty of stating such conditions in ordinary language, it may be useful to express them more formally. Let $\diamondsuit$ be the modal operator 'It is logically possible that'. Then we require that:

$$(A)(B)[\{R_+(A, B) \lor R_0(A, B) \lor R_-(A, B)\}$$
$$\equiv \{\diamondsuit R_+(A, B) \diamondsuit R_0(A, B) \diamondsuit R_-(A, B)\}]; \quad (1)$$

$$(A)(B)[\sim \{R_+(A, B)\ R_0(A, B)\} \sim \{R_0(A, B)\ R_-(A, B)\}$$
$$\sim \{R_+(A, B)\ R_-(A, B)\}]; \quad (2)$$

$$(A)(B)[R_+(A, B) \equiv R_-(B, A)],$$
$$(A)(B)[R_0(A, B) \equiv R_0(B, A)]; \quad (3)$$

$$(A)(B)(C)[\{R_0(A, B)\ R_0(B, C)\} \supset \{R_0(A, C)\}],$$
$$(A)(B)(C)[\{R_+(A, B)\ R_+(B, C)\} \supset \{R_+(A, C)\}],$$
$$(A)(B)(C)[\{R_-(A, B)\ R_-(B, C)\} \supset \{R_-(A, C)\}]; \quad (4)$$

$$(A)(B)[\{R_+(A, B)\} \supset \sim \{R_+(B, A)\}],$$
$$(A)(B)[\{R_-(A, B)\} \supset \sim \{R_-(B, A)\}]. \quad (5)$$

Formulae (1) and (2) express the alternative and mutually exclusive conditions respectively. (It will be noted that they are a kind of generalized form of the law of the excluded middle and the law of non-contradiction.) The formulae (3) express the converse and symmetry conditions, while (4) and (5) express the transitivity and asymmetry conditions. Now it will be seen that if $>_p$, $=_p$ and $<_p$ are substituted throughout for R_+, R_0 and R_- in the above formulae, they all become logically necessary. This is the basis for my claim that the existence of such a set of relationships is a necessary condition for the existence of a quantity.

But although these conditions may be necessary ones, it is not evident that they are also sufficient. And in order not to prejudge the issue, I will describe a set of relationships having the above formal characteristics as a *set of linear ordering relationships*. The reason for so describing them is simply that given such a set of relationships, it is always in principle possible to arrange the things that are connected by them in a linear order, so that the actual relationships which they bear to each other can be read off from their position in this order—things on the same level being connected by the R_0 relationship, and things higher in the order by the R_+ relationship to those below them. The question we must now ask is whether the existence of a set of linear ordering relationships entails the existence of a quantity.

This, of course, is not a factual question. Nor is it even a logical question. For what we are seeking is a suitable *explication* of the concept of a quantity. It is, therefore, primarily a question of decision. Nevertheless, we must demand that our criteria for the existence of quantities should correspond fairly well with ordinary usage. Otherwise, we shall have no grounds for claiming that we have explicated the concept of a quantity. Let us consider then some of the advantages and disadvantages of regarding the existence of a set of linear ordering relationships as being also a sufficient condition for the existence of a quantity. In other words, let us suppose that the existence of a quantity not only entails, but is also entailed by the existence of such a set of relationships.

The chief advantage of this suggestion is that it seems to give a satisfactory account of certain quantities that have always proved troublesome to students of the physical sciences. To illustrate this, consider the following examples:

Example 1. The various states of a freely swinging pendulum are connected by three possible, but mutually exclusive transformation relationships, having the properties of R_+, R_0 and R_-. They are:

(*a*) a state A may transform itself into a state B and conversely, when the pendulum is not subject to damping; but neither transformation may occur when it is subject to damping;

(*b*) a state A may transform itself into a state B, with suitable damping, but not conversely, or in the absence of damping;

(*c*) a state *B* may transform itself into a state *A* with suitable damping, but not conversely, or in the absence of damping.

These relationships have all of the required characteristics for linear ordering relationships. They are mutually exclusive and alternative. The second and third are the converse of one another. The first is symmetrical and transitive, and the second and third are each asymmetrical and transitive.

Now in fact we say that the various possible states of a pendulum have a certain quantity to different degrees, and we give it a name—'mechanical energy'. If two states *A* and *B* of a pendulum are related by (*a*), we say they are equal in mechanical energy. And if they are related to (*b*), we say that *A* is greater in mechanical energy than *B*.

These, of course, are not general ordering relationships for the quantity we call 'mechanical energy'. Other things besides the states of pendulums possess mechanical energy. But they are ordering relationships for the quantity we call 'the mechanical energy of a state of a pendulum'.

Example 2. The various possible states of an energetically isolated system may be connected by one or other of the following transformation relationships:

(*a*) *A* is transformable reversibly into *B*—a symmetrical and transitive relationship;

(*b*) *A* is only transformable irreversibly into *B*—an asymmetrical and transitive relationship;

(*c*) *B* is transformable irreversibly into *A*—an asymmetrical and transitive relationship which is the converse of (*b*).

The three relationships are mutually exclusive alternatives, and they have all of the characteristics of linear ordering relationships. Accordingly we say that the various states of an energetically isolated system have a certain quantity to different degrees. In this case the quantity is called 'entropy'.

In contrast to the previous case, these ordering relationships are general ordering relationships for entropy. Things can be compared in respect of entropy if and only if such ordering relationships connect them. That there are relationships of the kinds (*b*) and (*c*) (example 2) is, according to H. A. Buchdahl,* the most general form of the Second Law of Thermodynamics—the form

* Buchdahl (1949).

in which it was expressed by Carathéodory. Buchdahl expresses it in the following way:

In the neighbourhood of any arbitrary initial state $\mathcal{J}_0$ of a physical system, there exist neighbouring states $\mathcal{J}$ which are not accessible from $\mathcal{J}_0$ along adiabatic paths.... This principle thus takes as a starting point the empirical recognition that if two states, $\mathcal{J}_0$ and $\mathcal{J}$, of a given adiabatically enclosed thermodynamic system be prescribed and granted

(i) that the transition from $\mathcal{J}_0$ to $\mathcal{J}$ is mechanically possible, and

(ii) that such a transition would not violate the demands which the First Law of Thermodynamics already imposes upon it; then the transition from $\mathcal{J}_0$ to $\mathcal{J}$ may nevertheless be impossible, while at the same time the reverse transition is possible.

I have taken these two examples because of the conceptual difficulties they often present. The student wants to know what mechanical energy or entropy is; and he is given a formula—a means of calculating the measure of it from the results of other measurements. Either that, or he is given a theoretical interpretation; and what is this, but yet another way of calculating the measure of the given quantity from the results of other measurements? All the time, he may think he is being cheated. For he may feel that he does not yet know what he is supposed to be measuring or interpreting. His conception of a quantity is such that he wants to be shown some feature of the system itself which is its mechanical energy, or its entropy. And when his demands are consistently frustrated, he may feel it is not a genuine quantity at all, but a kind of logical construction out of the results of measuring operations.

This is precisely the view that Dingle takes—except that he consistently adopts this line of reasoning with regard to all quantities. He thus comes out with the arresting thesis that there are no quantities in nature (as usually conceived), only well-specified measuring operations. Nevertheless, it can now be seen that this course is not forced upon us. We must, it is true, reject the conception of a quantity which leads to the above dilemma. But in view of these examples, we can see that this conception might be replaced by a new one, which does not depend upon defining quantities in terms of measuring operations, and which does not produce the kind of conceptual difficulty that has been described.

It seems, then, that the view that the existence of a set of linear ordering relationships entails the existence of a quantity has much to recommend it, and that a satisfactory explication of the concept of a quantity is likely to be made along these lines. However, this criterion for the existence of quantities is not entirely satisfactory, and it is doubtful whether any such purely formal criteria for the existence of quantities can be given.

One reason for this is that linear ordering relationships vary enormously in their physical or psychological importance. People can be arranged in a linear order, for example, by taking the product of their height and age. Let us say that they are then arranged in order of 'hage'. But we do not think that 'hage' is the name of a genuine quantity like temperature or momentum. Hence, if the suggested formal criterion is adopted, we must be prepared to distinguish between genuine and artificial quantities. It seems better, therefore, to reject the existence of a set of linear ordering relationships as being alone a sufficient condition for the existence of a quantity, and impose certain further conditions. We might suppose, for example, that the linear ordering relationships must be determinable *without* recourse to measurement or calculation. For temperature, momentum, pressure, volume, area, entropy, and the vast majority of other indirectly measured quantities would still be classified as quantities according to this criterion, while 'hage' would be eliminated. If there are any so-called quantities which do not satisfy this criterion, we might cease to regard them as quantities.

But even this criterion is not entirely satisfactory. For although it works well with physical quantities, it seems particularly hard on psychological and sociological ones. Intelligence, brightness, loudness and favourability towards the church, for example, would not be quantities according to this criterion, since the process of arranging things in such orders always depends upon statistical analysis. To obviate this difficulty, we might make the further stipulation that even if a linear order is determinable only by recourse to measurement or calculation, it may yet count as a quantitative order, if it is highly correlated with some crude linear order recognized in ordinary discourse.

However, I am not quite sure that even this will do. For the general difficulty that we face is that of stating what makes a linear order an interesting one. It might be interesting because it is highly correlated with a crude order of ordinary discourse. It might be interesting for many other reasons. And if it is interesting for any reason, we are likely to invent a quantity name to enable us to talk about it. It is therefore extremely doubtful whether any precise criterion for the existence of quantities can be given, which will account for the use we actually make of quantity terms. Nevertheless, there is nothing to prevent us from making the following decision. We shall say that the existence of a quantity is entailed by the existence of a set of linear ordering relationships. Although, in saying this, we must recognize that many things must be regarded as quantities which would not ordinarily be described as such, and that many of these quantities would be so utterly uninteresting that it would be absurd to invent quantity names for them. Our final position, then, is that the existence of a quantity entails and is entailed by the existence of a set of linear ordering relationships. I leave it to others to give precise criteria for deciding which quantities are sufficiently interesting to warrant the invention of quantity names. The few criteria that I have given are, no doubt, only a first step in this direction.

B

The identity of quantities

The criteria I have offered for the existence of quantities must not be confused with those for their identity. It has not been claimed that for each quantity there must be one, and only one, set of linear ordering relationships, and I have carefully avoided saying that a set of linear ordering relationships defines a quantity.

I now wish to argue (*a*) that it is the *order* (and not the linear ordering relationships) which should provide our criteria for the identity of quantities; (*b*) that two or more logically independent sets of linear ordering relationships may refer to the *one* quantity; and (*c*) that our quantity concepts are generally *cluster* concepts, and so cannot always be defined by reference to particular sets of linear ordering relationships.

First, if we say that logically independent sets of linear ordering relationships always define different quantities, then we shall needlessly complicate our science. Consider the concept of mass. To begin with, we must distinguish between gravitational and inertial mass—a distinction that may have some advantage. But we must also distinguish many other kinds of mass; and these distinctions themselves must be broken down into yet finer distinctions, until we are so lost in the maze of distinctions that no concept of mass remains that is of any value.

Suppose we have a perfectly constructed beam balance with left- and right-hand scale-pans designated by L and R. Then it is not difficult to show that using such a balance, objects can be arranged in order of mass by either of two logically independent procedures, a balancing procedure and a substitution procedure. For we can say:

(a1) an object A is equal in mass to an object B if A can be substituted for B on one scale-pan without tilting effects;

(a2) an object A is greater in mass than an object B if when A is substituted for B on one scale-pan the scale-pan descends.

Or else we can say:

(b1) A is equal in mass to B if A on L balances B on R;

(b2) A is greater in mass than B if with A on L and B on R, A descends.

Now, since the relationships (a1) and (b1) are both in fact symmetrical and transitive, while the relationships (a2) and (b2) are both asymmetrical and transitive, then we are provided with two logically independent sets of linear ordering relationships. That they are logically independent will be seen if the attempt is made to derive one from the other. Accordingly, if we wish to say that each logically independent set of linear ordering relationships defines a different quantity, we shall have to distinguish between two kinds of gravitational mass—substitutional mass and balance mass.

But of course this is not the end of the process. The order given by either of these procedures on any one balance is logically independent of the order given on any other balance. Hence we must have a different kind of substitutional mass for each balance, and also a different kind of balance mass. Further, the order given at one place is logically independent of the order given at another. The order given in one kind of field (gravitational, say) is independent of the order given in another kind (electric, for example). And so we could go on subdividing our concept of mass indefinitely.

Now what applies to mass, also applies to other quantities. If

33

we suppose that there are as many quantities as logically independent sets of linear ordering relationships, we must say that there is not just one quantity that goes by the name 'temperature', but literally dozens of different quantities; not just one quantity called 'surface tension' (to use Dingle's own example), but ten or more different quantities. And the end result would be to create such a hopeless division and confusion of concepts that the point of using quantity names in the first place would be defeated. Moreover, we should not only have to multiply quantity names in this fashion, we should also have to multiply physical laws. For the fact that these various sets of, say, mass ordering relationships always generate the same order amongst the same particulars (under the same conditions) must be separately expressed.

It seems better, therefore, to say that it is the order which is important for the identity of quantities—not the ordering relationships. If two sets of ordering relationships, logically independent of each other, always generate the same order under the same conditions, then it seems clear that we should suppose that they are ordering relationships for the same quantity.* Of course, independent sets of ordering relationships which generate the same order in one field may not do so in another; but this only shows that two or more quantities may be shown to exist where previously we had thought that two or more ordering relationships served to identify the same quantity. Thus the process of subdividing out concepts may be useful in enabling us to explain anomalous results. But to subdivide without reason is simply to generate confusion.

It may be helpful to put this point in a wider setting. In an important article in a recent issue of the *Australasian Journal of Philosophy*, D. A. T. Gasking introduces and discusses the concept of a cluster.† The most important feature of a cluster is that it may be identified by any one of a large number of characteristics. But it has no definition in any commonly accepted sense of this word. For no one characteristic belongs essentially to a cluster. Our concept is formed by a continuing association of characteristics—an association which is relatively stable. And if there were no such stability we would have no concept.

---

* The concepts of 'same order' and 'same conditions' are discussed in ch. III, D.   † Gasking (1960).

Consider, for example, our concept of an individual—Tom Jones. Almost any statement that we may care to make about Tom Jones is empirical. That he was born at such and such a time, had such and such parentage, that he grew up in this or that town, that he was educated at Harvard, and even that he is called 'Tom Jones'. All such statements are corrigible. Any one or any combination of such statements may enable us to identify the individual referred to. But no one statement (or combination of statements) could be regarded as defining that individual. Our concept of that individual is therefore a cluster concept.

Consider also our concept of gold. Most statements about gold are empirical. That it has such and such specific gravity, that it has a certain kind of spectrum, that it is soluble in aqua regia, that it is yellow, malleable, and so on. No one of these characteristics is essential to the nature of gold. No one characteristic could be used as a defining characteristic, although any one or any combination of these characteristics may in certain circumstances enable us to identify a piece of gold.

The second case is somewhat less pure than the first. Certain characteristics of gold are theoretically more important than others. That it has a certain characteristic spectrum, for example, is theoretically linked with our concept of an element. And if we found some substance having this characteristic spectrum but different chemical properties, physicists (if not chemists) might well say that it is a species of gold. However, this is not a crucial point. Whether gold is a cluster concept or not is not at issue. If it serves to illustrate the conditions under which we should say that something is a cluster, it has served its purpose.

Now the point I wish to put is this. In my view our quantity concepts are usually cluster concepts. In general, no one set of ordering relationships belongs essentially to a quantity, although a quantity may usually be identified by any one of a large number of ordering relationships. And just as it may turn out that there are two individuals or two substances involved, where previously we had thought that only one existed, so it may turn out that there are two quantities present where previously we had thought there was only one. Thus I would maintain that it is usually an empirical question whether a given set of ordering relationships is a set of ordering relationships for a given quantity. They may or may not generate the same order as the other relationships by which this quantity may be identified.

If I am right in thinking that our quantity concepts are generally cluster concepts, then to subdivide them as Dingle does is both pointless and futile. It is pointless in that it gives us no insight which we could not get by considering the logic of clusters. And it is futile because if it were seriously followed through, we would be left with an unintelligible maze of partial concepts, and of laws relating to them.

Dingle's position concerning quantities is akin to that of certain Berkelean idealists who have wanted to say that there are no such things as physical objects or substances. And his grounds for saying what he does are very similar to theirs. For they have observed that there are various procedures which we may follow as a result of which we may usually conclude that a certain physical object or substance is present. But the results of following these various procedures are logically independent of one another. The results of using our eyes are logically independent of the results of using our feet. Further, no one or combination of such results entails that a certain sort of physical object or substance is present; so that if I see a stone and kick it I have a series of visual impressions followed by a certain sensation in my foot. But there is nothing which tells me that these events are connected via a physical object, namely, a stone. The stone is therefore an extraneous metaphysical thing. All I ever really observe are these sensations and sense-impressions. And I can never do more than note their occurrence, and what constant associations there may be between them.

Now this argument is almost entirely parallel to Dingle's argument that there are no such things as quantities, only various sorts of precisely specified operations which yield numbers. Taken seriously, this means that we should cease to talk about quantities, and talk only about relationships between the results of different sorts of operations (as Dingle recommends). Likewise, if Berkelean idealism is taken seriously, this means that we should cease to talk about physical objects. We should talk only in sense-datum language.

The main weakness of both of these arguments lies in the last step, when it is concluded that there are no such things as quantities, or that there are no such things as physical objects. The fact that the existence of a quantity is not entailed by the results of precisely specified operations which yield numbers, or that the presence of a physical object is not entailed by any statement about our own sensations or sense impressions does not imply that there are no such things. It only follows that logically sufficient conditions for saying that a quantity exists or that a physical object is present cannot be given in these terms. 'Empirically' sufficient conditions, however, can certainly be given in these terms. That is, we can state conditions under which we are *warranted* in saying that a quantity exists or that a physical object is present. And this is not a metaphysical hypothesis, for it has empirical consequences. If we say that a physical object, for example, a stone, is present, then we will expect that various other observations could be made, and would be confirmed by others. If some of these expectations fail, then this does not entail that no stone is present, for the relation is not one of entailment. But the more often they fail, the less confident we can be in the truth of our assertion. Likewise, if we say that a certain quantity is present we will expect that certain relations which we have shown to be approximately symmetrical and transitive or asymmetrical and transitive in a certain field will remain so in an extended field. Moreover, we will expect to find other relations which generate more or less the same order, and yet others which lead to a more consistent ordering of things. If no such expectations are fulfilled, we may doubt whether a quantity exists. If they are fulfilled, then the more logically independent ways we have of ordering things in a certain way, the greater confidence we will have that a quantity exists.

*　　　*　　　*

It should now be evident why I disagree with Dingle. For I hope that I have shown that it is possible to discover and identify a quantity without thereby discovering a means of measuring it. It also should be clear why I reject Dingle's criterion for the identity of quantities. To say, as Dingle does that there are at least ten different concepts of surface tension on the grounds that there are at least ten logically independent ways of measuring it, is to subdivide needlessly a useful physical concept, and to destroy the unity and simplicity which this concept generates.

37

It is interesting that Dingle's reasons for taking the line he does are basically the same as mine. For he also wishes to counter naïve realist conceptions of quantity and replace them by operationist conceptions. He says: 'Now it is obvious that this (the usual approach) is in no sense an "operational" approach. Bodies are assumed to have "properties" which have "magnitudes". All that "exists", so to speak, before we begin to measure....'*

Up to this point, I am in full agreement with him. I agree that it is wrong to start with the unquestioned and unanalysed assumption that bodies have properties which have magnitudes. Whether such assumptions make operational sense is a point that needs to be discussed. My own view, however, is that operational significance can be given to quantity names, without describing any measuring operations; and my aim in this chapter has been to justify this view.

Nevertheless, it must not be thought that this commits me to anything like the naïve realist view of quantity concepts with which we began. I have argued that the existence of a quantity is logically dependent upon the existence of a set of linear ordering relationships; and that being the case, all quantities have an essentially relational character. I would therefore reject the view that quantities have a kind of primary ontological status, and I would deny that it makes any sense to speak of a universe consisting of a single object possessing a variety of different quantities. For, as I understand it, this is to suppose that the imagined object enters into a variety of different relationships with other objects, which, by hypothesis is impossible. In my view, 'absolute mass', 'absolute volume', and 'absolute electrical resistance' are no more intelligible than 'absolute velocity'.

* Dingle (1950), p. 8.

CHAPTER III

THE CONCEPT OF A SCALE

The previous chapter concerned the concept of a quantity. We must now consider what it is to have a scale for the measurement of a quantity. To do this, we shall first examine the general concept of a scale. For, as we shall see, not all scales are designed for the measurement of quantities. We must try, first, to state necessary and sufficient conditions for saying that we have a scale of measurement and, secondly, to offer criteria for the identity of scales. This done, we shall try to say what further conditions must be satisfied, if a given scale is to be classed as one for the measurement of a given quantity.

A

The general concept of a scale

According to S. S. Stevens, 'measurement [is] the assignment of numerals to objects or events according to rule—any rule'.* And since, presumably, every measurement must be made on a scale, it follows that if we have a rule for making numerical assignments, we also have a scale of measurement. Moreover, it seems clear that if we have a scale of measurement, then we must at least have some rule for making numerical assignments. Hence, if Stevens' definition of measurement is accepted, it follows that we have a scale of measurement if and only if we have a rule for making numerical assignments. In other words, to have a scale of measurement is simply to have such a rule.

However, it is doubtful whether this definition of measurement is really satisfactory. There is no doubt that measurement always involves the assignment of numerals to things according to rule, but if no restrictions are placed on the nature of the rule, it seems to admit far too much. On my table at the present time, there is a child's tractor, an empty coffee cup, an ink bottle and an empty packet of cigarettes. Now suppose that I am instructed to take these various objects in turn and assign to each a number—the

---

* Stevens (1959), p. 19.

first that comes into my head; and suppose that the numbers I actually assign are 2, 2, 2, 3. In what respect can I be said to have measured these objects? On what scale were my measurements performed? There is no doubt that I have followed a rule, for I followed the instructions and wrote down the first numbers that came to me. But I do not think that anyone would wish to say that I have measured anything.

Again, suppose that I am instructed to take any monotonic increasing sequence of rational numbers, and assign the first number to the first book on the shelf in front of me, the second number to the second book, and so on. Can I then be said to have measured the books in any way? Clearly, the numerical assignments have been made according to a rule. But how should I express the results of my 'measurements'? Suppose that the second book is *A Textbook of General Botany* and that the second number in my sequence is 37·53. Should I now say that *A Textbook of General Botany* is 37·53? If so, what information does this statement carry—even to someone who knows the rule which led to this numerical assignment? It does not tell him that it is the second book on the shelf in front of me. For he has no way of knowing what sequence of rational numbers I chose. Moreover, there is no question of his being able to check the 'measurement'. If he too follows the rule, and makes a numerical assignment to *A Textbook of General Botany*, it is extremely unlikely that he will make the same numerical assignment. But clearly his 'measurement' would not conflict with mine.

The mere possession of a rule, therefore, does not ensure that we have a scale of measurement. For as the concept of a scale is usually understood, different measurements made on the same scale on the same particular under the same conditions are necessarily in conflict with one another. Moreover, when measurements are made on a particular scale, our statement of the results of these measurements must be informative. In the above examples, neither of these conditions is satisfied. Hence, even though the numerical assignments may be made according to rule, these do not represent the results of measurements. For there is no previously defined scale on which these 'measurements' may be said to be made.

For these reasons, then, it is necessary to modify Stevens'

definition of measurement. In particular, it is necessary to place some restriction on the kinds of rules that are permissible. For we require that the rule must be capable of defining a scale; and we have a scale of measurement only if the following conditions are satisfied:

(a) we have a rule for making numerical assignments;

(b) this rule is *determinative* in the sense that, provided sufficient care is exercised the same numerals (or ranges of numerals) would always be assigned to the same things under the same conditions;

(c) the rule is non-degenerate in the sense that it allows for the possibility of assigning different numerals (or ranges of numerals) to different things, or to the same thing under different conditions.

The conditions (b) and (c) are necessary to ensure that numerical assignments made according to the rule will be informative—the third condition being included in order to exclude such degenerate rules as: 'Assign the number 2 to everything.'

There is no argument which will show that these are also sufficient conditions for saying that we have a scale of measurement. For this is not an empirical, nor even a logical question. At best, we could only show that if this criterion is adopted, it yields a concept of a scale not too different from the one we are trying to explicate. Hence, without further argument, I offer the following definitions:

(a) Measurement is the assignment of numerals to things according to any determinative, non-degenerate rule.

(b) We have a scale of measurement if and only if we have such a rule.

Let us suppose, then, that we have a scale of measurement. The question now arises whether it is possible to make measurements on the *same* scale by following *another* rule. At first it may seem that our criteria for the identity of scales should be tied to the rules by which they are first defined. But it turns out that these are not the criteria we actually use. For we do allow that measurements can be made on the one scale by any of a number of logically independent procedures. We only demand that wherever they are agreed to be applicable they should always yield the same results. Measurements of mass, for example, can be made on the gram scale by any of a dozen or more logically independent procedures. It is, therefore, grossly at variance with our ordinary concept of a scale to tie our criteria for the identity of scales to specific measuring operations. It is much more in accordance with the way we ordinarily think about scales to link our criteria to the numerical assignments. Accordingly, I offer the following definition.

(c) Two procedures are procedures for measuring on the same scale, if and only if, wherever they are deemed to be applicable, they would always lead to the same numerical assignments being made to the same things under the same conditions.

There is an obvious parallel between our general concept of a scale, and our concept of a quantity. Just as it is the order which is important for the identity of quantities, and not the ordering relationships; so it is the numerical assignments which are important for the identity of scales, and not the procedures for making such assignments. Moreover, both concepts are cluster concepts. For just as it is generally an empirical question whether a given set of linear ordering relationships enables us to arrange things in the order of some given quantity; so also is it usually an empirical question whether a given procedure is one for measuring on a given scale. The range of applicability of a given measuring procedure, for example, is usually something which has to be determined empirically. It is seldom something which is determined simply by convention.

B

Scales for the measurement of quantities

The general concept of a scale described in the last section includes many kinds of scales that are not designed for the measurement of quantities. Nominal scales, for example, are merely scales for the measurement of identity and difference.* At the other extreme, we have various kinds of multi-dimensional scales for the measurement of such complex entities as colour and stress.† Our task now is to describe the class of scales used for the measurement of quantities, and to say what it is to have a scale for the measurement of a given quantity.

We have seen that the existence of a quantity entails the existence of a linear order, generable (usually) by any of a number

---

* See ch. IV, B.

† For an account of the techniques of multidimensional scaling, see Torgerson (1958), *Theory and Methods of Scaling*.

of logically independent sets of linear ordering relationships. We have also seen that to have a scale of measurement is to have one or more procedures for making numerical assignments which always in fact lead us to make the same numerical assignments to the same things under the same conditions (wherever they are applicable). The connection we seek, then, must be one between a linear order and a set of numerical assignments. The simplest plausible connection seems to be this:

(*d*) we have a scale S for the measurement of a given quantity q if, and only if:

(i) there is a procedure P for measuring on S such that for any object x which occurs in the order of q, x is measurable by P,

(ii) there is no object which is measurable on S which does not occur in the order of q,

(iii) if the objects measurable on S are arranged in the order of the numerical assignments, they are thereby arranged in the order of q

The condition (i) is included, although it may be doubted whether it is really a necessary one; for few quantities are in fact measurable over the whole of their range. Nevertheless, if we are to have what we may call a complete scale for the measurement of a given quantity, this condition is necessary. Most of our scales are in fact only partial scales. The inclusion of the condition (ii) seems obvious enough, and I do not anticipate any objections on this score. Most serious objections, however, are likely to be raised concerning condition (iii).

That condition (iii) is a necessary condition for saying that S is a scale for the measurement of q is not immediately obvious. For there are such things as nominal scales which could conceivably be used for the measurement of quantities; and on such a scale the order of the numerical assignments need not correspond to the order of the quantity q being measured. Nevertheless, it is doubtful whether we should describe this as a scale for the measurement of q. It seems more likely that we should say that it is a scale for the measurement of equality or inequality in q. However, since scientific language gives us no firm guide in the matter, we are at liberty to make whatever choice we please. My inclusion of condition (iii) as a necessary one is, therefore, rather arbitrary; but it is defensible on the grounds that the line has to be drawn somewhere, and this is a convenient place to do it.

A more serious objection, however, concerns whether (i), (ii) and (iii) should be regarded as jointly sufficient conditions for describing S as a a scale for the measurement of q. For if these conditions are so regarded, then we must admit the possibility of scales for the measurement of such quantities as mass, length, time-interval and volume which are *non-linear* with respect to our ordinary scales for these quantities. And it may be argued that our concepts of these quantities simply do not admit this possibility.

But here again, there is no decisive argument one way or the other. Every cosmologist is familiar with so-called 'non-linear' scales for the measurement of these quantities. Hence, a cosmologist is likely to accept conditions (i)–(iii) as being a set of sufficient conditions for describing S as a scale for the measurement of q. His concepts of these quantities do not differ essentially from mine. Most psychologists, on the other hand, speak of two different quantities—length and psychological length (or time and psychological time)—even though the criterion of sameness of order is satisfied. Hence a psychologist is likely to reject (i)–(iii) as being a set of jointly sufficient conditions.

We are presented, then, with yet another problem of choice. Whose lead shall we follow? If the lead of a psychologist is taken, then we are immediately presented with the following difficulties: (i) we must be prepared to make a distinction between different sorts of quantities—those for which sameness of order does provide a criterion of identity, and those for which somewhat more stringent criteria of identity are required; (ii) we must be prepared to offer appropriate criteria for the existence and identity of those quantities that cannot be characterized simply by a linear order.

If, however, the lead of the cosmologist is taken, then these two problems do not arise. The only change that must be made is that we should cease to speak of 'psychological length' and 'psychological time', as though these were quantities different from length and time, and make a distinction at the scale level instead. We should speak only of psychological scales for the measurement of length and time-interval, and contrast these with physical scales for the measurement of the same quantities. Of course, if the psychological length and time-interval orders were not the same as the physical ones, then a distinction between quantities would also have to be made. But then this would present no barrier to the acceptance of the conditions (i)–(iii) as sufficient conditions for describing S as a scale for the measurement of q.

It therefore seems that the acceptance of definition (d) is preferable to other alternatives. But in urging its acceptance, it must be made clear that I am recommending that we should make certain changes in our ways of thinking—especially about the so-called psychological quantities which occur in psychophysical measurements. In particular, where there is no essential difference between the psychological and physical orders, we should cease to speak of psychological quantities, and speak only of psycho-logical scales. A psychological scale of length is only one among many kinds of scales for the measurement of the *one* quantity, namely length.

C

Scales and fluents

The concept of a scale that has been developed here is in complete harmony with Karl Menger's concept of a fluent.* A fluent is conceived by Menger to be a kind of physical analogue of a mathematical function. It is clear that we have a mathematical function (of one variable) if, and only if, we have a determinate rule for replacing any given number in some given domain by some other number in that domain. Moreover, two mathematical procedures for making numerical replacements are procedures for determining the value of the *same function* if, and only if, they would always lead to the same replacements. Suppose, for example, that my procedure for making numerical replacements (in the field of real positive numbers) is to square the given number and take the cube root of the result. The corresponding function, in Menger's terminology, is $j^2.j^{\frac{1}{3}}$, where, for all n, j^n is the function such that for all x, $j^n(x) = x^n$. But if I were to reverse the order within this procedure, taking first the cube root and then the square, my results would be the same. The two *procedures* would not be the same, however, for the details of my mathematical calculations would differ. Nevertheless, we should describe them

* Menger (1959), pp. 97–128.

as alternative procedures for evaluating the same function, and we should say that '$j^2.j^{\frac{1}{3}}$', '$j^{\frac{1}{3}}.j^2$' and '$j^{\frac{7}{3}}$' are alternative designations for one and the same function.

The essential difference between a fluent and a function is that those elements which we may say form the arguments of fluents belong to some class of non-mathematical entities (for example physical objects or events). And, instead of numerical replacements, now, we must speak of numerical assignments. Menger's criteria for the existence and identity of fluents are then precisely the same as my criteria for the existence and identity of scales. Hence, we may say that we have a fluent if, and only if, we have a scale of measurement, and that two procedures are procedures for evaluating the same fluent if, and only if, they are procedures for measuring on the same scale. A fluent is, therefore, simply another name for a scale.

I am not sure whether Menger himself is clear about this. For he sometimes speaks of fluents as if they were quantities. Velocity and acceleration, for example, are both described as fluents.* Again, he sometimes speaks of a fluent as though it were the *measure* of some quantity on some particular scale. Thus 'pressure in atmospheres' and 'time in seconds' are regarded as the names of fluents.† But to be consistent, the names of fluents should be simply the names of scales. The 'atmosphere scale of pressure' and the 'second scale of time-interval' are the names he should have used.

However, it matters little what Menger conceived fluents to be. For it is clear that we may try to use his results for our own purposes, using the word 'scale' instead of 'fluent'. Now, in mathematics, a function f of one variable is defined thus: The function f is the class of pairs $(x, f(x))$ for all x within some specified domain called 'the domain of f'. (Of course, the definition is useless to anyone who does not know at least one procedure for calculating $f(x)$ for all x within the specified domain.) Likewise, then, we may try to define a scale S as a class of pairs $(A, S(A))$ for all objects A within some specified class (for example the class of objects possessing the quantity q for which S is a scale), $S(A)$ being the measure of A on S.‡

* Menger (1959), p. 108.   † Menger (1959), pp. 108–9.
‡ Cf. Menger's definition of a fluent (Menger, 1959, p. 109).

But this definition of Menger's (with the word 'scale' replacing the word 'fluent') is not without grave difficulties. For classes of physical objects or events are not really very like classes of mathematical entities. For one thing, their membership is variable. And this means that if a new object is created which belongs to the domain of S, the original scale S is no longer adequate. In other words, if S is a scale for the measurement of q, and a new object B possessing q is created, then it is logically impossible to measure B in respect of q on S. Hence the variability of class membership for extra-mathematical classes is utterly fatal to the proposed definition. Moreover, if any object changes in respect of q, and the required measurements are repeated, then we shall obtain a new class of pairs different from the first, and hence a new scale. But this conclusion is also absurd. Hence, the essential variability of the properties of extra-mathematical entities is also fatal to the proposed definition. These difficulties do not arise in the mathematical case because of the timelessness of mathematical entities.

The first of these arguments is also fatal to Suppes & Zinnes' definition of a scale as any ordered triple, consisting of an empirical relation system A, a full numerical relation system B, and a function f which maps A homomorphically on to a subsystem of B.* An empirical relation system is any finite sequence of the form: $A = < a, R_1, R_2, ..., R_n >$, where a is a non-empty set of extra-mathematical elements called the domain of A, and $R_1, R_2, ..., R_n$ are relations on a. Hence, if the membership of a changes, A must also change, and so too must the scale.

These difficulties, however, may not be fatal to the general approach that is being made. If a way can be found to overcome these objections, we may provide ourselves with some useful mathematical tools. In the efforts of Suppes, Zinnes and Menger, I recognize the existence of a very difficult and genuine problem; namely to supply a satisfactory denotation for scale names. If this problem can be solved, then very quickly we shall have a completely satisfactory denotation for dimension names. For as we shall see, dimension names may be regarded simply as the names of classes of similar scales.†

* Suppes & Zinnes (1962), p. 16.
† See ch. IX, E.

47

D

Some general remarks concerning scales and quantities

In this and the previous chapter, we have tried to explicate the concepts of 'scale' and 'quantity'. In doing so, however, we have passed over certain difficulties and made certain simplications. This is a convenient place to consider some of these points.

The first point concerns the concept of a quantity. We have said that two procedures are ones for ordering things in respect of the same quantity if and only if they would always generate the same order amongst the same particulars under the same conditions. But how should we in fact use this criterion? If it is taken too strictly, then it is useless, because states of the world, and hence the conditions under which objects exist, never really repeat themselves. Presumably, therefore, we must use our physical judgement and decide tentatively what differences are relevant, and what irrelevant. And then, if our procedures yield the same order, we may say, equally tentatively, that they are procedures for ordering things in the same respect.

But now this raises a question concerning sameness of order. If 'same order' is taken literally, then it follows that we cannot have different ordering procedures for the one quantity of different *range* or *refinement*—a conclusion which must obviously be rejected. Hence, 'same order' cannot be taken strictly, and somewhat looser criteria for sameness of order must be provided. To this end, we might suggest that two linear ordering procedures may be considered to generate the same order only if the orders which they generate show no inversions with respect to each other. For this allows for the possibility that things that are placed on the same level by the one procedure might be placed on different levels by the other—thus accounting for differences in both range and refinement.

However, it is doubtful whether even this will do. For it seems that we do allow occasional inversions of order—especially where there is a certain lack of objectivity in the ordering procedures, that is where the ordering procedures depend upon the psychological or physical make-up of those who carry them out. If, for example, I order things by means of heat sensation, we do not think that I am placing them exactly in the order of some quantity which is peculiar to me (although, according to the above revised criteria for the identity of quantities, this is what we should say). On the contrary, we say that I am attempting to arrange these things in the order of temperature; and my procedure would be described as a crude one for this purpose. Consequently, even the existence of occasional inversions of order cannot be taken as demonstrating that there is more than one quantity involved. If two ordering procedures yield linear orders that are highly correlated with each other (although not the same order, even when allowance is made for difference in range and refinement), we may yet consider that they are different procedures for ordering things in respect of the one quantity—the procedures differing only in their crudity or reliability.

In many cases, the recognition of a quantity begins with the recognition of crude subjective linear orders, which, though highly correlated with each other, are not the same even when differences of range and refinement are allowed for. Such quantities as weight, temperature, volume, pressure and length, for example, all have such beginnings. But instead of supposing (as logically we might) that each order defines a different quantity peculiar to ourselves, we in fact suppose that our various attempts at ordering yield linear orders that are only approximations to the real one. Such is the influence of Platonism in modern thought.

But now we may ask a more fundamental question. What is the real order of a given quantity? And, how do we know that there is any such order? Consider the first part of this question. The concept of a real order is, presumably, a kind of limit concept. It is conceived to be the order to which all physically obtainable orders (for a given quantity) approximate, however refined or universal in scope they may be. But then, if this ideal order is not physically obtainable, or otherwise knowable, it is also incomparable. Hence, the degree to which a physically obtainable order may be said to approximate to the ideal one cannot be ascertained by the sorts of procedures we may use for deciding how closely physically obtainable orders approximate to each other. Hence, if the supposition of ideal quantitative orders is not to remain a purely metaphysical dogma, alternative criteria for degrees of approximation must be provided.

The criteria we in fact use are hardly recognizable as having anything to do with approximation. And so, perhaps, this whole way of speaking about quantities should be rejected. In the absence of theoretical considerations (whose nature and relevance will be discussed later), we in fact prefer those linear ordering procedures which are most universal in scope, (that is have the greatest range), which are least dependent upon the peculiar properties of individual objects or substances, and which are most refined (that is which allow most distinctions of level). And, the linear orders which are generated by such procedures are supposed to be the closest approximations to the real ones. Hence, if there is any factual significance in the claim that a given linear order is a close approximation to the real order of a given quantity, it is simply that the procedure or procedures by which it is generated have the above characteristics—provided, of course, that we have no good theoretical explication of the quantity in question which upsets this conclusion.

Concerning the second part of the question, we may very well doubt whether there are any real orders of quantities (in the sense explained). For it is clearly possible that the simple linear orders which appear to exist in nature are really much more complex in structure. It is possible, for example, that as we attempt to refine our linear orders more and more, we should find that the simple one-dimensional picture that serves us well on the macroscopic level must be replaced by a much more complex picture; and that the real relationships between things are, in fact, much more complex than the simple linear ordering relationships which lead to our belief in quantities. Indeed, as I understand it, this is precisely the situation which has been shown to exist in matrix mechanics.

Now, a substantially similar set of points can be made concerning our criteria for the identity of scales. We have claimed that two procedures are procedures for measuring on the same scale if and only if they would always lead us to make the same numerical assignments to the same things under the same conditions. But, as before, neither 'sameness of conditions', nor 'sameness of numerical assignments' can be taken too strictly. We can only say that when the conditions are agreed to be the same (for the purposes of the experiment) the numerical assignments made by the different procedures must generally be the same to within prescribed limits of error deemed to be appropriate for those procedures. And only if this condition is not satisfied may we claim that the procedures define different scales of measurement.

Likewise, our scales for the measurement of various quantities are often considered to be only approximations to the true or ideal ones. Of course, we do not think that for each quantity there is only one true scale. Our Platonism does not extend that far. Nevertheless, some elements of Platonic idealism remain. For we do consider that some scales may more accurately represent quantities than others. And by 'accuracy' here, we mean not only to refer to the internal consistency of the results of our measurements, we also mean to refer to an external relationship between the scale and the quantity. It is often claimed, for example, that on a perfect scale for the measurement of such quantities as mass, length and time-interval, our numerical assignments would be 'proportional to the quantities themselves'.

This raises a very large and fundamental issue. Does it make any sense to speak of a real or true scale for the measurement of a given quantity? If so, by what criteria may such scales be recognized? If not, what sorts of considerations should guide us in our choice of scales? The detailed discussion of these questions, however, must be taken up at a later stage of the argument.

CHAPTER IV

THE CLASSIFICATION OF SCALES
OF MEASUREMENT

A system of classification gives us a way of looking at a group of phenomena, and it determines to some extent what general statements we can make about them. Usually, several systems of classification are possible, each with its own merits. For scales of measurement there are two main systems. The first, the classical system of Campbell,* depends upon an analysis of our measuring procedures. Our scales are grouped according to the kinds of procedures used in setting them up. The second, that of Stevens,† classifies our scales according to their mathematical properties. Both systems appear to have certain advantages. The Campbellian system gives us deeper insight into the conditions for the possibility of measurement. It enables us to see more clearly the significance of the numerals which we assign to things when we make measurements. We can see to what extent out scale choices depend on empirical facts, on theories concerning the quantities they measure, and on arbitrary conventions. Stevens' system may be more useful to the practical scientist; for if his claims are justified, then from a knowledge of the kind of scale on which a set of measurements is obtained, we can say what sorts of statistics are relevant to these measurements.

In addition to these, there is a third system of classification of scales, developed most notably by H. Coombs.‡ His approach is simply to classify our scales according to the kinds of applications of arithmetic they represent. In many ways, Coombs' system is loosely related to Stevens' (although the two systems are not identical). It will therefore be convenient to discuss these two systems under the one heading.

---

* Campbell (1920), part II.   † Stevens (1946), p. 677.
‡ Coombs (1952a).

A

Campbell's system of classification

Campbell's system depends on an initial distinction between two kinds of measurement—fundamental and derived. He observes that often the measurement of a quantity depends on the measurement of two or more other quantities. He says, for example, that to measure density we must be able to measure both mass and volume. But he points out that the measurement of mass does not (or need not) depend on the measurement of anything else. We could measure mass even if nothing else were measured. He therefore concludes that there are two kinds of measurement: that kind which does not depend on prior measurement he calls fundamental, the other he calls derived.

This distinction seems clear enough. But as it stands it is not exhaustive; for there are some quantities, not fundamentally measurable, whose measurement depends only on the measurement of one other quantity. Indeed I am inclined to think that most quantities can be measured in this way. To measure temperature, for example, we need only to be able to measure pressure, or volume, or electrical resistance, or any one of many other thermometric properties. Admittedly, we need criteria for equality in other respects, but we need these even for fundamental measurement; and in any case, if we have criteria for saying that two systems are equal in p, this is no guarantee that we can measure p. Hence the measurement of temperature need only depend on the measurement of one other quantity.

Even density may be measured by a procedure which is neither fundamental nor derived according to Campbell's definitions. For it is not true that the measurement of density necessarily depends on the measurement of both mass and volume. We could measure density if we could measure either one of these quantities and had only a criterion for equality in respect of the other. Hence if the distinction between fundamental and derived measurement is to be exhaustive, the wording must be slightly changed. We must say that a quantity is measured by derived measurement if this involves the measurement of one or more other quantities. Alternatively, we could retain Campbell's definition of derived measurement and introduce a new term to cover the case of temperature measurement.

As we shall see, there is some justification for this procedure, and I am sure that Campbell would wish to retain his original definition. For later he explains that derived measurement is 'measurement by means of constants in numerical laws'.* And the evaluation of such constants always requires the measurement of *two* or more quantities. If we measure temperature by measuring the volume of a given mass of gas at constant pressure we do not thereby determine the value of a constant in a numerical law. We would be able to measure temperature in this way even if no numerical laws were known. (That temperature is proportional to volume under these conditions is, of course, not a numerical law, but a more or less arbitrary stipulation.)

It should also be noticed that where a quantity is always measured by determining the value of a constant in a numerical law, we seldom speak of a scale of that quantity. We do not talk about scales of density or pressure or velocity. But we do speak of scales of temperature. Hence, if the ordinary usage of terms in scientific discourse is any guide, there should be some distinction between the measuring procedures, and the logical problems of temperature measurement should be somewhat different from those of, say, density measurement. I will therefore distinguish the two in my terminology. I will use the term *derived measurement* to refer to measurement by the determination of constants in numerical laws, and the term *associative measurement* to refer to the kind of measurement exemplified by temperature measurement. The term *indirect measurement* will be used to refer to any measurement of a given quantity which involves the measurement of one or more other quantities. Derived and associative measurement are thus both species of indirect measurement.

With Campbell's use of the term 'fundamental measurement' we find a similar ambiguity. He initially defines fundamental measurement as measurement which does not depend on prior measurement. But later it appears that he is using this term to refer to one particular species of such measurement. Fundamental measurement is measurement by a procedure which conforms to a certain pattern, and which is possible only because certain kinds of operations are possible. He observes that our scales of length, mass, electrical resistance, electrical potential,

* Campbell (1928), ch. VI.

area, volume, time-interval, and many other quantities, may be set up by logically similar procedures, and that these procedures are possible only because certain kinds of operations (called 'addition' operations) may be performed on systems possessing these quantities. But it is not difficult to show that there are or may be measuring procedures which are not indirect, according to the above definition, and which do not conform to Campbell's pattern, or depend on the possibility of performing 'addition' operations.

To illustrate this, suppose that all substances had the same specific heat capacity, and that this quantity was not temperature dependent. Then it would be possible to measure temperature directly by calorimetric mixing operations. We should need a criterion for equality of mass, but we should not need to be able to *measure* mass. To set up a scale of temperature, we could arbitrarily select two fixed heat states H_1 and H_2 and assign to them temperature numbers t_1 and t_2 respectively. Then, selecting equal masses of substances at temperatures t_1 and t_2, we could mix them calorimetrically and obtain a mass of substance whose temperature lies between t_1 and t_2. We could now agree to say, (arbitrarily), that its temperature is $\frac{1}{2}(t_1 + t_2)$, and calibrate our thermometer accordingly.

There is no need to develop this example fully. For it is obvious that a thermometer could be calibrated in this way as finely as we wish by performing a series of calorimetric mixing operations with equal masses of substance. The important point to note is that the scale so obtained would not be an 'additive' scale. For there would be no interpretation for the arithmetical operation of addition performed on temperature numbers. The only arithmetical operation which would be analytically interpreted would be the operation of taking the arithmetical mean. The scale would, therefore, not qualify as a fundamental scale in Campbell's terminology. But it would, nevertheless, be a scale set up by direct measurement. For temperature measurement on this scale would not depend on the measurement of any other quantity.

But we need not have taken such a fanciful case. The measurement of hardness on Mohs' scale provides us with a very simple example of a kind of measurement which is neither indirect nor fundamental. I therefore propose to use the term *direct measurement* to refer to the more general class, and to reserve the term *fundamental measurement* for the particular species described by Campbell. Direct measurement is any form of measurement which does not depend upon prior measurement. Fundamental measurement is one particular form of such measurement.

Our way of measuring hardness represents a particularly elementary form of measurement. For all quantities can be measured in this way. This is guaranteed by the conditions for saying that a quantity exists. If a quantity exists, then there is a set of linear ordering relationships, and it is at least theoretically possible to arrange things in a linear order by means of them. The existence of a quantity therefore entails the existence of an order, and this is all that is required for this kind of measurement. I will call such measurement *elemental measurement*.

There are then at least four kinds of measurement in practical use. The first, elemental measurement, is applicable to all quantities. The second, associative measurement, is possible only if there is an independently measurable quantity q, associated with the quantity p to be measured, such that if things (under certain specified conditions) are arranged in the order of q, they are also arranged in the order of p. The third, derived measurement, is possible only if:

(*a*) the systems which possess p (the quantity to be measured) possess other quantities q, r, s, ..., which are independently measurable;

(*b*) there are laws relating some of q, r, s, ..., in which constants occur which vary from system to system;

(*c*) there is at least one system-dependent constant c which is such that when the systems are arranged in the order of c, they are also arranged in the order of p.

The fourth kind of measurement, fundamental measurement, is the most restricted in application of all. For a quantity to be fundamentally measurable, at least the following conditions must be satisfied.*

(*a*) There must be some operation O of combining any two of the systems A, B, C, ..., possessing the quantity p to be measured, such that the resulting system also possesses this quantity.

(*b*) This operation O must be such that: *If* (i) $O(X, Y)$ is the

---

* These conditions are not, by themselves, sufficient conditions for the possibility of fundamental measurement. For a more complete statement, see ch. v.

name of the composite system formed by combining X and Y in that order *and* (ii) $>_p$ means 'is greater in p than', $=_p$ means 'is equal in p to', $<_p$ means 'is less in p than', *then*

$$O(X, Y) =_p O(Y, X),$$
$$O(X, Y) >_p X' \quad \text{where} \quad X =_p X',$$
$$O(X, Y) =_p O(X', Y') \quad \text{where } X =_p X' \text{ and } Y =_p Y',$$
$$O(O(X, Y), Z) =_p O(X, O(Y, Z)).$$

These four kinds of measurement thus form a sort of heirarchy. The conditions for their application become progressively more stringent, and their range of application becomes progressively less. If a quantity is in fact always measured derivatively, it is true that we rarely speak of a scale of that quantity. The reason for this, I believe, is that when our associative and fundamental scales have been fixed, the numerical values of the constants in our numerical laws relating these quantities can be uniquely determined. Hence there appears to be no freedom of choice in the adoption of a derivative scale. And where there is no choice it is odd to speak of a scale. Scales imply choice.

Nevertheless, quantities which are measured derivatively may be measured in various units, depending on our choices of associative and fundamental scales. And sometimes there may be two or more independent derived measuring procedures for the same quantity. For there may be more than one numerical law in which there occur system-dependent constants C_1, C_2, C_3, ..., such that when the systems are arranged in the order of each of these constants in turn, they are arranged in the same order—the order of p. In other words, the complex units in which a quantity may be measured derivatively may not even involve units of the same associatively or fundamentally measurable quantities. For these reasons we may speak intelligibly of derivative scales. There is a choice at one remove of associative and fundamental scales.

In the following chapters, we shall discuss some of the logical problems of fundamental, associative and derived measurement—for these are obviously the forms of measurement most important for the physical sciences. Sufficient has been said here to at least indicate the basis for classification. Before we proceed with this, however, let us turn to consider Stevens and Coombs' systems of classification.

B

The mathematical approach to the classification of scales

Stevens proposes that we should classify our scales of measurement according to 'their mathematical group structure'.* And he explains that the mathematical group structure of a scale is determined by considering what sorts of transformations leave its 'scale form' invariant. His system of classification therefore depends on his concept of a scale form. If it is to be a useful system, we must have clear criteria for saying that a scale form changes or does not change with any given transformation.

But first what is meant by transforming a scale? If measurements are made on a given scale then they are made in certain units. We cannot measure on the same scale in different units, or on different scales in the same units. For, as we shall see, unit names must be regarded as the names of scales. Now suppose that we have a set of measurements in the unit X, and another set of measurements of the same quantity (made on the same things under the same conditions) in the unit Y. Then if x is any such measurement in X and y is the corresponding measurement in Y, then presumably x and y are related by some function f such that $y = f(x)$. So that, if we know the function f, we can transform our measurements in X to measurements in Y, that is we can transform from the X-scale to the Y-scale.

In determining to which class a given scale belongs, Stevens asks us to consider what kinds of scale transformations would leave its scale form intact. And he says that a scale form is preserved under a given transformation if the new scale which it produces could serve 'all of the purposes' of the original one. No further explanation is given. And he evidently considers that none is necessary, for he proceeds immediately to his classification of scales. But when we examine the classification he produces we find that his criterion for invariance of scale form is somewhat ambiguous.

Stevens distinguishes four kinds of scales among those in common use, and a fifth kind that he considers a theoretical possibility. The four practical ones are called 'nominal', 'ordinal', 'linear interval', and 'ratio' scales. The fifth kind is his 'logarithmic

* Stevens (1946).

interval scale'.* He does not claim that these five kinds exhaust all possibilities. Indeed, he examines some other suggestions. But he does evidently consider that all scales in common use fall into one or other of the first four categories. It is not proposed to examine other possibilities here. For my immediate aim is to clarify Stevens' notion of scale form, and as no examples of logarithmic interval or other kinds of scales are given, such an examination would be beside the point.

In Stevens' view, 'measurement [is] the assignment of numerical to objects or events according to rule—any rule'.† Hence, even the numbering of football players is a rudimentary form of measurement. The rule is that each player in a given team must be assigned one and only one numeral, but no two players may be assigned the same numeral. It is perhaps somewhat strange to call this measurement. Certainly nothing other than sameness and difference could be said to be measured by this procedure. But, as we have seen, there is some point in extending the meaning of the word 'measurement', and hence of the word 'scale' to include this and similar cases.

For this discussion, the important point about the numbering of football players is that it does not matter in which order the numbering is carried out. So that if numerals are assigned to the various players of a given team according to the above rule, they may be permuted in any way we please, and we will still have a satisfactory numbering of the players. Hence, if we agree to say that the players are numbered on a certain scale, then this scale may be subject to any permutation transformation, and the purpose of the scale will still be served. That is, the scale form remains invariant under any permutation transformation. Stevens calls scales of this kind 'nominal scales'.

Ordinal scales are one stage richer than nominal scales. On such scales, the numerals not only serve as distinguishing marks, they indicate an order. Typical of this class is Mohs' hardness scale, where numerals are assigned to substances in such a way that if these substances are arranged in order of hardness they are also arranged in the order of the assigned numerals. Now, if we assume that this is the only purpose of our hardness scale, it follows that any order-preserving transformation will leave the scale form

* Stevens (1959), p. 31. † *Ibid.* p. 19.

intact. That is, hardness values may be transformed by any strictly monotonic increasing function. Ordinal scales, then, are characterized by functions of this kind.

Linear interval scales are so called because they may be subject to any order-preserving and interval-preserving transformation. And the only kind of transformation having these characteristics is a linear one of the form:

$$y = mx + c,$$

where $m > 0$.* As examples, he gives our date scales and the two temperature scales, Centigrade and Fahrenheit.

But now doubt begins to arise concerning Stevens' criterion for invariance of scale form. Why has he classified our Centigrade and Fahrenheit scales of temperature as linear interval scales? It is true that to convert Centigrade to Fahrenheit or vice versa we must transform by a linear function of the prescribed kind. But this does not show that they are linear interval scales in his sense. It only shows that they are linear with respect to each other. To show, by his criterion, that they are linear interval scales, he must show that the purposes of these scales could not be served by a scale which is non-linear with respect to either, for example Dalton's 'logarithmic' scale.† But what purposes could not be served by such a scale? What information do we fail to give if we give our measurements in °Daltonian instead of in ° C. or ° F.? What predictions could we not make? What laws could we not express?

Let us construct a scale of temperature by supposing that for a given mass of a perfect gas, $T = k \log V$. We are, as we shall see, free to make such an assumption since temperature is only associatively measurable.‡ Could we not use this scale for all of the

* For a proof of this, see appendix II.

† On Dalton's theory of temperature, the caloric or heat stuff occupies the spaces between the atoms and forces them apart. The temperature of an object is then the pressure of the caloric, and the heat capacity is the volume within which the caloric is compressed, that is, the volume of the interatomic space. Hence, since the change of volume which a substance undergoes is entirely due to the separation of the atoms, the change of volume must be proportional to the change of heat capacity. Hence, if the change of volume is proportional to the quantity of heat supplied (as is verified by calorimetry), the relationship between temperature and volume cannot be linear. Dalton supposed that the relationship should be of the form: $T = K(1 + (\Delta V/V))$. On the Centigrade and Fahrenheit scales it is assumed that: $T = K\Delta V$. For a further discussion of Dalton's scale, see appendix I, § 12.

‡ See ch. VI.

purposes of our Centigrade and Fahrenheit scales? Could we not calculate the resulting temperature in a calorimetric mixing experiment? Certainly. The method of calculation would not be the usual one. But what does this matter? Could we, using such a scale, have discovered the gas law of Gay-Lussac? Certainly. The form of this law would not be the usual one. It would be found empirically that $pV = Re^T$ (instead of $pV = RT$). But again, what does this matter? Isn't exactly the same information contained in both expressions? Finally, could we explain such a law on the kinetic theory? Yes, of course we could. We should have to assume that temperature is $\log(\overline{K.E.})$, instead of $\overline{K.E.}$ But what would be wrong with that? Our only reason for assuming that the temperature of a substance is the average kinetic energy of its molecules is that it enables us to explain the temperature laws that we have discovered using our ordinary temperature scales.

Stevens' use of his criterion for sameness of scale form is even more puzzling when he comes to his ratio scales. The defining characteristic of these scales is that they may only be subject to a transformation which is at once order, interval and ratio preserving. And the only kind of transformation which satisfies these conditions is one of the form:

$$y = mx$$

where $m > 0$. Hence ratio scales may only be subject to what he calls 'similarity' transformations.

As examples he cites our common scales of length, mass, time-interval, and other fundamentally measurable quantities. He also mentions our Absolute scale of temperature. We shall see later that it is possible to construct alternative scales for the fundamentally measurable quantities, which are *non-linear* with respect to our ordinary scales, and which may serve all of their purposes. We may even do this by fundamental measurement—by using an alternative fundamental measuring procedure.* Hence even our common scales of mass, length, and time-interval do not appear to be ratio scales by Stevens' criterion. They appear to be merely ordinal scales—or at best logarithmic interval scales; that is scales which may only be transformed by functions of the form:

$$y = mx^n \quad (m > 0, \quad n \neq 0).$$

* See ch. v.

But the really puzzling example is the Absolute temperature scale. I can see no good reasons other than reasons of mathematical simplicity why we should not transform our Absolute scale of temperature by any monotonic increasing function. Measurements on a new scale produced by any such transformation *must* contain exactly the same information as those on our original scale. The only reason that I can see which might be offered is not a valid one. It might be argued that if a scale is a ratio scale then we cannot arbitrarily change its zero. (This follows from the definition.) And if we assume that there are no other kinds of scales than the four which we have so far discussed, then from the fact that we cannot change the zero of a given scale without change of scale form, it follows that this scale is a ratio scale. Now, since we cannot change the zero of our Absolute scale of temperature and still have an Absolute scale, (that is a scale with the same zero as our Absolute scale), it might be thought to follow that our Absolute scale is a ratio scale.

But this argument is unsound. In the first place, there may be scales other than ratio scales which have fixed zeros. Stevens himself admits this possibility, and he in fact defines one such class of scales, namely, logarithmic interval scales. But even if we assume that there are no non-ratio scales with fixed zeros, the argument is invalid. For it conceals the false assumption that absolute scales (small 'a') have a peculiar job to do, a job which cannot be done by a scale of any other kind.

The fallacy of this argument can best be brought out by considering an analogous argument. Let us agree to call any scale of temperature on which the temperature interval between the ice point and the boiling point of water is 100° a 'centigrade' scale (written with a small 'c'). Then our ordinary Centigrade scale (capital 'C') is a centigrade scale. Now obviously our Centigrade scale may be transformed by any monotonic increasing function f, such that $f(100) - f(0) = 100$, and we shall still have a centigrade scale. But no other kind of transformation is permissible. Now, of course, it does not follow from this that our Centigrade scale has a unique and peculiar scale form. This would only be the case if there were some unique function which centigrade scales (small 'c') fulfilled.

Returning to the original argument, we may admit that only a transformation of our Absolute scale of temperature by some monotonic increasing function, f, such that $f(o) = o$, will yield another absolute scale, that is a scale on which the numeral 'o' is assigned to the lowest theoretically attainable heat state. But unless there is some special role which only absolute scales can play, it does not follow that transformation by other kinds of functions will alter the scale form. Much less does it follow that the Absolute scale is a ratio scale.

Now I am not sure that this fairly represents Stevens' reasoning, since he simply makes the classification as though the reason for it were self-evident. He does indicate that he accepts the presence of a fixed zero as a 'sure sign' that a scale is a ratio scale.* Moreover, he does say that ratio scales contain 'more information' than other kinds of scales. But the rest is guesswork. As we shall see, he may have had much better reasons than the ones that I have suggested. But if so, they need to be stated explicitly, and in much less ambiguous language.

Coombs' system of classification of scales is similar to Stevens', and by most writers it is considered to be merely a refinement of Stevens' system. For he too distinguishes nominal, ordinal, interval and ratio scales, although within some of these general classes, he distinguishes certain subclasses (for example nominal-interval and ordinal-interval scales). Yet, prima facie, Coombs' criteria for classification are different from Stevens', and it is not clear that the words 'nominal', 'ordinal', 'interval' and 'ratio' mean the same thing for the two authors. For Coombs proposes that we should classify our scales according to the kinds of applications of arithmetic they represent—saying nothing about scale transformations, or the preservation of scale form. According to Coombs, a *nominal scale* is any scale on which *only* arithmetical formulae of the form

$$a \gneqq b \tag{1}$$

have any analytic application. A scale designed for the numbering of football players is thus a nominal scale if the method of numerical assignment is such that the same number must always be assigned to the same player, and different numbers must always be assigned to different players.

---

* Stevens (1946).

An *ordinal scale* is any on which only arithmetical formulae of the form

$$a \gtreqless b \tag{2}$$

have an analytic application. An obvious example of such a scale is Mohs' hardness scale. For on this scale, the rules for numerical assignment are such that a substance A whose hardness is a will scratch and not be scratched by a substance B whose hardness is b if and only if $a > b$; while A will scratch and be scratched by B if and only if $a = b$.

An *interval scale*, according to Coombs, is any scale on which at least the following classes of arithmetical formulae have an analytic interpretation

$$a \gtreqless b \tag{3a}$$

$$|a-b| \gneqq |c-d|, \tag{3b}$$

but on which those of the form

$$a \gneqq nb \quad (n \text{ being any rational number}) \tag{3c}$$

have no such interpretation. In the case where only $(3a)$ and $(3b)$ are thus applied we have what he calls a *nominal-interval scale*; and in the case where formulae of the class

$$|a-b| \gtreqless |c-d| \tag{3d}$$

also have an analytic application, we have an *ordinal-interval scale*. Coombs' *ordered metric scale** is as Stevens clearly shows †simply an incomplete ordinal-interval scale.

Examples of ordinal-interval scales are fairly common. Our date scales (for example Jewish and Christian Calendars) are ordinal-interval scales according to Coombs' classification. For on these scales, it is evident that while arithmetical formulae of the class $(3a)$ may be analytically applied in terms of our time-ordering relationships (later than, at the same time as, earlier than), those of the class $(3d)$ may be analytically interpreted in terms of our *time-interval* ordering relationships (longer than, as long as, shorter than).

Finally, a ratio scale, according to Coombs, is any scale on which it is not only possible to interpret analytically arithmetical formulae of the classes $(3a)$ and $(3d)$, it is also possible to interpret arithmetical formulae of the form $(3c)$. Our ordinary scales of mass, length, and time-interval may be taken as examples.

---

* Coombs (1950).   † Stevens (1959), pp. 34–6.

Coombs thus appears to have achieved a system of classification remarkably similar to Stevens', even though his criteria for classification seem to be very different. However, the difference may be more apparent than real. For it may be (although the point is never made explicit) that when Stevens spoke of the purpose or function of a scale he had in mind simply the kind of application of arithmetic which it represents. If so, then Stevens' criterion for invariance of scale form under scale transformation may be formulated:

(C. 1) If a scale X is transformed into a scale Y, then Y has the same scale form as X if and only if propositions belonging to the same classes of arithmetical formulae may be interpreted in the same way on both X and Y—those formulae which are theorems yielding analytic statements under the given interpretations, and those which contradict theorems yielding self-contradictory statements.

Applying this criterion, we see that a nominal scale on Coombs' classification is necessarily a nominal scale on Stevens'. For if there is to be no change of scale form under scale transformation, we require only that the transformation function f be such that:

$$f(a) \gtreqqless f(b) \quad \text{according as } a \gtreqqless b.$$

That is, f may be any single-valued function with a single-valued inverse. (Permutation transformations are an important subclass of such transformations.)

Ordinal scales (Coombs' classification) are necessarily ordinal scales on Stevens' classification. For here we only require that:

$$f(a) \gtreqqless f(b) \quad \text{according as } a \gtreqqless b.$$

And this condition restricts f to the class of strictly monotonic increasing functions.

Again, both kinds of interval scales (Coombs' classification) turn out to be simply linear interval scales on Stevens' classification. For if we attempt to solve for the class of functions f which satisfy the following conditions

(i) $\qquad\qquad f(a) \gtreqqless f(b) \quad \text{according as } \quad a \gtreqqless b,$

(ii) $|f(a)-f(b)| \gtreqqless |f(c)-f(d)| \quad \text{according as} \quad |a-b| \gtreqqless |c-d|,$

we find that f is restricted to the class of linear increasing functions.[*] The additional stipulation that:

(iii) $|f(a)-f(b)| \gtreqqless |f(c)-f(d)| \quad \text{according as} \quad |a-b| \gtreqqless |c-d|$

[*] See appendix II.

imposes no further restriction.* Hence, both nominal-interval and ordinal-interval scales must be classified simply as linear interval scales in Stevens' system. The same is true of Coombs' ordered metric scale.

Finally, any scale which is a ratio scale in Coombs' classification is necessarily a ratio scale in Stevens'. For the additional requirement that:

$$f(a) \gtreqqless nf(b) \quad \text{according as} \quad a \gtreqqless nb$$

immediately restricts f to the class of similarity functions.

Consequently, if we adopt the criterion (C. 1) for invariance of scale form, then Stevens' classification system is readily derivable from Coombs'. Moreover, it immediately removes some of the difficulties we felt with Stevens' classification of the Absolute scale of temperature as a ratio scale. For this scale is based upon the formula for calculating the efficiency of a perfectly reversible heat engine, namely

$$e = \frac{T_1 - T_2}{T_1},$$

where T_1 is the temperature of the source, and T_2 is the temperature of the sink. If this relationship is taken to be an analytic one (thus defining a scale of temperature) then we have that the following classes of arithmetical formulae are analytically applied

$$a \gtreqqless b, \tag{4a}$$

$$\frac{a-b}{a} \gtreqqless e \quad (0 < e < 1). \tag{4b}$$

Then, if we solve to find the class of functions f such that:

(i) $f(a) \gtreqqless f(b)$ according as $a \gtreqqless b$,

(ii) $\dfrac{f(a) - f(b)}{f(a)} \gtreqqless e$ according as $\dfrac{a-b}{a} \gtreqqless e$,

we find that f can only be a similarity function. Hence, the scale must be classified as a ratio scale. The fact that the scale is not a ratio scale on Coombs' classification (since, for example, there is no analytic application for formulae of the class $(3d)$) is irrelevant. The words 'nominal', 'ordinal', 'interval' and 'ratio' do not indeed mean the same thing for the two authors.

---

* See appendix II.

We conclude, then, that despite the apparent differences in approach, the two classification systems are very closely related, provided that (C. 1) is adopted as a criterion for invariance of scale form. It is unfortunate that the relationship between the two systems has not been clearly understood. Nominal-interval and ordered metric scales do not belong 'midway between' ordinal and linear-interval scales (on Stevens' classification). They are simply linear-interval scales.

One final point. The concept of a ratio scale (Stevens' classification) does not preclude the possibility mutually dissimilar ratio scales for the measurement of the one quantity (that is ratio scales that are not related to each other by similarity transformations). To say that a given scale X is a ratio scale for the measurement of a given quantity q, is to say that X cannot be transformed into another scale X^1 for the measurement of the same quantity without change of scale form, unless X and X^1 are related by a similarity transformation. But this does not imply that there is no other scale Y for the measurement of q, which is dissimilar to X, and which is nevertheless a ratio scale. For the fact that X and Y are both ratio scales according to the criterion (C. 1) for invariance of scale form does not entail that X and Y are similar to each other.

A similar point has already been made concerning our temperature scales, Centigrade and Fahrenheit. The fact that these scales are linear with respect to each other tells us nothing whatever about their scale forms. Likewise, even if we know that our Centigrade and Fahrenheit scales are both linear-interval scales, it does not follow from this alone, that our Centigrade and Fahrenheit scales are linear with respect to each other. For this requires the additional information that the same classes of arithmetical formulae are analytically applied in the same way on both of these scales.

In the following chapter, we shall see in detail how mutually dissimilar ratio scales for the measurement of the same quantity can in fact be constructed.

5-2

C

The appropriateness of statistics

If Stevens' claims concerning his classification system are justified, then from a knowledge of the kind of scale used in obtaining a given set of measurements, we can say what sorts of statistical procedures are appropriate for the assessment of these results. It seems, however, that Stevens' criteria are not sufficiently restrictive, and that if a satisfactory solution to the general problem of the appropriateness of statistics is to be provided, somewhat more stringent criteria must be given.

Let x_1, x_2, ..., x_n be a set of results obtained on a scale X for the measurement of a given quantity q. Let us suppose that these results are all obtained by making measurements on the same particular under the same conditions. Our problem is to estimate what we may term the 'true' measure of q on X, and to indicate the range of likely error in this estimation. For this purpose, two kinds of statistical procedures are recognized—parametric and nonparametric. Non-parametric procedures, roughly speaking, are procedures which rely upon counting heads. For example, we may simply take the median, or the most frequently obtained result (that is the mode) to be our estimate of the true measure of q on X. Parametric procedures, on the other hand, take the actual numerical assignments directly into account, and our estimate of the true measure of q on X is formed by subjecting these results to some mathematical averaging procedure. If $\bar{x}_{(n)}$ is our estimate of the true measure of q on X, then

$$\bar{x}_{(n)} = A_{(n)}(x_1, x_2, ..., x_n), \tag{5}$$

where $A_{(n)}$ is a mathematical averaging function. What I have to say here concerns only the use of parametric techniques.

To my knowledge, no one has attempted to characterize mathematical averaging functions generally. But at least we should suppose that $A_{(n)}$ must be one of a sequence of functions

$$A_{(2)}, A_{(3)}, A_{(4)}, ..., \quad \text{of } 2, 3, 4, ...,$$

arguments respectively, each of which possesses the following characteristics.

(i) If x_i and x_j are the lowest and highest respectively of the n results obtained, then

$$x_i \leqq A_{(n)}(x_1, x_2, ..., x_n) \leqq x_j$$

($\bar{x}_{(n)}$ is thus confined to the range defined by the extreme results).

(ii) $A_{(n)}(x_1, x_2, ..., x_n)$ must be strictly monotonic increasing in each argument.

(iii) $A_{(n)}(x_1, x_2, ..., x_n)$ must be commutative with respect to each pair of arguments, that is

$$A_{(n)}(x_1, x_2, ... x_i ... x_j ... x_n) = A_{(n)}(x_1, x_2, ... x_j ... x_i ... x_n)$$
$$(i, j = 1, 2, ..., n, \quad i \neq j).$$

(This condition ensures that the order in which the results are taken is irrelevant.)

(iv) $x_{n+1} \gtreqless A_{(n+1)}(x_1, x_2, ..., x_{n+1}) \gtreqless A_{(n)}(x_1, x_2, ..., x_n)$

according as $\quad x_{n+1} \gtreqless A_{(n)}(x_1, x_2, ..., x_n).$

A function will here be described as *a mathematical averaging function* if and only if it satisfies the above four conditions.

Now, a sequence of mathematical averaging functions can always be generated from a single-valued function $f_{(2)}$ of two variables, which is defined for all values of these variables within some specified domain R, and which satisfies the following conditions for all values of these variables in R

(ia) $f_{(2)}(x_1, x_2)$ is strictly monotonic increasing in each argument.

(ii$a$) $f_{(2)}(x_1, x_2) = f_{(2)}(x_2, x_1).$

(iii$a$) $f_{(2)}[x_1, f_{(2)}(x_2, x_3)] = f_{(2)}[f_{(2)}(x_1, x_2), x_3] = {}_{df}f_{(3)}(x_1, x_2, x_3).$

Then finally, if

$$f_{(n)}(x_1, x_2, ..., x_n) = {}_{df}f_{(2)}[f_{(n-1)}(x_1, x_2, ..., x_{n-1}), x_n],$$

we require that there should be a unique $\bar{x}_{(n)}$ such that

(iv$a$) $f_{(n)}(\bar{x}_{(n)}, \bar{x}_{(n)}, ..., \bar{x}_{(n)}) = f_{(n)}(x_1, x_2, ..., x_n).$

Let $A_{(n)}(x_1, x_2, ..., x_n)$ be the function such that:

$$A_{(n)}(x_1, x_2, ..., x_n) = \bar{x}_{(n)}.$$

Then $A_{(n)}$ is the required mathematical averaging function.* The

---

* The proof that A_n satisfies the conditions (i)–(iv) is contained in appendix III.

function $f_{(2)}$ may be described as the *generating function* for $A_{(n)}$. To illustrate this, consider the following generating functions

(i) $f(x, y) = x + y$ (x and y real).

This generates the following mathematical averaging function

$$A_{(n)}(x_1, x_2, ..., x_n) = \frac{1}{n} \sum_{i=1}^{n} (x_i) \qquad (6a)$$

that is *the arithmetical mean*.

(ii) $f(x, y) = xy$ ($x > 0$ and $y > 0$).

The corresponding mathematical averaging function is

$$A_{(n)}(x_1, x_2, ..., x_n) = \left[\prod_{i=1}^{n} (x_i) \right]^{\frac{1}{n}} \qquad (6b)$$

that is *the geometric mean*.

(iii) $f(x, y) = x^2 + y^2$ ($x > 0$, $y > 0$).

In this case, the mathematical averaging function generated is

$$A_{(n)}(x_1, x_2, ..., x_n) = \left[\frac{1}{n} \sum_{i=1}^{n} x_i^2 \right]^{\frac{1}{2}} \qquad (6c)$$

that is *the root mean square*.

(iv) $f(x, y) = \frac{1}{x} + \frac{1}{y}$ ($x > 0$, $y > 0$).

This generates

$$A_{(n)}(x_1, x_2, ..., x_n) = \left[\frac{1}{n} \sum_{i=1}^{n} (x_i^{-1}) \right]^{-1} \qquad (6d)$$

that is *the harmonic mean*.

(v) $f(x, y) = e^x + e^y$ (x and y real).

In this case the corresponding mathematical averaging function has no accepted name. But it is defined by the formula:

$$A_{(n)}(x_1, x_2, ..., x_n) = \ln \left[\frac{1}{n} \sum_{i=1}^{n} e^{xi} \right]. \qquad (6e)$$

But these are only five of infinitely many generating functions, and hence of infinitely many mathematical averaging techniques. Indeed, for all $m \neq 0$,

$$f(x, y) = x^m + y^m \quad (x > 0, y > 0),$$

$f(x, y)$ is a generating function. And, to each there corresponds a unique mathematical averaging function. Hence there arises a genuine problem of choice. Why should we choose one procedure, rather than any other for estimating the true measure of q on X?

It is true that if we select a technique for measuring the spread or deviation of a given set of results from a given mean (for example calculating the R.M.S. deviation), and demand that our technique for estimating the mean be such as to minimize this deviation, then a mathematical averaging procedure may be determined. That is, for a given mathematical averaging procedure for determining the deviation there may correspond a unique procedure for determining the mean, and vice versa. In this sense, the arithmetical mean and the R.M.S. deviation are correlative techniques. But this does nothing to remove the problem. For why should we choose one set of correlative techniques rather than any other? There are, after all, infinitely many such sets of correlative techniques.

It was to this problem that Stevens directed his attention. And it is to his great credit that the answer he gave was non-circular. He did not, of course, claim to provide a complete answer to the problem. But he did have one very useful suggestion. He suggested that if a scale X may be transformed by a function ϕ to a scale Y without change of scale form, then if $\bar{x}_{(n)}$ is our estimate of the mean on X, $\phi(\bar{x}_{(n)})$ should be our estimate of the mean on Y, even when the individual results $x_1, x_2, ..., x_n$ are transformed first by the function ϕ. That is, $A_{(n)}$ must be such that

$$\phi(\bar{x}_{(n)}) = A_{(n)}[\phi(x_1), \phi(x_2), ..., \phi(x_n)]. \tag{7}$$

In the case of a ratio scale, for example, we should require that:

$$c\bar{x}_{(n)} = A_{(n)}(cx_1, cx_2, ..., cx_n), \tag{8}$$

for all $c > 0$. Hence, $(6a)$ to $(6d)$ are all permissible averaging functions for measurements made on ratio scales. But $(6e)$ is not permissible, since condition (8) is not satisfied.

In the case of a linear interval scale, we should require that:

$$m\bar{x}_{(n)} + c = A_{(n)}[(mx_1 + c), (mx_2 + c), ..., (mx_n + c)], \tag{9}$$

for all $m > 0$ and $c \neq 0$. And, of the averaging procedures listed, this leaves only the arithmetical mean. (Of course, this is not to say that the arithmetical mean is the only one permissible by this criterion.)

The power of Stevens' criterion for the appropriateness of statistics is evident. And its use is well justified on grounds of convenience. Nevertheless, it still leaves an extremely wide area of choice, and hence it would be useful to have some more stringent criterion.

With this end in view, we may make the following suggestion. Suppose that a given scale X for the measurement of a quantity q is additive, that is that there is a physical interpretation for the arithmetic operation of addition, when performed on measurements obtained on X. Let x_1, x_2, ..., x_n be a set of results obtained on X by making measurements on a particular object A under certain conditions. Let x'_1, x'_2, ..., x'_n be another set of results also obtained on X on some other object B under the same conditions. Let O be the physical addition operation, and let $O(A, B)$ signify the system which results from performing this operation on A and B. Then if $\bar{x}_{(n)}$ and $\bar{x}'_{(n)}$ are the respective means of the two sets of results, we should expect the measure of $O(A, B)$ in q to be given by $\bar{x}_{(n)} + \bar{x}'_{(n)}$. But we should also expect to get this same result by taking the mean of

$$(x_1 + x'_1), (x_2 + x'_2), ..., (x_n + x'_n).$$

At least, it would be very convenient if this were so. Hence, we might demand that our mathematical averaging procedure be such that:

$$\bar{x}_{(n)} + \bar{x}'_{(n)} = A_{(n)}[(x_1 + x'_1), (x_2 + x'_2), ..., (x_n + x'_n)]. \quad (10)$$

And this additional demand immediately eliminates the procedures $(6b)$, $(6c)$ and $(6d)$. Of those procedures listed, only $(6a)$ remains as an appropriate one.

Generalizing this, we might demand that if some arithmetical operation f has some physical interpretation on a given scale, then the chosen A_n must be such that:

$$f(\bar{x}_{(n)}, \bar{x}'_{(n)}) = A_{(n)}[f(x_1, x'_1), f(x_2, x'_2), ..., f(x_n, x'_n)]. \quad (11)$$

Hence, if the scale is multiplicative, $(6b)$ is an appropriate statistic, while $(6a)$ and $(6c)$–$(6e)$ are ruled out as inappropriate. Indeed, it seems (although I have no proof) if f is in fact a generating function, an appropriate statistic for a scale on which f has some physical interpretation can always be found by the procedure described on p. 69.

However, it is doubtful whether this criterion or Stevens' is really satisfactory. For grounds of convenience are not everything. Suppose I have a spring balance calibrated for measuring the weight of an object in dynes, and that the spring is peculiar in that the calibration marks are spaced thus:

Should we, even so, use the arithmetical mean and the R.M.S. deviation to assess the results of a set of measurements made on a given object using this balance? There is no doubt that the dyne scale is a ratio scale, and that these statistics would be considered appropriate by Stevens' criterion. But because of the distribution of scale markings, our errors of excess are likely to be considerably larger than our errors of deficiency (relative to those obtained on an ordinary balance), and, consequently, the calculated mean is likely to be considerably higher than it would be if an ordinary spring balance had been used instead. It seems reasonable, therefore, that in assessing these results, we should choose statistical procedures which give relatively greater weight to errors of deficiency, even if these procedures would be judged to be inappropriate by the above criteria.

CHAPTER V

FUNDAMENTAL MEASUREMENT

All measurement ultimately depends on certain basic forms of measurement. If, for example, we can measure length, then we can measure volume; and if we can measure volume, we can measure temperature. But length measurement need not depend on anything else. Like mass, time-interval, electrical resistance and potential difference, length may be measured directly. Now in fact, the procedures for measuring these and other quantities directly are formally analogous to one another; and accordingly we say that they are all samples of a particular kind of direct measurement. Following Campbell, we call such measurement *fundamental measurement*, and the procedures *fundamental measuring procedures*.

Our immediate problem is to describe fundamental measuring procedures in general terms, and to state the conditions for the possibility of fundamental measurement. When this is done, it will be seen that there are certain basic problems concerning fundamental measurement that need to be discussed.

A

Conditions for the possibility of fundamental measurement

There are two general conditions for the possibility of measuring a quantity p fundamentally.

First there must be criteria for quantitative equality and inequality of p which do not depend on prior measurement. That is, the relationships 'greater in p than', 'equal in p to' and 'less in p than' must be determinable independently of any measuring procedure. Let us signify these relationships by $>_p$, $=_p$ and $<_p$ respectively.

Secondly, there must be some operation O for combining any two systems S_1 and T_1 possessing p to form a composite system $O(S_1, T_1)$ which also possesses p. This operation must be such that

(i) $O(S_1, T_1) =_p O(S_2, T_2) =_p O(T_2, S_2)$

where $\qquad\qquad S_1 =_p S_2 \quad$ and $\quad T_1 =_p T_2$.

(ii) $O(S_1, T_1) >_p S_1$.

(iii) $O(O(S_1, T_1), U_1) =_p O(S_1, O(T_1, U_1))$.

(iv) If $S_1, S_2, S_3, \ldots$, is any set of systems equal in p, and T is any other finite system possessing p such that $S_1 <_p T$, then there is a number n such that if the systems $S_1, S_2, S_3, \ldots, S_n$ are combined successively by the operation O, the composite system thus formed is greater in p than T (Archimedean postulate).

These axioms are necessary conditions for the possibility of fundamental measurement. They are not alone sufficient, however. If fundamental measurement is to be possible, the universe must be sufficiently rich in objects possessing p, and bearing fixed p-relationships to each other, to enable us to construct what I shall presently call an extended system of standards, sufficiently refined to enable us to match any object in the universe which possesses p in this respect. If there are any objects which cannot be so matched, then our scale is only a partial scale. With this proviso, the axiom system is at least as powerful as that of Suppes;* for it takes care of both of the shortcomings which Suppes has noted in previous systems.† The relationships $>_p$, $=_p$, and $<_p$ have been independently axiomatized (ch. II), and the system is no stronger than it needs to be.

In view of the condition (iii), let us agree to signify the system which results from the successive combination by O of any systems, $S, T, U, \ldots$, by the expression $O(S, T, U, \ldots)$. Then, in view of (ii), we may express the last condition by saying that if

$$S_1 =_p S_2 =_p S_3 =_p S_4 \ldots,$$

and $\qquad\qquad S_1 <_p T,$

then there exists an N such that for all

$$n > N, \quad O(S_1, S_2, S_3, \ldots, S_n) >_p T.$$

In the case of length, the first of these conditions is satisfied by criteria involving overlap. We can say that two things A and B are equal in length, if A covers B without overlap, and vice versa. And the usual fundamental measuring operation O is simply that of

* Suppes (1951). † Hölder (1901).

placing things end to end. In the case of mass, the first condition is satisfied since we can decide whether two things A and B are equal in mass or not by comparison on a beam balance, and the second condition is satisfied by the operation of lumping together.

Consider now the quantity, potential difference. The first condition is satisfied since we can decide whether two batteries produce the same potential difference by connecting them into a circuit anode to anode and cathode to cathode, and using some instrument (for example a galvanometer) to detect whether there is any current flow. Further, we can decide which of the two batteries produces the greater potential difference by noting the direction of the current flow, that is by noting which way the galvanometer needle is deflected. (There is no need for us to be able to measure the current flow, we only need criteria for saying in which direction it is flowing.) The second condition is also satisfied since the operation of connecting the batteries in series anode to cathode is an operation of the required kind. Consequently, potential difference is a quantity which can be measured fundamentally.

The same is true of many other quantities. Electrical resistance, for example, can be measured fundamentally using a Wheatstone's Bridge apparatus. Force can be measured fundamentally and, no doubt, there are other quantities which could be added to this list.

Supposing then that the two general conditions on p. 75 are satisfied, let us see how, in detail, a scale for the measurement of p may be set up. The first step is to construct a system of standards. For this purpose, some system S_1, (usually a system having a relatively stable position in the order of p), is chosen as an initial standard. Another system $S_1' =_p S_1$ is found, and the composite system $O(S_1, S_1')$ is formed. This, or any system S_2 such that

$$S_2 =_p O(S_1, S_1')$$

may then be said to form a second member of the standard set. A third member may then be defined as any system S_3 such that

$$S_3 =_p O(S_2, S_1).$$

Similarly, $$S_4 =_p O(S_3, S_1)$$

and so on. In this way a sequence of standards $S_1, S_2, S_3, S_4, \ldots$, increasing in the order of p may be established. We shall call such a set a *standard set*. Besides this standard set, a *standard subset* is also needed. This may be constructed by finding two systems $S_{\frac{1}{2}}$ and $S'_{\frac{1}{2}}$ such that

$$S_{\frac{1}{2}} =_p S'_{\frac{1}{2}}$$

and

$$O(S_{\frac{1}{2}}, S'_{\frac{1}{2}}) =_p S_1,$$

and then three systems $S_{\frac{1}{3}}$, $S'_{\frac{1}{3}}$, and $S''_{\frac{1}{3}}$ such that

$$S_{\frac{1}{3}} =_p S'_{\frac{1}{3}} =_p S''_{\frac{1}{3}},$$

and

$$O(S_{\frac{1}{3}}, S'_{\frac{1}{3}}, S''_{\frac{1}{3}}) =_p S_1$$

and so on. The set $S_1, S_{\frac{1}{2}}, S_{\frac{1}{3}}, S_{\frac{1}{4}}, \ldots$ thus constructed forms a sequence of standards decreasing in the order of p, and may be called a standard subset.

Such a standard set and subset together constitute what I call *a system of standards*. Now we have already noted that the systems which belong to a system of standards may be combined by O or successive applications of O to form various complex systems. If $S_i, S_j, S_k, \ldots$, are members of a system of standards, then these can be combined by O two at a time to form the complex systems $O(S_i, S_j), O(S_i, S_k), O(S_j, S_k), \ldots$. These complex systems can in turn be combined by O with $S_i, S_j, S_k, \ldots$, to form further systems, and so on. A system of standards can thus be extended indefinitely. Let us call the whole set *an extended system of standards*.

Now it is not difficult to demonstrate the following theorems concerning such an extended system of standards.*

(i) That it is everywhere dense with respect to the relations $>_p$ and $<_p$, that is if S_i and S_j are any two members of an extended system of standards such that $S_i <_p S_j$, then there exists another member S_k such that $S_i <_p S_k <_p S_j$.

(ii) That if $O(S_i, S_j, S_k, \ldots, S_r)$ and $O(_x, S_y, S_z, \ldots, S_w)$ are any two members of an extended system, then

$$O(S_i, S_j, S_k, \ldots, S_r) \gtreqqless_p O(S_x, S_y, S_z, \ldots, S_w)$$

according as

$$(i+j+k+\ldots r) \gtreqqless (x+y+z+\ldots w).$$

From the second of these theorems, it follows that we can place any member of an extended standard system in the order of p by a numerical subscript which is the sum of the subscripts of the

---

* See appendix IV.

standards from which it was constructed. We can therefore drop the cumbersome notation, and indicate a member of an extended standard system simply by the expression 'S_n', where n is any positive rational number.

From the first of these theorems, together with the condition (iv) on p. 75, it follows that if T is any system possessing p, we can locate the position of T in the order of p as accurately as we choose. For it follows from (iv) that there are members of the system of standards S_i and S_j such that $S_i <_p T <_p S_j$. Hence any system T possessing p may be matched in p by this procedure as well as we think necessary.

But a procedure for matching is still not a measuring procedure. To measure p we must make a numerical assignment. And for this we need a scale of p. In practice this is usually obtained by assigning the numeral n (or Cn, where C is a constant) to a member S_n of the extended standard system. But it is important to realize that there is no need to follow this practice—that there is an area of choice here. This assignment does, of course, have the advantage of making the scale additive in the sense that on such a scale arithmetical formulae of the form

$$a+b \gtreqqless c$$

may now be interpreted as:

$$O(S_a, S_b) \gtreqqless_p S_c.$$

And this is a very simple interpretation to handle. But it is not the only kind of numerical assignment which is possible; and it is not necessarily the simplest. To see this, consider the following *mathematical* problem. It is required to find a function f and a domain R such that for all x and y in R:

(i) $$f(x, y) = f(y, x).$$

(ii) $$f(x, y) > x.$$

(iii) $$f(x, f(y, z)) = f(f(x, y), z).$$

(iv) *If* $$f(x, x) =_{df} f^{(1)}(x, x),$$
$$f(f^{(1)}(x, x), x) =_{df} f^{(2)}(x, x),$$
$$f(f^{(2)}(x, x), x) =_{df} f^{(3)}(x, x),$$
$$f(f^{(3)}(x, x), x) =_{df} f^{(4)}(x, x), \quad \text{and so on.}$$

Then there is an N such that for all

$$n > N, \quad \text{and} \quad y > x,$$
$$f^{(n)}(x, x) > y.$$

Note that in this problem the conditions are formally analogous to the conditions (i)–(iv)* imposed on any fundamental measuring operation O. Hence any solution of this problem will provide us with an arithmetical interpretation of the physical operation O.

Now $\qquad f(x, y) = x + y \quad (x > 0 \quad \text{and} \quad y > 0)$ $\qquad$ (1)

is certainly one solution. Hence the operation O may be interpreted as the arithmetical operation of addition. But it is not the only solution.

$$f(x, y) = x . y \quad (x > 1 \quad \text{and} \quad y > 1) \qquad (2)$$

is also a solution. Therefore, we can just as well interpret the operation O as the arithmetical operation of multiplication, and make our numerical assignments accordingly.

$$f(x, y) = \sqrt{(x^2 + y^2)} \quad (x > 0 \quad \text{and} \quad y > 0) \qquad (3)$$

is yet another solution. And this would yield yet another kind of scale.

Let us see what a multiplicative scale would look like. Suppose we assign the numeral 2 to the initial standard. Then if the scale is multiplicative, the numeral 2^2 must be assigned to the second member of the standard set, the numeral 2^3 to the third member, 2^4 to the fourth member, and so on. Generally, if S_n is any arbitrary member of the extended standard system, it must be assigned the numeral 2^n. Now such a scale would look very queer. For example, we should have to say that co-incident points were separated by unit distance. But who is to say that such a scale would not be advantageous in certain fields—lead to a simplification of the form of the laws relevant to those fields? This is not a matter than can be settled a priori.

Consider one last solution:

$$f(x, y) = (|\sqrt{x}| + |\sqrt{y}|) \quad (x > 0 \quad \text{and} \quad y > 0). \qquad (4)$$

In the corresponding scale we must simply assign the numeral n^2 to the member S_n of the extended standard system, thus yielding a scale which is, as it were, the square of our ordinary scale of p based upon the same initial standard. This kind of scale is of

* See p. 75.

special interest because it is not difficult to show how in the cases of length and force, scales like this may be constructed in another quite different way.

This is possible because at least for these two quantities there are alternative fundamental measuring operations. Consider the case of length. The normal fundamental measuring operation is that of placing objects end to end. But suppose instead we place them at right angles to one another. We can easily verify geometrically that this operation satisfies all of the conditions imposed upon fundamental measuring operations. Not only that, it satisfies every other axiom system that has ever been seriously canvassed—including the systems of Hölder, Menger and Suppes.

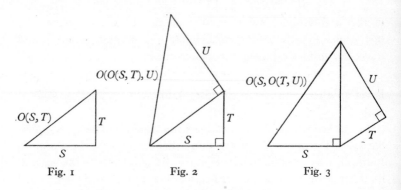

Fig. 1   Fig. 2   Fig. 3

For   (i) $O(S, T) =_l O(T, S)$ (see Fig. 1).

(ii) $O(S, T) >_l S$ (see Fig. 1).

(iii) $O(O(S, T), U) =_l O(S, O(T, U))$ (see Figs. 2 and 3).

And, of course, the fourth condition is also satisfied.

Now, if we take this 'right-angled addition' operation as our fundamental length measuring operation instead of the ordinary one, but start from the same initial standard, then we will obtain a scale which is, as it were, the square of our ordinary scale, provided that we adopt the usual procedure for correlating numerals with standards.

To illustrate this, suppose that we select some object as an initial standard, and let its length be 1 diagonal inch—a 'dinch' for short. And suppose that

$$1 \text{ dinch} = 1 \text{ inch}.$$

If we now combine two standard dinches by the right-angled addition procedure we shall obtain the second member of our standard set. And according to the usual practice in fundamental measurement we should say that its length is 2 dinches. But a line of length 2 dinches is the diagonal of a square of side 1 inch. Accordingly:

$$2 \text{ dinches} = \sqrt{2} \text{ inches.}$$

The third member of our standard set, a line of length 3 dinches is the diagonal of a rectangle of sides 2 inches and 1 inch. So

$$3 \text{ dinches} = \sqrt{3} \text{ inches.}$$

And, of course, generally

$$n \text{ dinches} = \sqrt{n} \text{ inches.}$$

Hence, to obtain measurements in dinches given measurements in inches, we must simply square the numbers concerned.

We are now in a position to state the two problems concerning fundamental measurement. The first is the problem of choice of fundamental measuring operation. What reasons may there be for choosing one fundamental measuring operation rather than another? The second is the problem of choice of principle of correlation.* We have seen that there are many different principles which we could use to correlate numerals with members of an extended standard system. Why should we choose one principle rather than another? What reasons, logical, theoretical or practical could there be for making a particular choice?

B

Two basic problems of fundamental measurement

The two problems of choice involved in fundamental measurement are, of course, very closely linked together. For to choose a fundamental scale for the measurement of any quantity, both of these choices have to be made. Consequently, they are both parts of the more general problem of choosing a scale, and the same considerations are likely to be relevant to both choices. I will proceed by considering the problem of choice of fundamental measuring operation.

* For a discussion of these two problems, see Ellis (1960).

Why should we choose the fundamental measuring operations that we do? The obvious answer that no one, except Campbell,* have ever suspected the existence of alternatives does not satisfy me. For this makes our choices look like historical accidents. In the case we have discussed, there can be no doubt that the ordinary length-measuring procedure is easier to follow. But can this be the only reason? If it is, then it certainly makes our length scale look very arbitrary. Grounds of convenience are not usually regarded as important. The mercury scale of temperature is easier to set up than the thermodynamic scale. But grounds of convenience are completely overruled by other grounds. However, if it is not a matter of convenience, what is it? What justifies our feeling that the kind of scale that we use is the only natural one, and that any other scale is forced and unnatural?

It may be, partly, that from childhood we have learned to estimate distances by procedures very like those used in ordinary fundamental length measurement. We estimate distances by counting the number of steps necessary to get from one place to another, by the number of telegraph poles, the number of city blocks, and so on. And the whole of our thinking about distance must to some extent be coloured by our upbringing. But this is only to explain our feeling, not to justify it.

Perhaps a satisfactory solution of this problem is to be found by considering the role of distance variables, in physical theory. If we change our scale to the diagonal one, we shall have to say that a body moving without friction on a smooth horizontal plane covers a distance proportional to the square of the time interval. We must also say that a freely falling body travels a distance proportional to the fourth power of the time-interval. In general, wherever r (the ordinary distance) appears as a variable in a physical equation, we must substitute $\sqrt{s}$ (where s is the diagonal distance); and it may be argued that this would complicate our physics. But this argument needs to be worked out in detail. I can see reason to suppose that in some fields of physics the use of the dinch or a similar diagonal scale would simplify our working. For if the rectangular co-ordinates of points were always given on dinch-type scales, the distance of any point from the origin would always be given the arithmetical sum of these co-ordinates—a somewhat

* Campbell (1920), ch. XII.

simpler relationship than the square root of the sum of the squares of the co-ordinates. However, whether this leads to simplification or not does not affect the argument. If it does not lead to simplification, and there are no other length-measuring procedures which do lead to simplification, then according to this argument our present length scale is justified by simplicity—not by the simplicity of the procedures used in setting up the scale, but by the mathematical simplicity of the laws involving distance which are expressed in terms of such a scale.

Now this, if it were true, would be an important conclusion. But as a justification it would not, I think, be acceptable to most people. For it would mean that if a dinch or any other kind of scale could simplify the mathematical form of physical laws involving distance variables, then such a scale should be adopted. Many people, I am sure, would say that such considerations of simplicity are irrelevant. They would say that we should adopt the kind of length scale we do no matter what mathematical simplicity could be achieved with the use of any other kind of scale. For they have at the back of their minds the belief that only our ordinary length scale reflects reality. They would insist that the notion of 'twice as long as' has a significance which is independent of measuring operations—a kind of absolute significance.

My own view, however, is that this is the only kind of justification that can be given. It seems to me that only reasons of mathematical simplicity can guide us in the choice of a fundamental scale. The only way that I can see of arguing against this conclusion is to challenge my description of fundamental measuring procedures. It could be argued that I have left out an essential element from my description, that the higher members of our standard sets must be literally composed of the lower members. Thus an object, the length of which is 2 inches, can be literally decomposed or split into two objects, the lengths of which are each 1 inch. An object, the mass of which is 2 grams, can be literally divided into two objects, the masses of which are each 1 gram, a process, the duration of which is 2 seconds, can be subdivided into two sub-processes, the durations of which are each 1 second, and so on. But an object, the length of which is 2 dinches, cannot be thus split up into two objects, the lengths of which are each 1 dinch. If I have two objects, the lengths of which are each 1 dinch, there is no way of uniting these two objects together so that I obtain an object of the same sort, the length of which is two dinches. If I join two straight rods at right angles, I no longer have a straight rod at all, but an L–shaped structure—although of course it is true that the distance between the extremities of such a structure is 2 dinches.

But we may surely question why such an addition to the description of fundamental measurement should be made. Sufficient conditions for the application of certain classes of arithmetical formulae have already been described. Any additional requirement can, therefore, only place restrictions on the way in which these formulae may be interpreted. And why should we make such restrictions? Unless compelling reasons can be given, we should allow scientists the maximum liberty in the application of arithmetic.

Furthermore, even if we add the requirement of literal divisibility to our description of fundamental measurement, we can still set up the dinch scale by an alternative fundamental measuring operation. So that one of the premisses of the argument is false. To set up the dinch scale, we need only choose an initial standard of a different shape from the usual straight rod. If we take a right-angled isosceles triangular-shaped object as our initial standard and agree to call the distance between the terminal points of the diagonal the length of such an object, then two such objects, each 1 dinch in length, can be literally combined to form a composite object of the same kind, the length of which is 2 dinches. Indeed, two such objects, the lengths of which are each n dinches can be combined by the same procedure to form a composite object of the same kind, the length of which is $2n$ dinches. Thus, the objects A and B may be combined in the following way:

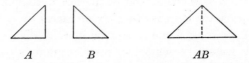

A B AB

The object AB will then be twice the length (on the diagonal scale) of the objects A and B. Hence, the premiss of the argument which I am attacking, namely that there is no way of literally joining together two objects, each of length 1 dinch, so as to form a composite object of the same sort, the length of which is 2 dinches, is false. This premiss seems plausible only if we assume that the objects with which fundamental length measurement is to be carried out must be of a certain sort, and must be literally joined together in a certain way. But why should we assume this? The arbitrariness of fundamental length measurement, which this argument seeks to remove, reappears in these assumptions. And so there is still a problem of choice of fundamental measuring operation.

Perhaps the basic reason why philosophers fail to recognize this problem is that they have a misconception of a unit. It is thought that if one object possesses a unit of a certain quantity and another object also possesses a unit of that quantity, then the two objects together must possess two units—just as, if one leopard has one spot, and another leopard has one spot, the two leopards together must have two spots. It is true that not all units are conceived in this way. The units of those quantities which Campbell calls 'qualities' and which Cohen and Nagel call 'intensive magnitudes' are thought of differently. But those of the so-called 'extensive magnitudes' have always been so regarded. Thus, it is thought that fundamental measurement is simply a matter of counting units. The notion of 'twice as much', when it is applied to such quantities, thus needs no explanation. To say that a given physical system is twice as great in q, where q is the name of a fundamentally measurable quantity, is according to this view, simply to say that it contains twice as many units of that quantity. Hence it is felt that there can be no room for ambiguity in statements of relative magnitude.

But units of length, for example, are not like spots on a leopard, or eggs in a basket. A physical object, or group of physical objects, cannot be said to contain so many units of length (inches, say) in the sense that a basket may be said to contain so many eggs. I can point to a part of a physical object and say that it is 1 inch long. But I cannot point to an inch, or say how long it is. I can say that a given physical object can be split up in a certain way so that I will obtain so many physical objects each 1 inch long. But I do not thereby obtain so many inches. And if I get, say, ten *things* each an inch long, it does not follow that the original object was 10 inches long. It depends how the splitting up was done. It may have been only 10 dinches long; or it may have had some other length. The trouble lies with the usual conception of units. If we think of unit names as referring to physical or quasi-physical objects (that is as things which can be counted), then we shall think that the number of such units in any physical system is pre-determined. We shall regard measurement as simply the determination of that number; and we shall consider, with Campbell, that the only arbitrary element in fundamental measurement lies in the choice of unit size.*

I conclude then that the two fundamental problems of choice involved in fundamental scaling can only be resolved satisfactorily by considering the roles of the various quantities in physical theory. If a new scale leads to a simplification of the mathematical form of physical equations, or to simpler working, then the new scale should be adopted whether or not it is additive. Only considerations of this sort of simplicity can have any bearing on the choice of fundamental measuring operation, or on the kind of correlation principle which we should adopt.

C

The choice of initial standard

We have seen that there are two fundamental problems of choice involved in setting up a fundamental scale. But behind these there lies an even more fundamental one. This is the problem of choice of initial standard. At first it may be thought that this is completely trivial, and that only considerations of convenience have any bearing here. But the choice of initial standard is by no means arbitrary and the reasons for choosing one kind of standard rather than another may not be simply reasons of convenience.

In discussing the nature of quantity we gave the conditions which must be satisfied before we can speak of one system being greater than, equal to or less than another in respect of some quantity p, But we did not discuss the conditions under which we can say that a given system changes or does not change in p. It might be suggested that we could arbitrarily select any system S_1, which possesses p, stipulate that S_1 is constant in p, and then refer all other systems to S_1 to determine whether or not they are

* For a full discussion of the concept of a unit, see ch. IX, A–C.

changing in p. But clearly this will not do. If S_1 is to be used as the initial standard for the fundamental measurement of p, then it must be possible to find (or construct) as many systems S_1', S_1'', S_1''' ... as we want, all equal in p to S_1 under certain specified conditions. It must also be possible to find (or construct) various members of an extended system of standards which are related to one another by fixed p relationships under these conditions. In other words, if S_1 (under the conditions c_1) is a possible initial standard for the fundamental measurement of p, then it must be possible to construct from S_1 a stable extended system of standards of sufficient richness to enable us to match any given object possessing p with sufficient precision. Conversely, if this is possible, then S_1 (under the conditions c_1) is a possible initial standard.

Now clearly, this will usually rule out many systems which possess p as possible initial standards. However, there may still be a wide area of choice. In practice, the choice appears to be relatively unimportant. Given two possible initial standards S_1 and S_2, the same fundamental measuring operation, and the same principle of correlation, then usually we get similar fundamental scales for the measurement of p. That is, the numerical assignments made on the one scale will be related to those made (on the same particulars under the same conditions) on the other scale by a constant multiplying factor. And hence we are faced with the kind of choice which Campbell described as the choice of 'unit size'. And this choice, it seems, is trivial.

However, we can easily imagine a world in which this choice would appear to be anything but trivial. Suppose, for example, that the world contained two sets of objects, A and B, such that the members of each of these sets always retained stable length (or mass, or volume etc....) relationships to each other, but that the length (or mass, or volume, etc....) relationship of any member of set A to any member of set B changed continually. Then it would clearly be of some importance whether a member of set A or a member of set B were chosen to act as an initial standard for the fundamental measurement of length (or mass, or volume, etc....). For depending on which choice we make, we would have to say that different things were changing or remaining the same. And this would obviously affect the form of our physical laws, and hence the complexity of our physics. In such a world, we could have two scales of length which at any instant are similar to one another, but which are, as it were, dynamic with respect to each other.

As in the case of the other problems of choice, it seems clear that the only reasons we could have for choosing between such relatively dynamic scales are reasons of formal simplicity. I can think of no other sorts of reasons which even appear to be relevant. A naïve realist may think that only one such scale could be the Real or True scale of, say, length. But then the only criteria which he could have for saying which scale is the True one would be criteria involving the formal simplicity of laws expressed with respect to such scales.

The possibility of relatively dynamic scales of fundamental measurement no doubt raises some important issues concerning units and dimensions. For if X_1 and Y_1 are two relatively dynamic scales for the fundamental measurement of some quantity q which are similar at any instant, then if x_1 is the result of any measurement on the scale X_1, and y_1 is the measure of the same particular under the same conditions made at the same time on the scale Y_1, then

$$x_1 = f(t)y_1$$

where t is the time (date) of the measurements. And hence it appears that the scale X_1 is dimensionally different from the scale Y_1. However, I do not propose to discuss relatively dynamic scales any further. My remarks in the following chapters are meant to apply only to relatively static scales.

D

Summary

In conclusion, let me summarize the central points in this chapter.

There are certain conditions for the possibility of fundamental measurement.

If these conditions are satisfied, then various kinds of applications of arithmetic are possible. Hence there arises the first problem of choice, namely which kind of application of arithmetic are we to make? I have called this the problem of choice of principle of correlation.

The conditions for the possibility of fundamental measurement may be satisfied in more than one way, that is there may be (and are in fact) alternative fundamental measuring operations for the same quantity. Hence there arises the problem of choice of fundamental measuring operation.

If fundamental measurement is possible, a class of relatively stable systems must exist. That is, there must be a subclass of the systems which possess p (the quantity to be measured), the members of which exhibit fixed p relationships to one another. But in general there may be more than one such subclass. Hence there arises the third fundamental problem—that of choice of initial standard.

The only considerations relevant to the solution of these problems are ones of formal simplicity. The best fundamental scale is the one which most simplifies the forms of the expressions of our laws of nature.

CHAPTER VI

ASSOCIATIVE MEASUREMENT: I

As illustrated by the case of temperature measurement

In our preliminary discussion of the classification of scales, we distinguished two forms of indirect measurement—associative and derived. Associative measurement was said to depend on there being some quantity p associated with the quantity q to be measured, such that when things are arranged in the order of p, under certain specified conditions, they are also arranged in the order of q. An associative scale for the measurement of q is then defined by taking $f(M_p)$ as the measure of q, where M_p is the measure of p on some previously defined scale, and f is any strictly monotonic increasing function.

Our problem now is to discuss what considerations should guide us first in the choice of p and secondly, in the choice of f. Following Mach,* we shall call these problems:

(i) the problem of choice of associated property p,

(ii) the problem of choice of principle of correlation.

To fix our ideas, we shall consider the special case of temperature measurement. Any quantity p associated with temperature in the above way will be called a *thermometric property*.

A

The choice of thermometric property

Objects can be arranged in a crude order of temperature without instrumental aids; the basic ordering relationships being 'feels hotter than', 'feels as hot as', and 'feels colder than'. But the order given by these relationships is extended and refined by our knowledge of what makes a body hotter or colder, and of the effects of heating and cooling. Consider: 'Today must have been colder than yesterday—there was ice on the ground', and 'The temperature of melting lead is less than that of melting aluminium, because lead melts before aluminium'.

* See appendix I.

Objects can also be arranged in more or less the same order in at least two ways by means of thermometric properties. The most straightforward of these is to arrange the objects in the order of some thermometric property p, taking care that the conditions under which p is a thermometric property are satisfied. If, for example, we have a number of pure gas samples whose masses are proportial to their molecular weights, and which exist at the same pressure, then to arrange them in order of temperature, we need only arrange them in order of volume; for under these conditions, volume is a thermometric property. But the conditions under which a given property p is a thermometric property for a given set of objects are seldom realized in nature, and less straightforward methods must be used.

The most common method is to use what we call a thermometer. For this, we select some particular object T which possesses a quantity p, which may serve as a thermometric property for the objects under consideration: (*a*) when T is placed in contact with these objects; and (*b*) when thermal equilibrium has been reached.

The use of a thermometer thus depends on the concept of thermal equilibrium; and we must first say something about this.

It is an empirical fact that when objects are placed in contact with each other for a sufficiently long time away from heat sources and sinks (for example fires and refrigerators), their various thermometric properties cease to vary. We say that they come to a state of *thermal equilibrium.* Now thermal equilibrium is taken to imply *temperature equality*—although this is conventional. There is no logical reason why we must say that objects in thermal equilibrium are equal in temperature. In fact, if the lead of electrostatics were followed, we should deny that thermal equilibrium implies temperature equality, just as we deny that electrical equilibrium (absence of current flow) implies equipotentiality. Thus we could, if there were any good reason for doing so, admit the existence of contact temperature differences in much the same way as we admit the existence of contact potential differences.

It is a further empirical fact that if objects in thermal equilibrium are re-arranged in any way, then the equilibrium is not disturbed. Thus, if A is in contact with B, and B with C, and equilibrium has been reached, then if A is brought into contact with C, the equilibrium will not be disturbed. Hence, we may say that thermal equilibrium is a transitive relationship; and the fact that thermal equilibrium is a transitive relationship is sometimes known as the Zero'th Law of Thermodynamics. This fact is important for the following reason: If the Zero'th Law did not hold, we should have no criteria for equality of temperature which did not involve reference to a particular thermometer.

To explain this, consider what would happen if thermal equilibrium were not a transitive relationship. Suppose that three objects A, B and C are placed together thus: $\boxed{A \mid B \mid C}$, and that in these circumstances their thermometric properties do not vary. But suppose that on changing A and B around, the equilibrium is disturbed. Now if B is chosen as a thermometer, then (under the usual conventions) we must say that A, B and C are all at the same temperature (since B is in thermal equilibrium with both A and C). But if A is chosen as a thermometer, then the experiment reveals that while A is in thermal equilibrium with B, A and C are not in thermal equilibrium. Hence we must say that A and C are at different temperatures. Thus, if thermal equilibrium were not a transitive relationship, temperature equality, as defined by a thermometer, would depend on the choice of thermometer. The existence of the Zero'th Law of Thermodynamics thus guarantees that we may set up criteria for temperature equality which do not depend on the choice of any particular thermometer, that is which are thermometer-independent.

Of course, this criterion for temperature equality applies only to coexistent objects. For only coexistent objects can be in thermal equilibrium. To say that the temperature of an object remains the same over a period of time, or under transport, we need additional criteria. However, it is an empirical fact that when the various thermometric properties of objects vary, they do so, as it were, in harmony; that is, there are simple functional relationships relating the measures of the various thermometric properties. Hence, without ambiguity, we may stipulate that the temperature of an object remains the same if, and only if, its various thermometric properties do not vary. If there were no such harmony, then a particular thermometric property would have to be specified before we could give criteria for saying that the temperature of an object remains the same.

It seems then that as far as our criteria for temperature equality are concerned, there are no problems of choice of thermometric property. For, whichever thermometric property we choose, we shall make the same judgements, whether these judgements concern coexistent or non-coexistent objects. The problem of choice of thermometric property only arises when we come to set up a scale of temperature.

The simplest kind of scale for temperature would be an elemental or rank-order scale. To set up such a scale, we should only have to specify a number of fixed and reproducible heat states to serve as standards, and make numerical assignments to these indicating their temperature order—where, by a 'fixed heat state', I mean any independently identifiable state of an object which always exists at the same temperature. (Melting ice, and boiling water may serve as examples of fixed heat states.) This procedure would at least have the merit of avoiding the problem of choice of thermometric property. But to adopt such a scale would be to forego all hope of expressing quantitative temperature laws.

If an associative scale of temperature is required, then the problem of choice of thermometric property cannot be escaped. The best we can hope is to select a thermometric property whose measure on a given scale under given circumstances is independent of the nature of the substance which possesses it, that is a thermometric property which is, in this sense, a universal property of matter. For if such a property could be found, then at least the problem of choice of thermometric substance would be avoided. A more important reason, however, is that we are inclined to think that a scale based on the selection of a universal thermometric property is more likely to be a significant one. For it seems that a scale based on the peculiar properties of particular substances is likely to impose these peculiarities on to the mathematical form of any temperature law we may discover using this scale; thus complicating our physics. It was for this reason, for example, that Gay-Lussac chose to base his scale of temperature on the properties of gases, rather than such liquids as mercury or alcohol. For gases at least seem to show less individual thermal properties; and the scale he eventually devised was, to a high degree, independent of the choice of gaseous substance.

Moreover, if a universal property of matter could be chosen to serve as a thermometric property, we may feel that this would go some way towards finding a theoretical interpretation of temperature. For the first step towards finding a theoretical interpretation of a given quantity is often simply to find some universally applicable criteria for ordering things in respect of that quantity. The second, and more important step, is then to explain why these criteria succeed in ordering things in the way that they do.

Now in fact there is at least one quantity, namely, the efficiency of a perfectly reversible heat engine, which qualifies by the above criterion as a universal property of matter, and which is clearly in some sense a thermal property. It is a universal property in the required sense, because the efficiency of a perfectly reversible heat engine is independent of the nature of the working substance, and of the structure of the machine; and it is a thermal property in the sense that the efficiency of such an engine depends on the fixed heat states between which it operates. But, as it stands, it is clearly not a thermometric property; for the efficiency order would correspond to no temperature order.

However, for a given heat source, the temperature order of the heat sinks is the inverse of the efficiency order; and for a given heat sink, the temperature order of the heat sources is the same as the efficiency order. Moreover, if the source and sink are at the same temperature, the efficiency of the heat engine is zero. Hence, in setting up a scale of temperature, using the efficiency of a perfectly reversible heat engine, as a criterion, we should at least require that

$$f(t_1, t_2) = e \quad (0 < e < 1),$$

where t_1 and t_2 are the temperature numbers to be assigned to the source and sink respectively, where f is strictly monotonic increasing in t_1, and strictly monotonic decreasing in t_2, and where $f(t_1, t_2) \equiv 0$. The relation actually chosen in defining the thermodynamic scale is

$$1 - \frac{t_2}{t_1} = e, \tag{1}$$

although in fact, any relation of the form

$$1 - \frac{f(t_2)}{f(t_1)} = e, \tag{2}$$

where f is any strictly monotonic increasing function which passes through the origin, would also serve to define a temperature scale.

But even this does not solve the problem. We may admit that a universal property, like the efficiency of a perfectly reversible heat engine, is to be preferred to a property of a particular substance (for example volume of a given mass of mercury at constant pressure); but there are, in fact, several such universal properties. The laws of black-body radiation, for example, are also substance-independent, and associative scales of temperature could obviously be defined on the basis of these. And if it is objected that there are no perfectly black bodies, it may also be objected that there are no perfectly reversible heat engines. I can see no reasons, other than reasons of mathematical simplicity, why we should prefer to define a scale of temperature on the basis of the efficiency of a perfectly reversible heat engine rather than on the basis of the kind of radiation emitted from a perfectly black body.

But perhaps this question is only of secondary importance. The important question, after all, is: 'What kind of scale shall we use for the measurement of temperature?' If the problem of choice of thermometric property is solved, this still leaves a wide area for choosing a scale. From relation (2), for example, it can be seen that infinitely many thermodynamic scales could be based on the efficiency of perfectly reversible heat engines. The problem of choice of principle of correlation thus remains to be solved.

B

The choice of principle of correlation

As the argument has been presented so far, it would appear that good reasons may be given for accepting the thermodynamic scale of temperature in preference to others without it being necessary to mention specific theories about the nature of heat and temperature. This may suggest that such theoretical considerations have no role in the choice of temperature scale. Yet, theoretical considerations (as well as practical ones) led Black to adopt the mercury scale; and theoretical considerations were behind Dalton's rejection of it.* Also, theoretical considerations gave strong support to the adoption of the gas scale. Historically, theories about heat and temperature have played a decisive role in the choice of temperature scales. Logically, however, the only kinds of con-

* See p. 60, footnote †.

siderations that should have any bearing on the choice of temperature scales are considerations of mathematical simplicity. For as we shall see, there is an essential arbitrariness in our choice of temperature scale on which theories of heat and temperature have very little bearing. This arbitrariness lies in the choice of principle of correlation.

The principle of correlation, as it is here understood, is the functional relationship between the temperature number assigned to an object and the measure of its chosen thermometric property; that is the function f such that $\theta° = f(p)$. The only restrictions which must be placed upon f are that θ must be defined for every value which p may in fact assume, and the numerical order of the temperature numbers assigned to objects according to this principle must correspond to the temperature order. If these conditions were not fulfilled we should not be justified in calling the number θ assigned to an object a measure of its temperature.

The second of these points I take to be sufficiently clear. The first may be illustrated by the following example. Suppose we were to adopt the principle of correlation $\theta = \log(l - l_{ice})$ where l is the length of the mercury column in an ordinary mercury thermometer, and l_{ice} the length at the ice-point; θ is then defined in the field of real numbers for values of $l > l_{ice}$. But there would, of course, be conditions under which $l \leq l_{ice}$, and according to this principle, when $l = l_{ice}$, $\theta = -\infty°$. But what should we say is the temperature of a certain mixture of ice and salt which gives a reading of $l < l_{ice}$? It must have a temperature since it can be placed in a unique position in the temperature order. It would seem, then, that if we were to adopt this as a principle of correlation, we should have to say that its temperature is less than $-\infty°$. The only alternative is to reject the principle of correlation; and this is certainly the course that would be taken.

Granting these restrictions, there are nevertheless infinitely many possible principles of correlation between temperature and the measure of a given thermometric property. Historically, most but not all of these have been linear in form. Amontons used a linear relationship of the form $\theta \alpha p$, where p is the pressure of air held at constant volume. Celsius and Fahrenheit calibrated their scales by taking equal increments in the volume of a sample of mercury to correspond to equal temperature intervals. But linearity was rejected by Dalton who took equal increments in volume to correspond to equal increments in heat capacity. He suggested that the relationship between volume and temperature was a logarithmic one.

The initial reasons for adopting a linear correlation principle were no doubt reasons of simplicity. Why assume a complicated relationship when a simpler one will do? But Black at any rate considered that his calorimetric experiments confirmed the assumption of linearity, and Dalton, considering similar experimental results, concluded that the assumption of linearity must be false. It is clear that both Black and Dalton believed that good reasons other than reasons of simplicity could be given for choosing one principle of correlation rather than another. If they were right, then the whole problem of choice of thermometric property could be circumvented. For it would matter very little which thermometric property or substance were chosen for use in a standard thermometer, if this thermometer could be calibrated on the basis of, say, calorimetric mixing experiments.

But there is a fundamental weakness of all theoretical arguments for adopting one principle of correlation rather than another. It is, that the very difficulty which these arguments seek to overcome, crops up again in the theory. The problem is that of choice of principle of correlation, that is of a functional relationship between thermometric property and temperature. A theory of temperature proceeds by saying what temperature is. On the caloric theory, temperature is a measure of the pressure of caloric. On the kinetic theory, temperature is a measure of the average kinetic energy of the molecules. But why should we make such assumptions? Only because they enable us to predict the experimental results or laws obtained on scales using a linear principle of correlation. If, for example, a logarithmically calibrated instrument has been used from the start, that is if $\theta \alpha \log V$ had been used as a principle of correlation in the eighteenth century, then the empirically discovered gas law of Gay-Lussac would have been of the form $PV = Re^{\theta}$. To account for this law, it would then have been necessary to assume in the kinetic theory that temperature is the logarithmic of the average kinetic energy of the molecules. And this could have been taken to support the original logarithmic correlation principle.

The only argument which I can see against the adoption of a non-linear correlation principle is not a theoretical argument at all, but an argument from simplicity. It could be argued with some justification that $PV = R\theta$ is a much simpler mathematical form for the gas law than $PV = Re^\theta$, and that the results of calorimetric mixing experiments would be much easier to predict on the assumption of linearity than otherwise. But although this may be, there is yet no guarantee that a linear scale is the simplest possible temperature scale. Indeed, it seems that from the point of view of the mathematical simplicity of temperature laws, the substitution of $-1/\theta$ for θ (the Absolute temperature) would achieve some further simplication. It would mean that instead of the gas law: $PV = R\theta$, we should have: $PV\theta = $ const.; and instead of the Second Law of Thermodynamics as it applies to thermodynamically reversible processes: $\Sigma(Q/\theta) = 0$; we should have: $\Sigma(Q\theta) = 0$. At any rate, it is by no means evident that temperature laws assume their simplest mathematical form when a linear correlation principle is adopted. If they do, then it is only an historical accident. But whether or not they do, is not a question which theory can decide. Thus, whatever theoretical considerations we may make, there remains an essential arbitrariness in the choice of principle of correlation. Only reasons of simplicity can guide us in this choice.

But surely, it will be said, theories do determine at least some aspects of our temperature scale? Is there not an Absolute Zero of temperature? And is this not a theoretical prediction? Yes, this is certainly true. But let us see what it means and what it does not mean. It does not mean that there is a lowest member of the sequence of possible heat states. Indeed, the Third Law of Thermodynamics suggests that this is not the case. It does not mean that there is, or might be, a heat state with which the association of the number zero is particularly appropriate in view of the special mathematical properties of zero. The proposition $n \pm 0 = n$ cannot be used to predict the result of any physical operation involving objects at temperatures $n°$ A and $0°$ A. To say that there is a natural zero for temperature, therefore, cannot be quite like saying that there is a natural zero for, say, distance. What it does mean, however, is that the temperature in $°$ C. always appears in fundamental temperature laws together with a constant $(+273)$, and that a simplification of the form of these laws can therefore be achieved by a change of variable, that is a change to the Absolute scale. And this is an argument of precisely the kind we have discussed. It is an argument from mathematical simplicity.

It also means that on the Absolute scale there is a lower limit to the temperature numbers which are significant, and this conveniently is the lower limit of the real positive numbers, namely, zero. To suppose that there is an object, the temperature of which is less than 0° A is to make a supposition which can only be true if certain accepted temperature laws and theories are false. For instance, the substitution of a negative number for t_0, the temperature of the sink (condenser) in a reversible heat engine, is to give a value for the efficiency of this engine greater than 100%. Moreover, a negative temperature number on the Absolute scale would have no interpretation on the kinetic theory of temperature.

Theoretical considerations, then, do influence us in the determination of certain features of our temperature scale. For if on any arbitrarily chosen temperature scale there are theoretical limits to the temperature numbers which are significant, we find it convenient to change the principle of correlation so that these limits are reflected by the properties of the number system.

But even when this is done we must, as Mach has pointed out,[*] always be careful about drawing inferences from the properties of the number system. From the fact that the set of real positive numbers is everywhere dense, it does not follow that the sequence of heat states is everywhere dense. From the fact that this set of numbers is bounded below, but unbounded above, it does not follow that the set of heat states is bounded below and unbounded above. This is an important point, and we need to be constantly reminded of it, not only in connection with temperature measurement, but in connection with other kinds of measurement as well.

Consider the effect on our thinking of a change to a non-linear correlation principle, where the numbers assigned to objects according to this principle are related to the Absolute temperature by a relationship of the form $T = k \log A$, where A is the Absolute temperature, and T is the new temperature. Then 0° A would be represented on this scale by $-\infty°$ T. Now it seems to me that if we had been brought up to use such a scale, the Third Law of Thermodynamics would have been taken as self-evident. 'Of

---

[*] See appendix I, § 20.

7-2

course, we cannot reach $-\infty°$ T', it would be said. Moreover, the question of whether there could be an object, the temperature of which is $< -\infty°$ T would have been rejected as absurd. But, obviously, there is nothing self-evident about the Third Law, and it is not absurd to ask whether there could be an object which is colder than one at $0°$ A, or $-\infty°$ T.

The psychological effect of adopting one principle of correlation rather than another is clearly illustrated by this example. And although, from a mathematical point of view, a change of principle of correlation amounts simply to a change of variable, which may or may not simplify the mathematical form of temperature laws, the whole effect of such a change is likely to be much greater than this. It is likely to change quite radically our thinking about the subject of temperature. And this is so because we easily and naturally think that the properties of the sequence of heat states are reflected in the properties of the numbers by which we designate them.

C

The choice of scale form

It appears then that the only good reasons for choosing one associative scale rather than another are reasons of formal simplicity. My conclusions concerning associative scales are, therefore, very similar to those concerning fundamental scales. This being the case, if there is a choice between an associative and a fundamental scale, we may expect to find that, at least sometimes, an associative scale is preferred to a fundamental one on grounds of simplicity.

I believe that this is in fact the case. Other things being equal, we should no doubt prefer a fundamental scale to an associative one. For measurements on fundamental scales are more informative. But where a fundamental scale would lead to complex laws, and an associative scale to relatively simple ones, I believe that we should prefer the associative scale to the fundamental one.

Consider the measurement of temperature interval. It is in fact possible to give direct criteria, that is criteria which do not depend on previous measurement for the quantitative equality or inequality of temperature interval, and further, to measure this quantity fundamentally on a ratio scale. And just as we can base an interval scale on time (a date scale) upon a ratio scale of time interval, we could base an interval scale of temperature upon this ratio scale of temperature interval. Yet I have no doubt that we should prefer to use an associative scale for temperature, and to have no independent scale at all for temperature interval. The reason for this will become clear. Measurements on the new scale would yield extremely complex temperature laws, and extremely complex theoretical correlations would have to be made to account for them. Reasons of mathematical simplicity, therefore, may not only determine what sort of fundamental, associative or other scale we should employ, they may even determine the scale form. In other words, we may prefer mathematical simplicity to information. Measurements on a weaker scale form contain less information, but if these measurements yield simpler laws, this may be an overriding consideration.

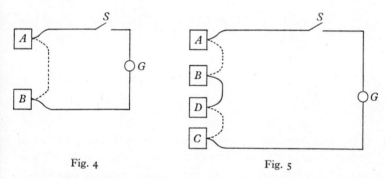

Fig. 4   Fig. 5

Suppose that we have two objects A and B in fixed heat states. Let us insert thermocouples into them and connect them through a galvanometer G according to the design of Fig. 4. Suppose that when the switch S is closed, the galvanometer needle is deflected to the right, remains stationary, or is deflected to the left according as the temperature of A is greater than, equal to, or less than the temperature of B. We could then use the deflection of the galvanometer needle as a criterion for quantitative equality or inequality of temperature.

Next, suppose that we have four bodies, A, B, C and D, in fixed heat states increasing in order of temperature, and that we connect them with thermocouples and a galvanometer as in Fig. 5. We may now stipulate that the temperature-interval between A and B is greater than, equal to, or less than the temperature interval between

C and D according as the galvanometer is deflected to the right, remains stationary, or is deflected to the left. For the sufficient conditions of transitivity, symmetry, asymmetry and so forth would be found to be satisfied. We could thus interpret arithmetical formulae of the form

$$a \gtreqless b.$$

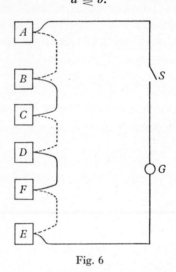

Fig. 6

Using this criterion, we could then set up a standard set of temperature intervals. Suppose that the initial standard is the pair of objects (A, B), and that the temperature interval between C and D is found to be equal to that between A and B. If we now switch the objects C and D around in Fig. 5, it will be found that the galvanometer needle is deflected to the right. But it will usually be possible to find another pair of objects E and F in fixed heat states such that when they are connected as in Fig. 6 no deflection occurs. The pair of objects EF, may then serve as the second member of our standard set. And so we could proceed using E and F in place of C and D to find a third member of our standard set, and so forth. It is obvious that a standard subset could also be formed, and thus a whole fundamental scale of temperature interval set up.

But, in spite of this, we should not feel happy with such a scale, or with the temperature scale which could be based upon it. In the first place, there would be a completely arbitrary choice of thermocouple materials. In the second, there are no close theoretical links between temperature and electrical phenomena. But perhaps most important, the use of such a scale would lead to extremely complex temperature laws. If it led to simple temperature laws, it would have very strong claims indeed; but just because it would not do so, we should prefer a temperature scale set-up by associative measurement where this requirement is satisfied.

CHAPTER VII

ASSOCIATIVE MEASUREMENT: II

As illustrated by the case of time measurement
in extreme ranges

No magnitude is directly and fundamentally measurable over the whole of its range. Inter-atomic distances are not fundamentally measurable; nor are intergalactic distances. Sub-atomic masses are not directly measurable; nor are the masses of the stars or planets. To measure such distances or masses we need to adopt a quantitative criterion, and a principle of correlation. Does this mean that in these extreme ranges the measurement of length and mass should be regarded as a form of associative measurement?

There are, I think, certain differences between the logical problems of measurement in extreme ranges and those of associative measurement. But it is my view that these differences are superficial, and that the measurement of very large or very small distances or masses is logically very like temperature measurement. If I am right, then the question of whether space is infinite in extent or infinitely subdivisible, is logically very like that of whether there is an upper or lower limit to temperature. It is ambiguous in the same sort of way, and it contains similar traps. I now propose to consider the problem of time measurement in extreme ranges, and to apply my analysis to the question of whether the universe has a beginning in time. But what I have to say should also apply to whether space is infinitely subdivisible, whether it is infinite in extent, or whether there are 'atoms' of time interval.

A

Timing and dating

If we are timing an event—a foot-race, for example—we count the number of pendulum swings necessary to match the given event. We may judge, for example, that the time for the race was equal to the time for ten pendulum swings. This suggests that time-interval should be regarded as a directly and fundamentally measurable quantity, like length.

But there is a difficulty in this; for once the race is over, we cannot 'go back' and time it in this way. Only present, not past events, can be timed directly. Hence, while *present* time-intervals are directly measurable, *past* time-intervals are not. I shall therefore distinguish between what I shall call *dating* and *timing* procedures. By a timing procedure, I shall mean what is ordinarily meant by this term; and according to ordinary usage, it makes no sense to speak of timing now a past event. I cannot intelligibly say that I am now timing the 100 metres final in the last Olympic Games. By the term 'dating procedure', I wish to include any procedure for measuring the time-interval between two past events, or between a past and a present event. This is a special use for these words, and it is not connected very closely with their ordinary usage.

First we should notice that most of the dating done by historians cannot, properly speaking, be described as measurement. In most matters, historians have to rely on the reports of witnesses, or upon reports of these reports. They use techniques of sifting them for consistency, of checking them off against one another, of building up a coherent picture of the course of events. But none of this is measurement. I cannot be said to have measured the length of a table if I have merely considered the reports of three people who claim to have measured it, no matter what investigations I may make concerning the character or the circumstances of the individuals concerned. It does not matter how well founded my judgement as to the length of the table may be as a result of these considerations, I cannot be said to have measured its length, unless I have myself carried out an appropriate measuring procedure. Similarly, I wish to argue, an historian who relies upon diaries, reports, and so on in assigning a date to an occurrence, cannot be said to be measuring anything.

However, there is something I do wish to describe as the measurement of past or past-present time-intervals. The geologist who takes the salinity of the sea as a criterion for the age of the solid earth may, by measuring salinity, measure the age of the solid earth. If, in a less simple way, he takes the quantities of radioactive substances in the earth's crust as a criterion for the age of the earth, he is measuring the age of the earth by an alternative means. Similarly, the archaeologist may measure the age of something by employing radioactive carbon criteria. The cosmologist may measure what he calls 'the age of the universe' by measuring the red shift of distant nebulae. A man may measure the age of a tree by counting the number of annular rings. And so examples may be multiplied.

In each case, something is accepted as a quantitative criterion for the age of something—that is, for the length of a past-present time-interval. In each case, a principle of correlation between this quantitative criterion and age must be adopted. In each case, age is determined by measuring this quantitative property and employing the adopted principle of correlation. The measurement of age, therefore, seems to involve similar problems to the measurement of temperature. There is a problem of choice of temporal property, and a problem of choice of principle of correlation. Thus it seems that age, like temperature, must be regarded as an associatively measurable quantity.

But there is at least one very striking difference. This difference lies in the existence of a sort of 'correspondence' principle. That is, there must be a correspondence between the results of timing and dating. Otherwise, we should say that one or the other is inaccurate. Suppose, for example, that a certain process has been timed. Then if, afterwards, the beginning of this process can be dated, the results of these two investigations must agree. If they do not agree, then we should say that a mistake must have been made, or eliminating this, that the dating procedure or principle of correlation employed is inappropriate.

Hence it may be argued that neither of the above problems really exist. For whichever quantitative property we choose as a criterion for age, an individual principle of correlation can be determined experimentally by using this 'correspondence' principle. That is, we can time the changes in this property, and by this means determine how the measure of this property varies with age. And further, it may be argued, this is just what we do. We time changes in radioactivity, extrapolate the curve and obtain empirically a principle of correlation between degree of radioactivity and age of sample. There is nothing arbitrary about this principle of correlation: it is fixed and determinate. Hence, in age measurement, there is no problem of choice of principle of correlation.

I believe that this argument is sound. Principles of correlation between temporal property and time-interval can be established by direct timing procedures—but only over very limited time ranges. A principle of correlation is a mathematical conversion formula. In this case it must be of the form

$$A = f(p),$$

where A is the age of a given event-type, p is the measure of a temporal property and f is a strictly monotonic function. But the validity of this formula can only be established for very small values of A—at most a few thousand years. In the dating of very distant past events we must extrapolate this relationship; and there arises, in place of what I have called the problem of choice of principle of correlation, a new problem which, for convenience, I shall call the problem of choice of *principle of extrapolation*. For all that is required of the extrapolated principle of correlation is that for very small values of A, it merges into the principle

$$A = f(p).$$

Thus any principle of correlation

$$A = \phi(p)$$

which is such that as $A \to 0$, $\phi \to f$ will do as an extrapolated principle of correlation.

Consider an analogy: suppose that temperature were directly measurable between 0 and 0·1° C. It would then be the case that, over this range of temperature, any principle of correlation between a thermometric property and temperature could be checked by direct measurement. But it would be fantastic to suppose that because a given principle of correlation can be shown to hold in this temperature range, it would hold over the whole temperature range. It would indeed place some restrictions on the choice of extrapolated principle of correlation. But there would nevertheless remain a very wide area of choice.

Thus I would maintain that in the discussion of such questions as the age of the earth, of the solar system, or of the universe, age must be regarded as an indirectly measurable quantity—more like temperature than like length. Dating is not, of course, exactly like temperature measurement; the existence of the 'correspondence' principle does make dating logically somewhat different. But, at the same time, it is logically very different from fundamental measurement, and it is less misleading to consider dating to be a form of associative measurement.

B

The age of the universe

To show the importance of this conclusion, consider the question of the age of the universe.

When we say 'the temperature of this object is 400° C.', just what do we mean? We mean that by following any of a number of well-specified temperature-measuring procedures with sufficient care, anyone would be led to assign the number 400 to the object in question. When we say that there is a lower temperature limit at −273° C., we mean that no matter which object is taken under whatever circumstances, we shall never be led to assign a number < −273 to it, provided that we follow a recognized temperature-measuring procedure with sufficient care. It does not matter for the moment what reasons we may have for saying such a thing; this is what we ordinarily mean.

There is, however, a second sense in which we may speak of a lower temperature limit. In this sense there exists a lower temperature limit if, and only if, an object can be found or produced such that no colder object can be ever found or produced. Mach, for example, thinks of the possibility of a lower temperature limit like this: 'Whether the range of heat states has an upper or a lower limit can only be decided through experience. The existence of a limit is only proved if, having a body with a definite heat state, we cannot find one which is either hotter or colder.'* A little reflection soon reveals that these two senses are quite distinct from one another. There is no contradiction in saying that we can always produce an object which is colder than any given object, and at the same time, that no matter which object is taken, under whatever circumstances, we will never be led to assign to it a temperature number less than, say, −273. That is, there may be a lower temperature limit in the first sense, but not in the second. Also, it is possible that there should be no lower temperature limit in the first sense, but nevertheless a lower temperature limit in the second. This

* Appendix 1, § 21.

would be the case where the coldest possible object is assigned the temperature number $-\infty$. If an object at absolute zero could be produced, and we used a logarithmic correlation principle, this would be true. Now there is a similar distinction to be drawn between different senses of the question: 'Has the universe a beginning in time?' In one sense it is the question: 'Is there a maximum age for events?' That is: 'Is there, for whatever reason, a lower limit to the number which can be assigned to an event as the date of its occurrence?' But in the second sense it is the question: 'Was there an event before which no other events occurred?'

Now, these two questions have usually been taken together as though they were one and the same. But there is, I think, no contradiction in saying 'Yes' to one and 'No' to the other. It is logically possible that the universe should have a beginning in time in one sense, but not in the other. That is, it is logically possible that there should be no theoretical limit to the number which may be assigned to an event as its age, but that nevertheless there should be a first event. Also, it is logically possible that there should be a theoretical limit to the age numbers of events, and at the same time that there should be no first event.

This now seems to me so obvious that I wonder why it has not been commonly accepted. I think the answer must be that we all, naturally, think of time from the time-keepers' point of view. Dates are thought of as dependent on time-keeping. We thus fail to see that prehistoric dating depends very little on time-keeping. It depends upon the discovery of temporal properties and the adoption of a principle of correlation between temporal property and age—in almost, but not quite the same way, as temperature measurement depends upon the discovery of thermometric properties and the adoption of suitable principles of correlation. When we adopt the latter point of view, this ambiguity in the question: 'Has the universe a beginning in time?' becomes almost self-evident. When, however, we fail to adopt it, and adopt instead the point of view of a recording angel, the ambiguity mentioned becomes unintelligible. It becomes nonsense to suppose that the age of the universe is infinite but that there was nevertheless a first event; and nonsense to suppose that there was no first event but that the age of the universe is finite. For, from such a viewpoint, either there was a first event or there was not. If so, then the age of the universe cannot be infinite—for even a recording angel cannot count an infinite number of events. If not, then the age of the universe must be infinite.

But for whatever reasons this distinction may have been overlooked, it *has* been overlooked; and the result has been confusion. For once this distinction is recognized, it becomes clear that the question: 'Has the universe a beginning in time?' may be either of two distinct questions:

(*a*) Is there a theoretical maximum to the age of an event as determined on any given scale?

(*b*) Was there an event before which no other events occurred?

The answer to the first question will depend upon an examination of our prehistoric dating techniques, upon the kinds of temporal properties employed, and the choice of extrapolated principle of correlation. The second question is, I think, in principle undecidable. Not even a recording angel, if there were such a being, and he were a part of the universe, could decide this question.

CHAPTER VIII

DERIVED MEASUREMENT

To make a derived measurement, we must determine the value of a constant in a numerical law. A discussion of the nature of derived measurement must therefore depend on a discussion of numerical laws. We must try to say what a numerical law is, what sorts of facts are contained in the statement of such a law, and how else these same facts may be described. It will be seen that there are many different ways, in which a given numerical law may be expressed, leading to a variety of different kinds of derivative scales. However, there are certain conventions governing the expression of numerical laws which are tacitly adopted; and our derivative scales have the properties they do in virtue of these conventions.

A

The expression of numerical laws

A numerical law is usually stated as a relationship between two or more quantities under specified conditions. Thus Ohm's law is usually stated: 'Current flow along a wire is directly proportional to the potential difference along the wire and inversely proportional to its electrical resistance'. The law of gravitation is stated: 'Every body attracts every other body with a force directly proportional to the product of their masses and inversely proportional to the square of the distance between them'. Occasionally reference is made to particular scales. Thus Charles' law would usually be stated: 'If a given mass of gas is maintained at constant pressure, then its volume is proportional to its *Absolute* temperature'— specific reference being made to the Absolute scale of temperature. But generally speaking, our expressions of numerical laws make no such references; they are expressed as though they had nothing to do with scales of measurement.

But this is surely misleading. Three quantities cannot be related in the way that the usual expression of Ohm's law suggests; for the notion of proportionality is necessarily foreign to that of a quantity. If three quantities p, q and r are possessed by a number of systems, then we can say that if we arrange those systems which are equal in r in the order of p, they are also arranged in the order of q; or, that if we select those systems which are equal in q, and arrange them in the order of p, then we also arrange them in the inverse order of r. But we cannot say (other than elliptically) that p is proportional to q and inversely proportional to r. For there is nothing in the notion of a quantity to make such expressions intelligible. Yet Ohm's law is obviously more informative than the corresponding statement relating to the orders of current flow, potential difference and electrical resistance. It enables us to predict fairly precisely the results of certain measurements. A numerical law is not, therefore, simply the statement of a relationship between quantities—although the existence of such relationships is a necessary condition for the existence of numerical laws. We shall see that a numerical law relates the results of measurements of two or more quantities, these measurements being made on certain scales or classes of scales.

Let S_1 and T_1 be any two scales for the measurement of two quantities p and q possessed by a given system A_1 which meets certain general specifications M. Thus, A_1 might be the name of a particular sample of gas, and M might be the specification that it is maintained at constant pressure. Let s_1 and t_1 be the results of any two measurements made on A_1 on the scales S_1 and T_1 respectively. Let us also suppose that the conditions under which A_1 exists may be modified so that the measures of p and q are seen to vary, while A_1 still meets the general specifications M. Then if it is found that

$$f(s_1, t_1) = k_1 \qquad (1)$$

holds for A_1 under all such conditions, where k_1 is a constant, then we may say that we have discovered a numerical law pertaining to the system A_1. And the formula (1) constitutes the expression of this law with respect to the particular scales S_1 and T_1.

There is, however, no need to express this law with respect to the particular scales S_1 and T_1. Let S_2 and T_2 be any two scales similar to S_1 and T_1, respectively, that is which are related by similarity transformations to S_1 and T_1.* Then if s_1 and s_2 represent the results of any two measurements made on the same parti-

* Similarity transformations were defined in ch. IV. See especially p. 61.

cular under the same conditions on the scales S_1 and S_2 respectively, we have that

$$s_1 = ms_2,$$

where m is a constant called the *conversion factor* from S_1 to S_2. Similarly

$$t_1 = nt_2,$$

where n is the conversion factor from T_1 to T_2. Hence, if the scales S_2 and T_2 had been used initially, the empirically discovered law would have been:

$$f(ms_2, nt_2) = k_1. \tag{2}$$

But since S_2 and T_2 are any arbitrary scales similar to S_1 and T_1, we may express this law more generally. For if $[S]$ and $[T]$ designate the classes of scales similar to S_1 and T_1 respectively, an equation of the form (2) must hold whichever scales are chosen from within these classes.

Let s and t be the results of any measurements made on A_1 on *any* scales of the classes $[S]$ and $[T]$ respectively. Then we have that

$$f(\alpha s, \beta t) = k_1, \tag{3}$$

where k_1 is the same constant as in *equations* (1) and (2), and α and β are what we may call *scale-dependent constants*, since the numbers they represent depend on the choices of scales from within the classes $[S]$ and $[T]$. The equation (3) may be called the expression of the law (1) with respect to the classes of scales $[S]$ and $[T]$.

Now there is no reason why we should stop here. Still more general forms of expression can easily be achieved. We might, for example, express the law with respect to the classes of scales linear with respect to S_1 and T_1. Then we should obtain an expression of the form

$$f\{(m_1 s + m_2), (n_1 s + n_2)\} = k_1, \tag{4}$$

where m_1, m_2, n_1, and n_2 are all scale-dependent constants. Or again, we could express the law with respect to the power groups of scales centred around S_1 and T_1.* Then we should have

$$f(m_1 s^{m_2}, n_1 t^{n_2}) = k_1, \tag{5}$$

where again, m_1, m_2, n_1 and n_2 are all scale-dependent constants.

In fact, such forms of expression are never used; and it is our

---

* The concept of a power group is explained in Stevens (1959), pp. 31–4.

universal practice to express our laws either with respect to particular scales, or else with respect to classes of similar scales; although the practice varies somewhat in different areas of science. In mechanics, for example, we nearly always express our laws with respect to classes of similar scales. The formula

$$f = G\,\frac{m_1 m_2}{r^2},$$

which is the usual expression of the law of gravitation, is valid for all choices of scales within the classes of scales similar to our dyne, gram and centimetre scales; and G is a scale-dependent constant which depends in a complex way on the choices of force, mass and length scales from within these classes. In electrical and magnetic theory, on the other hand, our laws are usually expressed with respect to particular scales (compare equation (1)), and we indicate these particular scales by the use of such expressions as 'e.s.u.' and 'e.m.u.'. Thus, scale-dependent constants often do not seem to appear in the expressions of such laws; or, where they do, they are seen to depend only on the choices of scales for the measurement of such 'mechanical' quantities as mass, length and time-interval, which may happen to be involved. Ohm's law, for example, seems to contain no scale-dependent constants; and this is because we have chosen to express this law with respect to our Volt, Ampère and Ohm scales. To express it more generally, however, with respect to the classes of scales similar to out Volt, Ampère and Ohm scales, we should have to write:

$$E = kIR,$$

where k is a scale-dependent constant exactly like G in gravitation theory.

Sometimes we use mixed expressions. Our laws of temperature for example, are usually expressed with respect to particular temperature scales, but with respect to classes of similar scales for the measurement of whatever 'mechanical' quantities may be involved. Thus, the scale-dependent constants which occur in the expressions of these laws are apparently dependent only on the choices of scales for the measurement of these mechanical quantities. Again, our laws of mechanics which involve the quantity, angle, are always expressed with respect to particular scales of angle (usually the Radian or Degree scales), but with respect to classes of similar scales for the measurement of other quantities. Hence our scale-dependent constants in mechanics are never seen to depend on the choice of angle scale.

It is hard to see why we have adopted the particular conventions we have concerning the expression of numerical laws. There is no doubt that other forms of expression could be used. Some of these, it is true, would be mathematically more complex. Yet, empirically, they would contain precisely the same information; and what is lost in formal simplicity should be compensated for by a gain in formal content. For the more complex expressions should yield information concerning a wider class of scale transformations. Now it may be argued that this would be poor compensation, since we are usually not interested in the result of such transformations— mutually dissimilar scales for the measurement of the one quantity not being in common use. But then, this only shifts the question. Why should mutually dissimilar scales not be used? I find that I am quite unable to offer any rationale for the choices we have made concerning the expression of numerical laws. In fact, I believe, there are no rational grounds for them. Certain conventions have evolved concerning the expression of numerical laws, and scientists have quite unwittingly adopted them.

The law (1) referred to a particular system A_1 which met certain general specifications M. Most laws, however, do not relate to particular systems, but concern all systems which meet certain general specifications. Let $[A]$ be the class of systems satisfying the specifications M, and let A_i be any arbitrary system belonging to the class $[A]$. Let S_1, T_1, U_1, ... be any arbitrary scales for the measurement of the quantities p, q, r, ... respectively possessed by all systems of the class $[A]$. Let s_{1i}, t_{1i}, u_{1i}, ... be the results of any simultaneous measurements made on the system A_i on the scales S_1, T_1, U_1, ... respectively.* Now, suppose it is found that

$$f(s_{1i}, t_{1i}, u_{1i}, ...) = k_{1i} \quad (i = 1, 2, ...) \tag{6}$$

holds under all conditions in which A_i meets the general specification M, k_{1i} being a constant characteristic of the system A_i. Then we may say that we have discovered a numerical law pertaining to the systems of the class $[A]$.

* We could, of course, have laws relating non-simultaneous measurements. But this complication is of little importance here.

8-2

To express this law more economically, we may introduce the concept of a *system-dependent constant*. Instead of k_{1i}, we may simply write k_1, and let it be known that the value of k_1 will depend on the choice of system from within the class $[A]$. Thus, for the system A_i, $k_1 = k_{1i}$. This understood, we may now write

$$f(s_1, t_1, u_1, \ldots) = k_1, \tag{7}$$

where $s_1, t_1, u_1, \ldots$ refer to the results of measurements made on any system of the class $[A]$, on the scales $S_1, T_1, U_1, \ldots$ respectively, and where k_1 is a system-dependent constant.

As before, we may express this law more generally. Equation (7) is the expression of the law with respect to the particular scales $S_1, T_1, U_1, \ldots$. Let $[S], [T], [U], \ldots$ be the classes of scales similar to $S_1, T_1, U_1, \ldots$ respectively. Then if $s, t, u, \ldots$ are the results of measurements made on any scales of the classes $[S], [T], [U], \ldots$ we have that

$$f(\alpha s, \beta t, \gamma u, \ldots) = k_1, \tag{8}$$

where $\alpha, \beta, \gamma, \ldots$ are all scale-dependent constants, and k_1 is the same system-dependent constant as in equation (7).

Usually, however, our system-dependent and scale-dependent constants are not so neatly separated. If, for example, the function f in equation (8) is such that

$$f(\alpha s, \beta t, \gamma u, \ldots) = \phi(\alpha, \beta, \gamma, \ldots) f(s, t, u, \ldots), \tag{9}$$

then (and only then) may we write

$$f(s, t, u, \ldots) = k, \tag{10}$$

where $k\phi(\alpha, \beta, \gamma, \ldots) = k_1$. In this case, k is generally both a system- and a scale-dependent constant; for k will usually depend both on the choices of scales from within the classes $[S], [T], [U], \ldots$ and on the choice of system from within the class $[A]$.

Now it is an interesting fact that most of our physical laws are expressed by means of equations like (10), where k is the only system- and/or scale-dependent constant that occurs. This means that most functions f relating the measurements on particular scales must satisfy the condition (9). And it is easily proved* that this condition is satisfied if and only if f is a function of the form

$$f(s, t, u, \ldots) = C s^a t^b u^c \ldots. \tag{11}$$

* See appendix v.

where $C, a, b, c, \ldots$ are neither system- nor scale-dependent constants. Hence there follows the general and all-important theorem:

Theorem 1. If a law is expressed with respect to certain classes of similar scales, and there occurs in the expression of this law one and only one system- and/or scale-dependent constant, then this law must be expressible with respect to these classes of scales in the form

$$Cs^a t^b u^c \ldots = k. \tag{12}$$

Let us call this the *standard form* for the expression of numerical laws.

It is not clear, however, why so many of our physical laws should be capable of assuming this form. Obviously, no a priori restrictions can be placed on the form of the function f in equation (8). Let us consider the case of a simple 'unorthodox' law. Suppose that for the particular scales S_1 and T_1, the equation

$$s_1 = k_1 \ln t_1 \tag{13}$$

is found to hold for all systems of a class $[A]$, where k_1 is a purely system-dependent constant. To express this law with respect to the scale classes $[S]$ and $[T]$, similar to S_1 and T_1 respectively, we must write

$$\alpha s = k_1 \ln \beta t. \tag{14}$$

But since this equation is not reducible to standard form there is no way of bringing these various constants, α, β, k_1 together into a single system- and scale-dependent constant.

Faced with this situation, I suppose we should often choose to express the law with respect to the particular scale T_1, and with respect to the class of scales similar to S_1, that is that we should use the mixed mode of expression that we do for our temperature laws. There is, however, no need to follow this procedure. For we might simply transform the expression of the law into standard form by making appropriate scale transformations. In the above case, for example, we might adopt a scale T_1' related to T_1 by a transformation function of the form

$$t_1' = \ln t, \tag{15}$$

and then, in place of (13), we should have

$$s_1 = k_1 t_1'. \tag{16}$$

And now, if this law is expressed with respect to the classes of scales $[S]$ and $[T']$ similar to S_1 and T'_1 respectively, we obtain

$$s = kt', \tag{17}$$

where k is the only system- and scale-dependent constant.

Thus, we can always express a law in standard form if we wish to. Hence it is not simply an empirical fact that laws usually assume this form. Rather, it is a fact about the way we choose to express them. There is, however, an important empirical fact for which I have no explanation. It is the fact that different laws can often be expressed with respect to the same classes of similar scales, and yet all assume standard form. This degree of coherence between various laws of nature is not something that can be explained in terms conventions alone.

The possibility of reducing 'unorthodox' numerical laws to standard form by means of scale transformations may have an important bearing on our choices of scales. For even if the scale T_1 were a fundamental scale, we may nevertheless prefer to express our laws with respect to the class $[T']$ rather than the class $[T]$, on the grounds that when our laws are expressed in this way, they assume a simpler mathematical form. And this illustrates, in a way that we were unable to do previously, how considerations of formal simplicity may guide us in the choice of even fundamental scales.

B

Derivative scales

We are now in a position to say more precisely what is meant by derived measurement. Derived measurement is measurement by the evaluation of the single system- and/or scale-dependent constants which occur in numerical laws expressed in standard form.

Let us suppose that

$$Cs^a t^b u^c \ldots = k \tag{18}$$

is a numerical law expressed in standard form with respect to the classes of scales $[S], [T], [U], \ldots$ and pertaining to the systems of a class $[A]$. Let any system A_i belonging to $[A]$, and any set of scales $S_1, T_1, U_1, \ldots$ belonging to $[S], [T], [U], \ldots$ be chosen. Then if the appropriate measurements are made, the value of k for the system A_i may be determined. Now it is clear that this procedure may be repeated for the various systems of the class

[A], and the appropriate values of k determined. We have, therefore, a determinate rule for making numerical assignments to the systems of [A]; hence we may say that we have a scale for measuring these systems. Moreover, the k-order must be a linear one. Hence we must have a scale for the measurement of some quantity possessed by the various systems of the class [A]. In some cases (for example refractive index), the quantity measured on such a scale is not previously defined. In other cases (for example density, pressure) the quantity is already known to exist in virtue of other independent sets of linear ordering relationships.

Any scale defined in the above way will be called a *derivative scale*. Let us now consider some of the properties of such scales.

First, it is clear that derivative scales are, in some sense, dependent scales. We cannot choose a derivative scale in the way that we may choose a fundamental or associative scale. We may choose scales of mass, length, time-interval, temperature and many other quantities, make measurements on these scales, and discover laws in which scale- and system-dependent constants appear. We may then take the value of such a constant for a particular system, and for a particular choice of independent scales, as the measure of some quantity. But the scale thus defined depends on the initial choices of independent scales.

What, then, is the manner of this dependence? Let k_1 be the value of k in equation (18) for the system A_i and independent scales S_1, T_1, U_1, ... Let k_2 be the value of k for the same system when the independent scales are S_2, T_2, U_2, ..., these scales being similar to S_1, T_1, U_1, ... respectively. Let $m, n, o, ...$ be the conversion factors from S_1 and S_2, T_1 to T_2, U_1 to U_2 ... respectively. Then if $s_1, t_1, u_1, ...$ are the results of any measurements made on S_1, T_1, U_1, ... respectively, and $s_2, t_2, u_2, ...$ are the results of measurements made on the same particulars under the same conditions on the scales S_2, T_2, U_2, ... respectively, we have that

$$\left. \begin{array}{l} s_1 = ms_2, \\ t_1 = nt_2, \\ u_1 = ou_2. \end{array} \right\} \tag{19}$$

But, from (18), we have that

and
$$\left. \begin{array}{l} Cs_1^a t_1^b u_1^c \dots = k_1, \\ Cs_2^a t_2^b u_2^c \dots = k_2. \end{array} \right\} \tag{20}$$

Hence, substituting (19) in (20), we get

$$k_1 = m^a n^b o^c \ldots k_2. \tag{21}$$

Hence, if K_1 is the name of the derivative scale defined by the choices of $S_1, T_1, U_1, \ldots$ as independent scales, and K_2 is the scale which results from the choices of $S_2, T_2, U_2, \ldots$, it follows that K_1 and K_2 are similar scales, and the conversion factor from K_1 to K_2 is a product of powers of the conversion factors from S_1 to S_2, T_1 to T_2, U_1 to U_2, ...

From this, one may be tempted to conclude that derivative scales for the measurement of any given quantity must always be similar to each other. But this would be a mistake. In the first place, there are always infinitely many ways in which a given numerical law can be expressed in standard form. There is never any need to express it with respect to any *particular* set of classes of similar independent scales. Hence, mutually dissimilar derivative scales for the measurement of the one quantity can always be defined by expressing the law with respect to different classes of similar scales. In the second place, even if the same classes of similar independent scales are chosen, we may yet define mutually dissimilar derivative scales for the measurement of the one quantity by choosing a different numerical law. For there is no a priori reason why the orders of different system-dependent constants appearing in different laws should not coincide.

Suppose, for example, that

$$\begin{aligned} f_1(s, t) &= k_1, \\ f_2(u, v) &= k_2, \end{aligned} \tag{22}$$

and

are two numerical laws expressed in standard form with respect to the classes of scales $[S]$, $[T]$, $[U]$, $[V]$, that these laws pertain to the same class of systems $[A]$, and that the order of k_1 coincides with the order of k_2. Then according to our criteria for the identity of quantities, the choice of the particular scales S_1, T_1, U_1, V_1 would define two different derivative scales for the measurement of the one quantity. But clearly, there is no necessity that these scales should be similar to each other.

However, let us agree to say that two derivative scales are similarly defined if and only if they are defined on the basis of the same numerical law expressed in standard form with respect to the same classes of similar independent scales. Then we may state a second important theorem concerning derivative measurement:

Theorem 2. Similarly defined derivatives scales for the measurement of the one quantity are always similar to each other.

This theorem is very important, because it means that if sufficiently many numerical laws are known to apply, in any given field of science, then classes of similar derivative scales, for the measurement of most quantities in that field, may be defined on the basis of an initial choice of classes of similar fundamental or associative scales. Therefore, it will be possible to construct an interconnected system of scales of measurement; and as we shall see, such a system has advantages over a disconnected system.

C

Universal constants

Numerical laws often contain what are called universal constants, and these are thought to have peculiar significance. It is not realized, however, that the existence of universal constants is more a matter of convention than anything else. For, first, it is not difficult to prove that universal constants can *always* be made to appear in any given universal law, provided we choose a suitable mode of expression; and, secondly, that universal constants can usually be eliminated from any particular law, although not necessarily from the whole of science.

A universal constant appears in the following way. Let $[A]$ be any class of systems satisfying certain general specifications M. Let

$$f(s, t, u, \ldots) = k \qquad (23)$$

be any numerical law expressed in standard form with respect to the classes of similar scales $[S]$, $[T]$, $[U]$, ... and pertaining to the systems of $[A]$. Then, generally speaking, k will be a system-dependent as well as a scale-dependent constant. It sometimes happens, however, that k is not system-dependent, that is that the value of k is independent of the choice of system from within the class $[A]$. In that case, k becomes a purely scale-dependent constant. Now if, further, $[A]$ is neither spatially nor temporally restricted, and the general specifications M make no reference to particular objects, events or substances, then we may say that k is a universal scale-dependent constant. (Normally, we should say that k is a universal dimensional constant—the term 'dimensional' having roughly the same significance as my term 'scale-dependent'.)

Moreover, it sometimes happens that a universal constant is not even scale-dependent. For it sometimes happens that whichever choices of scales are made from within the given scale classes, the value of k is unaffected. This occurs when the product of powers of the conversion factors $\equiv 1$. In that case, we have a universal constant which is neither system- nor scale-dependent (or, as we should normally say, a *dimensionless* universal constant).

Now universal constants can always be made to appear in any universal law. Suppose that k in equation (23) is a system-dependent constant. Let d be the name of the quantity of which k is a measure, and let $[K]$ be the class of similar derivative scales defined on the basis of this law. Then instead of expressing the law with respect only to $[S]$, $[T]$, $[U]$, ..., let us express it with respect to $[S]$, $[T]$, $[U]$, ... *and* $[K]$. Then, clearly, we must write

$$f(s, t, u, \ldots) = ck, \qquad (24)$$

where c is a purely scale-dependent constant. Hence, if the law has the required universality, it follows at once that c is a universal constant.

To illustrate this, consider Newton's second law of motion. Expressed with respect to the classes of scales similar to our gram and centimetre scales, it assumes the form

$$ma = f, \qquad (25)$$

where f is a system- and scale-dependent constant, which we say provides a measure of the force acting. If, however, we choose to express this law in such a way that it shall be valid for all choices of scales within the classes of scales similar to our gram, centimetre and dyne scales, we must write

$$ma = kf, \qquad (26)$$

where k is a universal scale-dependent constant. And, as we shall see, it may properly be called a 'dimensional' constant.

Again, consider Ohm's law. Conventionally, it is expressed

$$E = IR. \qquad (27)$$

But this expression is obviously not valid for all choices of scales similar to our Ohm, Volt and Ampère scales. We could, of course, regard say R as the measure of electrical resistance on a derivative scale defined via this law. Then equation (27) would be valid for all choices of scales within the classes $[E]$ and $[I]$ similar to our Volt and Ampère scales. But we could also express it with respect to $[E]$, $[I]$ *and* $[R]$, and then we should have to write

$$E = kIR, \tag{28}$$

where k is a universal dimensional constant. It should be clear, then, that universal constants can always be made to appear in any law with the requisite universality.

The second point that universal scale-dependent constants can always be eliminated from any particular law is almost as obvious. It can be achieved by simply reversing the above procedure. Let

$$f(s, t, u, \ldots) = k \tag{29}$$

be a universal law expressed in standard form with respect to the scale classes $[S]$, $[T]$, $[U]$, ..., k being a universal scale-dependent constant. Then since k is scale-dependent, its value must depend on the choices of scales from within the classes $[S]$, $[T]$, $[U]$, ... To eliminate k, we need only use this law to define a class of similar derivative scales for the measurement of one of the quantities previously measured independently. Thus, if $[S]$ is a class of similar scales for the measurement of a quantity q, a class of similar derivative scales for the measurement of q may be defined simply by expressing the law in standard form with respect to $[T]$, $[U]$, ... and taking the value of the scale- and system-dependent constant which now appears to define a class of similar derivative scales for the measurement of q.

Consider, for example, Newton's law of gravitation. Expressed with respect to the classes of scales $[M]$, $[L]$ and $[F]$ similar to our gram, centimetre and dyne scales, it has the form

$$f = G \frac{m_1 m_2}{r^2}, \tag{30}$$

where G is a universal scale-dependent constant. To eliminate G, we need only express the law with respect to, say, $[M]$ and $[L]$. Then we should have that

$$f' = \frac{m_1 m_2}{r^2}, \tag{31}$$

where f' is a scale- and system-dependent constant which may be taken to measure the force acting between the gravitating bodies on a derivative scale dependent only on the choice of mass and length scales. G is thus successfully eliminated from this particular law.

However, although G may be eliminated by this technique, the convention that we should always express our laws with respect to similarly defined derivative scales for the measurement of the one quantity would produce other universal constants in other laws. In particular, a universal constant would have to appear in Newton's second law of motion. Hence, it may be argued that while universal scale-dependent constants may be elimited from particular laws, there total number in physics cannot be reduced.

But the case is stronger than that. Many universal scale-dependent constants can in fact be eliminated *without remainder* simply by the adoption of new conventions. The reason why the above elimination of G from the gravitation law led to the creation of a new universal constant in the second law of motion is simply that force is already measured on a derivative scale defined via the second law of motion.

Let us consider the case in more detail.* For convenience, let us adopt the c.g.s. (centimetre, gram, second) system of measurement. Then, according to the law (31), f' must be measured in g.^{2} cm.$^{-2}$ (by the usual conventions). Hence, when we come to express the second law of motion with respect to these particular scales, we must write

$$f' = kma, \tag{32}$$

where k is a universal scale-dependent constant determined in the units g. cm.$^{-3}$ sec.^{2}.

However, if instead of using the law (30) to define a derivative scale of force, we had used it to define a derivative scale of *mass*, then no universal constant would have appeared in the second law. In place of (31), we should have

$$f'' = \frac{m_1' m_2'}{r^2} . \tag{33}$$

And in place of (32), we should have

$$f'' = m' a, \tag{34}$$

---

* The remainder of this section will be better understood after ch. IX has been read.

m'_1 and m'_2 being system- and scale-dependent constants defined via equation (33) and f'' being a system- and scale-dependent constant defined via equation (34). In the c.s. (centimetre, second) system, m' would be determined in the units cm.^{3} sec.$^{-2}$. and f'' in the units cm.^{4} sec.$^{-4}$. The reader can readily verify that this leads to no 'dimensional' anomalies.

We may conclude, then, that simply by adopting different conventions concerning the expression of numerical laws, universal scale-dependent constants may be created or eliminated at will. We cannot, therefore, attach to these constants anything other than a conventional existence; and it is quite absurd to suppose that these constants represent the magnitudes of peculiar invariant properties of space or of matter.

D

Some unsolved problems of derived measurement

We have seen that there are many conventions involved in derived measurement. There are, first of all, several conventions involving the expression of numerical laws. It is clear that there are many different ways in which a given numerical law may be expressed. It may, for example, be expressed with respect to particular scales of measurement, with respect to particular classes of similar scales, or with respect to more general classes.* The different expressions do not differ at all in empirical content; they differ only in formal content, that is in the formal information they contain concerning the results of scale transformations. Why then should some forms of expression be generally preferred to others? Why, in particular, should we choose to express our laws of mechanics with respect to classes of similar scales?

I know of no justification for this convention. Indeed, as far as I know, it has never been discussed. Bridgman apparently suspected that there was such a convention when he wrote:

Now there is a certain definite restriction on the rules of operation which we are at liberty to set up in defining secondary quantities. We make the same requirement that we did for primary quantities, namely,

---

* R. D. Luce has investigated the problem of what kinds of laws were possible when they are expressed with respect to more general scale classes; although he did not conceive his task in this way (Luce, 1959).

that the ratio of the numbers measuring any two concrete examples of a secondary quantity shall be independent of the size of the fundamental units used in making the required primary measurements.*

Translated into my language, this means that our derivative scales for the measurement of any quantity must be similar to one another, just as our fundamental and associative scales for the measurement of any quantity must be similar to each other.

But Bridgman himself gives us no indication as to why we are not at liberty to use dissimilar scales. What forces us to use similar scales? Is it the force of some argument? If so, what argument? Is it the force of logic? No, for he himself admits that 'this requirement is not necessary in order to make measurement itself possible'.* By what, then, is our liberty constrained?

In considering this question, I have done no more than push it back to a deeper level. What I have shown is that if we adopt the convention always to express our laws with respect to classes of similar independent scales, and if we always use similarly defined derivative scales for the measurement of all other quantities, then the various derivative scales for the measurement of any given quantity must be similar to each other. But that is as far as I have been able to go. I can see no reason why we should adopt either of these conventions.

However, let us suppose that this question has been answered. Our choices of derivative scales are still not determined. For why should we choose to express our laws with respect to the particular classes of similar scales that we do? Other reference classes could certainly be used; and our laws would receive different mathematical expressions if they were. What then (if any) is the peculiar advantage of expressing our laws in just the way that we do? Many writers, I am sure, would say that only these scales truly represent the quantities concerned, and that these choices are, as it were, forced upon us by nature. But I simply cannot accept that answer, for I do not see how we can recognize 'truly representative' scales. It seems that if any answer can be given to this question, it must be in terms of the formal or mathematical simplicity of the expressions of our numerical laws.

* Bridgman (1931), p. 19.

CHAPTER IX

UNITS AND DIMENSIONS

When we give the result of a measurement on something, we usually say that it is aX in q, where a is a numeral, X is a unit name, and q is a quantity name. In previous chapters we have discussed the meaning of quantity names, and considered in what ways numerical assignments may be made. But so far we have made little mention of unit names. We must now consider what these terms signify, and what conventions govern their use.

A

The concept of a unit

Two sorts of units are usually recognized—fundamental and derived. The fundamental units are usually considered to be the names of certain physical or quasi-physical objects, and the derived units to be any units defined in terms of the fundamental ones. Thus, the metre is often said to be length of a certain rod maintained under special conditions in Paris, and the gram to be the mass of a cubic centimetre of pure water at certain conditions of temperature and pressure. These are usually called fundamental units. The dyne, on the other hand, is usually said to be a derived unit. For it is defined in terms of the units of mass, length, and time-interval as the force necessary to give a mass of 1 g. an acceleration of 1 cm./sec.^{2}.

When I say that the fundamental units are considered to be physical or quasi-physical objects, I mean that they are regarded as countable entities. It is thought that if something has mass, then it must contain so many units of mass, if it has length, then it must contain so many units of length. The mass or length of any given body is regarded as being made up of so many units of mass or length. Also, it is usually supposed to make sense to speak of the sizes of the various fundamental units. One unit of length may be twice or three times as big as another, one unit of time-interval n times as long as another.

I need not quote extracts to establish these points, for this manner of conceiving units is quite universal. There is no book, no article on the logic of measurement which does not make use of expressions like 'the size of the fundamental units' or 'the number of units'.

Yet I believe that this way of regarding units is fundamentally wrong. Consider the proposition: 'This unit of length is twice the size of that one'. What could the phrase 'twice the size of' mean in this context? Presumably it means 'twice the length of'. But what is to say that one unit of length is twice the length of another? For it makes little sense to say that the length of one thing is twice the length of the length of another. We can say that one object A is twice as long as another object B (with respect to a given class of similar length scales). But can we also say that the length of A is twice as long as the length of B? And if we can, then should we not also be able to speak of the length of the length of A, and the length of the length of the length of A, and so on?

It seems clear that while there are physical objects in nature, and that these physical objects are connected by various sorts of relationships—amongst them, mass and length ordering relationships—the length of some object A is not the name of a quasi-physical object which occurs along with A in the order of length. So that if a unit of length is defined to be the length of some standard object, or of some object which meets certain specifications, then it makes no sense to compare units of length for length. We cannot say that one unit of length is twice the size of another, or even that it is greater or less than another.

Of course, we can say that one initial standard for the fundamental measurement of length is longer or shorter than another. For an initial standard of length is merely one object among others in the length order (usually an object which bears very stable length relationships to certain other objects). But an initial standard is not a unit. For all sorts of different fundamental scales may be based upon the same initial standard—depending upon the choices of fundamental measuring procedure and principle of correlation. No one would wish to say, for example, that the unit names 'inch' and 'dinch' are synonymous.

In my view, a unit name merely specifies the particular scale on which a given numerical assignment is made. Our ordinary usage of the terms 'scale' and 'unit' confirms this. If we can say that two measurements are made on the same scale, we can also say that they are made in the same units, and if on different scales, then also in different units. Sameness of scale is, therefore, a necessary and sufficient condition for sameness of units. If you like, a unit name is simply the name of a scale. Consequently, the criterion for the identity of units is simply the criterion for the identity of scales. And if by any means we can specify a particular scale, then by that means, we can define a unit. Nothing less than the complete specification of a scale will satisfactorily define a unit. If we merely refer to a particular object to be used as an initial standard for the fundamental measurement of some quantity, we have not defined a unit for the measurement of that quantity. In addition, we must describe the fundamental measuring procedure, and nominate the principle of correlation.

It must not be thought, however, that a unit name for a fundamental scale indicates which particular choices of measuring procedure, initial standard, and principle of correlation have been made in setting up that scale. For just as the same person may be identified by alternative descriptions, the same scale may be specified by alternative means. For example, we may measure the mass of something in grams by performing certain operations on a beam balance with certain standard objects. But we may also measure mass in grams by subjecting the object concerned to a given force, measuring this force fundamentally in dynes, the acceleration it produces in cm./sec.², and calculating the ratio of these two results. The two procedures are totally different, but in either case we may express our final result as the measure of the mass of the given object in grams. We should say that they are alternative procedures for measuring on the same scale.

The reason for this is simply that as far as we know the two procedures would always lead to the same numerical assignments. Of course, it is possible that they should not always do so. And then we should have to invent a new scale name if we are to continue to use both kinds of measuring procedures.

This then points to the criterion which we actually use for sameness of units. If we have two procedures P_1 and P_2 for the measurement of a given quantity, and if we have reason to believe that with sufficient care P_1 and P_2 would always lead to the same numerical assignments under the same conditions, then we also have reason to believe that P_1 and P_2 are alternative procedures for measuring in the same units.

B

Conventions governing the use of unit names

So much for the general concept of a unit. Let us now consider the conventions which govern the use of unit names.

First, we should note that in setting up a system of scales of measurement for any particular field it is usual to centre the system around certain scales (usually fundamental or associative scales). In mechanics, for example, it is usual to centre our scale systems around scales for the measurement of mass, length and time-interval, and to name the particular scale system by referring to the scales used for the measurement of these quantities. Thus we have the m.k.s. (metre, kilogram, second), the c.g.s. (centimetre, gram, second) and the f.p.s. (foot, pound, second) systems of scales.

These scale systems are systems of interconnected scales, and there are procedures for deciding whether a given scale for the measurement of some quantity does or does not belong to a given system. Let us agree to call the central scales of a given scale system the *independent scales* of that system, and all other scales of the same system the *dependent scales*. Also, let us agree to say that a quantity is measured in *independent units* if it is measured on an independent scale, and in *dependent units* if it is measured on a dependent scale.*

We must now try to clarify this distinction between dependent and independent units. It is best to proceed by example. Suppose that L is the unit chosen as the unit of length, and that we now wish to define the unit of area. There are three quite distinct procedures which we could adopt:

(i) We could arbitrarily select some particular object (maintained under special conditions and kept in a Bureau of Standards), and treat it as an initial standard for the fundamental measurement of area, and then define a fundamental area scale.

(ii) We could make our unit of area depend upon our choice of

---

* I use the terms 'dependent' and 'independent' rather than 'derived' and 'fundamental' because an independent scale need not be a fundamental one. Associative scales are usually independent.

unit of length, so that if a new unit of length is chosen, a new unit of area must be introduced. Thus we could prescribe that the initial standard for the fundamental measurement of area by such and such a procedure is a square* whose sides are of unit length. Then if we change the length unit from L to L', the area unit A must also be changed to some other unit A' if we are to continue to measure in the same system.

(iii) We could specify the unit of area in terms of *specific* length units and in future always measure area in these units whatever scale of length is chosen. Thus we could say that the initial standard for the fundamental measurement of area (by a given procedure) is a square whose sides are 1 cm. in length. Then, no matter what length unit is chosen in our scale system, the unit of area must be unaffected by this choice.

If we adopt either of the procedures (i) or (iii), then clearly our area scale is independent of our length scale. But if we adopt the procedure (ii) our area scale will depend upon our choice of length scale. Now it is this which distinguishes the dependent from the independent scales in a given scale system. The dependent scales are the scales which depend on the choices of other scales. The independent scales are the scales which do not depend in any way upon such choices. All derivative scales, of course, must be dependent scales,† but a dependent scale need not be a derivative scale. It is possible for a fundamental scale to be dependent within a given scale system if the initial standard is specified after the fashion of (ii).

In mechanics, for example, we may say that the initial standard for the fundamental measurement of force is that which will give unit mass unit acceleration. The dyne is therefore a dependent unit in the c.g.s. system. But we do not say that the initial standard for the fundamental measurement of mass is a sample of pure water occupying unit volume at standard conditions of temperature and pressure. No, it is a sample of pure water occupying 1 or 1000 c.c. under these conditions. The gram and the kilogram are therefore independent units. Of course, we could specify the unit

* There is, of course, no need for the initial standard to be a square. For some purposes an equilateral triangle may be more convenient. There is no more difficulty in measuring area in triangular inches than in square inches.

† The Radian scale is apparently an exception to this. But it is a special case which will be discussed later.

of mass in the way we specify our unit of force. And then we should have a more highly centred scale system than the one we actually use. It would be simply a c.s. (centimetre, second), an m.s. (metre, second) or an f.s. (foot, second) system. To mention the mass unit as well would be superfluous.

We could indeed carry this a stage further. There is no reason in the logic of measurement why we should not have single-centred scale systems. The initial standard for the fundamental measurement of length, for example, could be specified as the distance travelled by light in unit time (in a vacuum). Then, of course, our whole scale system would be centred around a single scale, and it would be sufficient to indicate our system of measurement merely to specify our scale of time-interval. On the other hand, there is no reason why we should not have less highly centred systems. We could if we wished have independent scales for every quantity which is fundamentally or associatively measurable.

Why we usually choose to centre our scale systems for mechanics around scales of mass, length and time-interval need not concern us for the moment. The fact is that we do; and we indicate this fact by our use of unit names. For the independent scales we use simple unit names, for example, 'gram', 'metre', 'second'. For the dependent scales we may use complex unit names, for example 'g. cm.$^{-3}$', 'cm. sec.$^{-1}$', 'sec.$^{-1}$', 'g. cm. sec.$^{-2}$', and so on. Sometimes, it is true, we use abbreviations for these complexes, for example 'erg', 'dyne', 'poundal'. But such unit names may always be replaced by complex names without change of meaning.* For 'erg' we may write 'g. cm.^{2} sec.$^{-2}$', for 'dyne', 'g. cm. sec.$^{-2}$', and so on.

There are, therefore, two kinds of unit names, simple and complex, corresponding to the distinction between dependent and independent scales. The significance of the simple unit names has been sufficiently discussed already. We must now turn to consider the meaning of the complex names.

* Once again, the term 'radian' is apparently an exception to this rule. But we shall see that in one way our Radian scale is independent, while in another it is dependent.

C

The significance of complex unit names

In the chapter on derived measurement we saw how derivative scales depend on other scales. We showed that if $[X]$, $[Y]$, $[Z]$, ... are classes of similar scales, and

$$f(x, y, z, ...) = k$$

is a numerical law expressed with respect to these classes of scales, where k is a system- and scale-dependent constant, then k may be taken as the measure of some quantity on a derivative scale dependent on the choices of scales within the classes $[X]$, $[Y]$, $[Z]$, ... We also showed that if k is the only scale-dependent constant which appears, then owing to the convention that our numerical laws be expressed with respect to classes of similar scales, this law must be of the form

$$x^\alpha y^\beta z^\gamma ... = k.$$

And, finally, if X_1 and X_2, Y_1 and Y_2, Z_1 and Z_2, ... are any pairs of scales from the classes $[X]$, $[Y]$, $[Z]$, ..., and $m, n, o, ...$ are the conversion factors for X_1 to X_2, Y_1 to Y_2, Z_1 to Z_2, ... respectively, then

$$k_1 = m^\alpha n^\beta o^\gamma ... k_2,$$

where k_1 and k_2 are the values of the system-dependent constants, determined for any system with respect to the scales X_1, Y_1, Z_1, ... and X_2, Y_2, Z_2, ... respectively. Hence if K_1 and K_2 are the two derivative scales, the conversion factor for K_1 to K_2 is $m^\alpha n^\beta o^\gamma ...$.

Now we can readily indicate the manner in which similarly defined derivative scales of the class $[K]$ depend upon the choices of other scales by writing $X_1^\alpha Y_1^\beta Z_1^\gamma ...$ and $X_2^\alpha Y_2^\beta Z_2^\gamma ...$ in place of K_1 and K_2 respectively. That is, we may substitute complex unit names for the simple unit names K_1 and K_2 and thereby show how K_1 and K_2 depend upon other scales. And I believe that this is precisely the significance of the complex unit names which are used for the dependent scales in our various scale systems. They indicate in just this fashion how these dependent scales rest on the independent ones.

Consider, for example, the unit of force in the c.g.s. system. This is given the complex name 'g. cm. sec.$^{-2}$'. Now according to the above, this means that if we change our length, mass and time-interval scales to similar scales by the conversion factors m, n, and o respectively, our force scale must also be changed by the conversion factor mno^{-2} if we are to continue to measure force in units of a similar scale system, that is a system which is centred around similar scales for the measurement of the same quantities, and in which the derivative and dependent fundamental scales are similarly defined.

Complex unit names therefore give us certain information about the results of transforming from one scale system to any other similar scale system. But why is this information worth giving? What is so important about similar scale systems? The answer to this lies in the convention that we have adopted for the expression of laws, namely, that they be expressed with respect to classes of similar scales. If two scale systems are similar in the above sense, then the independent scales of these systems must be similar, and the derivative scales, being similarly defined, must also be similar. It is not necessary that the dependent fundamental scales be similar. But it is always possible to make them so by suitable choices of fundamental measuring procedures and principles of correlation. Then, supposing that such choices have been made, it follows that on similar scale systems, the same quantity is always measured on similar scales.

Consequently, we may express all of our numerical laws in a given field with respect to a class of similar scale systems, and there will be no need to specify individually the classes of similar scales with respect to which a given numerical law holds. It will be enough if we know the class of similar scale systems to which all of our laws are referred in the relevant fields.

D

Units and numerical laws

The above view of the significance of complex unit names is not without difficulties. First, it seems over-sophisticated. Surely, when I say that a body is travelling at 1 cm./sec., all I mean is that provided its speed remains constant, it will travel a distance of 1 cm. in 1 sec. Secondly, why is it that the complex unit names which we employ are always of the form $X^{\alpha} Y^{\beta} Z^{\gamma} \dots$ where

$X, Y, Z, \ldots$ are simple unit names? If these names merely express the conversion factors for dependent scales as functions of the conversion factors for independent scales, why must these functions all be of the same form? Why should we not have scales with units like 'log cm.', 'sin (g.^{2})', or 'e^{sec^3}'? Thirdly, what about those scales, like the Radian scale of angle, which do not have complex unit names, but which are universally regarded as dependent scales? How do they fit into the above account?

Regarding the first point, it is true that for the simplest derivative scales a much less sophisticated account of the significance of complex unit names seems plausible. If we say that a body is travelling at I cm./sec. we certainly imply that it will cover a distance of I cm. in I sec. or n cm. in n sec., provided that its speed does not change. But when we consider other derivative scales, it is hard to see what sort of account could be given in such terms. When, for example, we measure momentum in g. cm./sec., or force in g. cm./sec.^{2}, what naïve interpretation for these complex unit names can we give? It appears that while the naïve account seems adequate for the most elementary derivative scales it is quite inadequate for the more complex ones.

The reason for this is not immediately obvious, but it is nevertheless important. For it brings out another important function of complex unit names. Suppose that we are provided with the following information. We are told that for a certain class of systems under certain conditions there is a numerical law relating the independently measurable quantities p, q, and r, in which only a single system-dependent constant appears. Let X, Y and Z be three independent scales for the measurement of p, q, and r. Then if we are told that the system-dependent constant has the units $X^\alpha Y^\beta Z^\gamma$, where X, Y, and Z are chosen as independent scales, we know that this law must be of the form

$$x^\alpha y^\beta z^\gamma = \text{const.},$$

when it is expressed with respect to classes of scales similar to X, Y and Z. That is, our complex unit names contain a certain amount of empirical information. They not only give us information concerning the conversion factors for dependent scales, but in certain circumstances they also enable us to predict the standard forms of numerical laws.

Now let us return to the original objection. If we are merely told that some object is 107 cm./sec. in q, where q is a quantity name we cannot identify, then this gives us no information at all about the world. We know, of course, that it is also 1·07 m./sec. in q, or 1·07 × 60 m./min. in q. But these are the only sorts of inferences we can draw. We certainly cannot say that the body is moving with a speed of 107 cm./sec. For q might not be another name for the speed of anything. It might be the case, for example, that whenever a top is set spinning on a circular table, the product of the angular velocity of the top and its distance from the centre is a constant. Then this product would evidently assume some importance in physics, and we should try to find out how this constant changed with changing conditions. To do this, we should need to determine it under various circumstances, and give its value in appropriate dependent units. In the c.g.s. systems these units would be cm./sec.* But the quantity defined by this system-dependent constant would *not* be a velocity.

Consequently, we cannot accept the naïve view that '1 cm./sec.' means '1 cm. every second'. There is no such intimate connection. But if we know that a measurement v cm./sec. is a measure of the speed of a body, then we also know that provided that the body is subject to no resultant forces

$$lt^{-1} = v$$

is a numerical law, and consequently, that the body will travel v cm. in 1 second.

The second difficulty concerns the form which complex unit names always assume. Why must they apparently always be of the form $X^{\alpha} Y^{\beta} Z^{\gamma} \dots$ where $X, Y, Z, \dots$ are the names of independent scales? The answer is that so long as we wish to express our laws with respect to classes of similar scales, we must develop scale systems suitable for this purpose. And this places certain restrictions on the kinds of dependent scales we may employ; for the dependent scales for the measurement of the same quantity, in similar scale systems, must themselves be similar. And this is possible only if the dependent scales depend on the independent scales in certain ways.

Suppose, for example, that $f(x, y, z, \dots) = k$ is a numerical law

* For in the c.g.s. system, angular velocity is measured in the units sec.$^{-1}$.

expressed with respect to the scale classes $[X]$, $[Y]$, $[Z]$, ... Then this law must be of the form

$$x^\alpha y^\beta z^\gamma \ldots = k$$

if k is the only system-dependent constant. Consequently, if $X, Y, Z, \ldots$ are chosen as independent units, and the value of k is determined for various systems, then we must say that the scale on which k is determined is the derivative scale

$$X^\alpha Y^\beta Z^\gamma \ldots.$$

But, of course, it is possible that a numerical law may not be expressible in this form, or that we may choose other conventions for the expression of numerical laws. In either case, we may need to use other sorts of complex unit names—depending on how the law is expressed. Suppose we were to find that

$$y_1 = k_1 \log x_1,$$

where x_1 and y_1 are measurements made on the scales X_1 and Y_1 respectively under certain conditions. Then, with respect to the classes of similar scales $[X]$ and $[Y]$, we could express the numerical law in many different ways. For example, we could write

$$y = k \log k'x,$$
or $$y = k (\log x + k').$$

If we use the first mode of expression, there is no difficulty. If K and K' are the derivative scales corresponding to k and k', for the independent scales X, and Y, K may be given the complex unit name Y, and K' the complex name X^{-1}. But, if we choose the second mode of expression, we find that it is impossible to refer to the scale K' by an ordinary complex unit name. For suppose that for a particular system

$$y_1 = k_1 (\log x_1 + k_1') \tag{1}$$

on the scales X_1 and Y_1, and

$$y_2 = k_2 (\log x_2 + k_2') \tag{2}$$

on the scales X_2 and Y_2.

Let $$x_1 = mx_2,$$
and $$y_1 = ny_2. \tag{3}$$

Then from (1) and (3)

$$ny_2 = k_1 (\log x_2 + \log m + k_1').$$

Hence from (2)

$$k_1 = nk_2,$$
$$\text{and} \qquad k_1' = k_2' - \log m. \qquad (4)$$

Consequently, if we know the value of k_1 and k_1' for a particular system, in derived units dependent upon X_1 and Y_1, then we can predict the value of k_2 and k_2' for the same system, when the units depend on X_2 and Y_2. But there is no simple conversion factor for K_1' to K_2'. For the two scales are dissimilar. To convert from one to the other would require a linear transformation which is not merely a similarity transformation.

However, it is always possible to express our laws with respect to classes of similar scales in such a way that this problem does not arise. And it is an unwritten convention that we should always do so. If we should find that for a particular set of scales, the results of measurements made on particular systems are related by

$$f(x, y, z, \ldots) = k_1.$$

Then, whatever the function f, we may write

$$f(ax, by, cz, \ldots) = k$$

as a numerical law, where $a, b, c, \ldots$ are all scale-dependent constants. Then, if $A_1, B_1, C_1, \ldots$ are the corresponding derivative scales in the scale system $X_1, Y_1, Z_1, \ldots$, then A_1 has the complex unit X_1^{-1}, B_1 the complex unit Y_1^{-1}, C_1 the complex unit Z_1^{-1}, and so on.

Finally, we must say something about the Radian and other so-called dimensionless scales, which from one point of view seem to be dependent scales, and from another independent. They are dependent in the sense that they are defined by the evaluation of system-dependent constants in numerical laws. But they are independent in the sense that the values of these constants are independent of the choices of independent scales within a given class of similar scale systems.

Let us take a simple example to illustrate this. Suppose that $A, B, C, \ldots$ are similar right-angled triangles and that α is a common acute angle of these various triangles. Let l_1 be the length of the side opposite to α, and l_2 the length of the side (not the hypotenuse) adjacent to α. Then we should find that for this class of similar right-angled triangles

$$l_1 = kl_2$$

is a numerical law. But for similar scale systems k would not be scale-dependent. For clearly l_1 and l_2 would always be determined on the same scale whichever scale system is chosen, and if k is to be assigned any complex unit name, it must be LL^{-1}, where L is the name of the length scale chosen. But now this means that if our length scale L is changed by the conversion factor m to the similar scale L^1, the derivative scale defined by this numerical law must be changed by the factor $mm^{-1} = 1$. That is, the numerical assignments on the new derivatives scale will be the same as on the old.

Of course, k would be system-dependent. For a different set of similar right-angled triangles, we would generally get a different value for k. Hence, k must be the measure of some quantity (angle) on a derivative scale. But the Tangent scale of angle, which it defines, would not depend upon the choices of independent scales within any given class of similar scale systems. Like the Radian scale for the same quantity, it is in one sense an independent scale, and in another a dependent scale.

E

The concept of a dimension

It must by now be evident that classes of similar scales have an extremely important role in the logic of measurement. For it is to such classes of scales that most of our numerical laws are referred. It is important, therefore, that we should have some simple way of referring to these classes. Just as we need names for particular scales, we need names for classes of similar scales.

Now, in fact, we do not have any such names—or, at least, names which are conceived in this way. We do, however, have the term 'dimension', and speak of the dimensions of length, mass, time-interval and so forth. And it seems to me that if the theory of dimensions is to have any validity, these terms must be conceived as the names of particular classes of similar scales for the measurement of quantities.

It is difficult to say how dimensions are usually regarded. For no one seems to have any clear conception. In a vague way, I suppose, we may say that dimensions are thought to be some sort of intrinsic characteristic of quantities. Quantities are supposed to have either unique dimensions of their own, or complex dimensions expressible as functions of the dimensions of other quantities. And, accordingly, to ask what are the dimensions of a given quantity, is thought to be a complete and intelligible question. But in my view this question, taken out of context, is nonsensical. The same quantity may be measured on scales of many different dimensions.

Consider, for example, the measurement of length. We have shown how this quantity may be measured on dissimilar scales. Thus we may measure in inches or we may measure in dinches. Now measurements in dinches are invariably the squares of measurements on the same particulars in inches, so that according to our usual criteria, we should say that our measurements in dinches have the dimensions of area. But, of course, they are measurements of length, not area, so that whatever the relations between the two sorts of length scales, it seems that we should say that they have the dimensions of length.

This confusion only arises because dimensions are misconceived. If we consider dimensions to be classes of similar scales then the paradox is resolved. For there is no reason whatever why the same quantity should not be measured on scales of different dimensions. Adopting this view, then, let us consider its implications.

First, let us introduce the square bracket [ ] as a device for naming dimensions and agree to use the term $[X]$ to mean 'the class of scales similar to X'. Then two scales of the same dimension $[X]$ will be similar scales, and two scales of different dimensions $[X]$ and $[Y]$ will be dissimilar. Now an important property of dimensions is that within any dimension, relative magnitude is invariant. For suppose that X and X' are two scales of the class $[X]$, that x_1, x_2 are the results of any two measurements on the scale X, and x'_1, x'_2, are the results of measurements on the same particulars, under the same conditions, on the scale X'. Then according to the definition of similar scales

$$x_1 = mx'_1$$

and
$$x_2 = mx'_2,$$

where m is a constant, depending only on the choices of X and X'. Consequently
$$\frac{x_1}{x_2} = \frac{x'_1}{x'_2},$$

that is, relative magnitude is invariant with iso-dimensional changes of scale.

It is not difficult to show that this condition of the invariance of relative magnitude is also a sufficient condition for saying that two scales are similar. Hence, we may use this as a criterion for sameness of dimension. We may say that two scales X and X' belong to the same dimension if and only if the ratio of any two measurements on X is the same as the ratio of the same measurements on X'.

There is nothing very new in this result. Bridgman, for example, has observed that, for all scales of measurement in scientific use, the ratios of measurements on concrete particulars have 'absolute significance'. But it is not clear that Bridgman understood why this should be so. He did not conceive it as a direct consequence of the convention that our numerical laws be expressed with respect to classes of similar scales, and of the fact that, in most fields of science, we always use scales of the same dimension for the measurement of the same quantity. Rather, he took the absolute significance of relative magnitude as the starting point for his theory of dimensions. And he thus appears to make his theory rest upon the kind of realist dogma which he of all people took most trouble to eliminate.

As I view the matter, there is no absolute significance of relative magnitude. Relative magnitude does not, indeed, depend on the choice of scale within a given dimension. But it does depend upon the choice of dimension. If we were to decide always to measure, say, length, on scales of a different dimension from the usual one, then we may do so if we wish, and express our numerical laws with reference to this new dimension. And, within this dimension, relative length would be independent of the choice of length scale. But our relative length measures would change, with a change of scale from one dimension to another. Relative length is itself a quantity which can be measured on a variety of different sorts of derivative scales.

These remarks, however, in no way undermine Bridgman's theory of dimensions. Rather, they serve to place it on a more acceptable foundation. The rejection of the postulate of the absolute significance of relative magnitude in no way destroys the theory which depends on it. For the necessary invariance of relative magnitude, within a given dimension, will serve every purpose of the original postulate. We may therefore accept the algebra of dimensions, which Bridgman develops, without further argument. Only, we should now be able to see more clearly the scope and limitations of this theory.

If this account of the nature of dimensions is correct, then dimension names may be regarded as generalized unit names. For just as a unit name refers to a particular scale, so a dimension name refers to a particular class of similar scales. Accordingly, we may distinguish within a given system of measurement between independent and dependent dimensions—the independent dimensions being the classes of similar independent scales, to which our numerical laws are referred, and the dependent dimensions, the classes of similar dependent scales.

Moreover, we may adopt similar conventions for the naming of dimensions. For the independent dimensions we may use simple dimension names like $[X], [Y], [Z], \ldots$ and for the dependent dimensions, complex dimension names or dimensional formulae. If $X^\alpha Y^\beta Z^\gamma \ldots$ is a complex unit name for the measurement of some quantity on a given scale system, then we may write $[X]^\alpha [Y]^\beta [Z]^\gamma \ldots$ as the complex dimension or dimensional formula of that quantity in our system of measurement, and thereby indicate that, if $X_1, Y_1, Z_1, \ldots$ are chosen as independent scales of the dimensions $[X], [Y], [Z], \ldots$ respectively, then this quantity must be measured on the dependent scale $X_1^\alpha Y_1^\beta Z_1^\gamma \ldots$. And, as we have seen, this gives us a certain amount of information—both empirical and formal.

F

The nature and scope of dimensional analysis

The theory of dimensions has always been an enigma to the physical scientist. For it appears that here is a genuinely a priori method of obtaining empirical knowledge. We are invited to ask ourselves what quantities could conceivably be involved in a numerical law, to write down their dimensional formulae, perform a few artful manipulations, and hey presto! we have the form which this law must assume. By dimensional analysis, for example, we may arrive at the conclusion that the period of swing of a pendulum

(T) is independent of the mass of the bob, and depends only upon its length (l), the gravitational acceleration (g), and possibly the amplitude of swing (θ), according to the following formula:*

$$T = f(\theta) \sqrt{l/g}. \tag{5}$$

But surely it is obvious that the period of swing of a pendulum *could* depend upon the mass of the bob, and it *could* depend in quite a different way upon its length and the gravitational acceleration. How could such information possibly be contained in mere dimensional formulae?

The answer is, of course, that this information is not contained in the dimensional formulae—although, as we have seen, dimensional formulae are not empirically empty. The period of swing of a pendulum could depend in any way at all upon the mass of the bob, its length, the gravitational acceleration, and any other factors one cares to think of. But if such were the case, a scale-dependent or 'dimensional' constant would have to appear in the expression of this law. And for quite separate reasons, we do not believe that there is any such constant. For we should assume that the law, concerning the period of swing of a pendulum, is a derivative one, that is that, given the boundary conditions, this law could be derived from the basic laws of Newtonian mechanics. Now, since no such dimensional constant appears in these laws, we may conclude that there will be no such constant in any laws derivable from them—the law of the pendulum included. It is not absurd, therefore, that against this background of knowledge we may be able to say something about the form which this law must assume, especially when we take into account the empirical information about the forms of our basic numerical laws contained in our dimensional formulae.

This, basically, is the way that dimensional analysis works. It is not, as it appears to be, a genuinely a priori way of doing physics. Empirical information comes in at several points. First, there is a judgement based upon experience in the selection of likely factors. (It is not always possible to eliminate wrong selections by dimensional analysis.) Secondly, there is the assumption that we have included all of the relevant dimensional constants. (This is usually based upon a well-informed guess as to the detailed analysis.)

* See Bridgman (1931), ch. 1.

Thirdly, there is the information concerning the standard forms of the basic numerical laws contained in the dimensional formulae themselves. With this understanding, dimensional analysis seems much less mysterious. It is, as Bridgman says, 'an analysis of an analysis'.*

It follows that dimensional analysis is completely useless as a tool for the discovery of *basic* numerical laws. For, since we cannot assume that these laws are derived from other laws, no information whatsoever can be gained concerning the form of these laws. To Galileo, looking for the form of the law of free fall, a knowledge of dimensional analysis would have been about as valuable as a knowledge of the rules of cricket. Newton, in looking for the law of gravitation, could not have obtained any guidance at all from dimensional analysis. For these laws were fundamental laws— fundamental in the sense that they were not derivable, and could not be assumed to be derivable, from any previously known laws.

Imagine yourself in the position of Newton. You suspect that there is a law of gravitational attraction. You do not know the precise form of this law, but you try dimensional analysis. In the usual way, you make a list of the quantities you feel may be relevant, and write the dimensional formulae alongside.

Quantity	Dimensional formula	Symbol
Force	$[M][L][T]^{-2}$	f
Mass of A	$[M]$	m_a
Mass of B	$[M]$	m_b
Distance AB	$[L]$	r
Relative velocity AB	$[L][T]^{-1}$	v

Now if the law is valid for similar scale systems, you reason that the law must be of the form

$$f = \text{const. } m_a^{\alpha} m_b^{\beta} r^{\gamma} v^{\delta}.$$

Since the situation is symmetrical, you assume $\alpha = \beta$

$$\therefore f = \text{const. } m_a^{\alpha} m_b^{\alpha} r^{\gamma} v^{\delta}.$$

You now suppose that the constant is dimensionless, and then you have

$$2\alpha = 1,$$
$$\gamma + \delta = 1,$$
$$-\delta = -2,$$
$$\therefore \alpha = \tfrac{1}{2}, \quad \delta = 2, \quad \gamma = -1.$$

* Bridgman (1931), p. 52.

Hence the law must be of the form:

$$f = \text{const.}\; \frac{m_a^{\frac{1}{2}} m_b^{\frac{1}{2}} v^2}{r}.$$

Your result, of course, is quite incorrect. And the reason is, simply, that you have no grounds whatever for assuming the constant to be dimensionless. For you are not dealing with a law which you can reasonably assume to be deducible from the three laws of motion.

G

The power of dimensional analysis

If my views concerning the nature of dimensional analysis are correct, then the power of dimensional analysis must be a function of the empirical content of our dimensional formulae. And this, in turn, must depend on what conventions we adopt for the expression of numerical laws. If we express our laws with respect to particular scales, then, since no classes of similar scales are (tacitly) referred to, no dimensional formulae can be assigned. Dimensional analysis only becomes possible, if we adopt the convention always to express our numerical laws with respect to classes of similar scales. It is no accident, therefore, that the usefulness of dimensional analysis is chiefly confined to mechanics. For this is the only field of science where this practice is widely adopted.

Even in mechanics, the power of dimensional analysis could be considerably increased. Our laws involving the quantity, *angle*, for example, are always expressed with respect to particular scales of angle (usually the Radian scale). Hence angle is said to be a 'dimensionless' quantity, and dimensional analysis is powerless to yield any information at all about the way that this quantity enters into quantitative expressions. But it is only powerless, in this regard, because we choose to express our laws in the way that we do. If we always chose to express our laws with respect to the class of scales of angle similar to our Radian scale, the power of dimensional analysis would be increased.

To illustrate this, consider the law of torsion. In a wire of circular cross-section, of radius r, and of length l, the couple (or torque) T required to produce a twist θ (in Radians) is given by the relation

$$T = 2\pi \frac{\eta r^4}{l}\, \theta, \tag{6}$$

where η is the modulus of rigidity of the material. The law is, of course, expressed with respect to the usual dimensions of length and torque. But note that θ, unlike the other variables, is specifically stated to be in Radians. That is, the law (6) is expressed with respect to classes of similar scales for the measurement of length and torque, but with respect to a particular scale for the measurement of angle.

Now, the modulus of rigidity (or shear modulus) η is a scale- and system-dependent constant which occurs in another law involving angle. If a homogeneous cube of material is subjected to a uniform shearing stress S, parallel to one of the faces of the cube, then the cube will be transformed into a parallelepiped, with the faces originally parallel to S, now being parallelograms. And if ϕ (in Radians) is the angular displacement of the sides, resulting from this transformation, then

$$S = \eta\phi, \tag{7}$$

where S is determined on any stress scale of the usual dimension, and η is a system- and scale-dependent constant, characteristic of the material of the cube. Accordingly, since the dimension of S is denoted by $[M][L]^{-1}[T]^{-2}$, on the usual analysis, η is also assigned this same dimensional formula (since ϕ is said to be dimensionless).

Now, since any element of a wire in torsion is subject to a pure shear stress, we may reasonably assume that the law of torsion is derivable from the law relating shear stress and shear strain. Moreover, since the problem is a static one, we have no reason to suppose that the fundamental laws of dynamics (for example Newton's second law of motion) would be involved in the detailed analysis. There is no need, therefore, to use a dimensional formula for stress, which gives information concerning the fundamental laws of dynamics. In place of $[M][L]^{-1}[T]^{-2}$, therefore, we may simply write $[F][L]^{-2}$, where $[F]$ denotes the class of scales similar to our dyne scale. Hence, we may make the following dimensional analysis shown at the top of p. 147.

Now, since we require the law to be expressed in a form, which is valid for all choices of scales from within the classes similar to

Quantity	Dimensional formula	Symbol
Torque	$[F][L]$	T
Length of wire	$[L]$	l
Radius of wire	$[L]$	r
Angle of twist	—	θ
Rigidity modulus	$[F][L]^{-2}$	η

our usual scales for the measurement of torque, length and rigidity modulus; and since, moreover, we have no reason to believe that there is any other scale-dependent constant besides η involved in the expression of this law, then the law of torsion must be expressible in the form

$$T = \eta^{\alpha} l^{\beta} r^{\gamma} f(\theta).$$

No restriction can be placed on the form of the function f. Now, making the dimensional analysis, we find

$$[F][L] \equiv [F]^{\alpha} [L]^{-2\alpha} [L]^{\beta} [L]^{\gamma}.$$

Hence, $\alpha = 1$ and $\beta + \gamma = 3$. Thus the law must be of the form

$$T = \eta l^{\beta} r^{\gamma} f(\theta), \quad \text{where } \beta + \gamma = 3. \tag{8}$$

Comparison with (6) reveals that this is in complete agreement with the empirical formula.

But why have we not been able to obtain any information at all about the way θ enters into the expression? Only because we chose to express the law of shear stress and shear strain with respect to a particular scale of angle (namely the Radian scale). To obtain more information regarding the law of torsion, we need only express the law (7) with respect to the class of scales similar to our Radian scale. Let ϕ' be the result of any measurement on any scale similar to our Radian scale. Then, in place of (7), we should have

$$S = \eta' \phi', \tag{9}$$

where η' is a new scale-dependent constant dependent not only on the choice of stress scale, but also on the choice of angle scale.

Let $[A]$ denote the class of scales similar to our Radian scale. Then η' must have the dimensional formula $[F][L]^{-2}[A]^{-1}$. Now, let us repeat the dimensional analysis, using η' and θ' in place of η and θ.

Quantity	Dimensional formula	Symbol
Torque	$[F][L]$	T
Length of wire	$[L]$	l
Radius of wire	$[L]$	r
Angle of twist	$[A]$	θ'
Rigidity modulus	$[F][L]^{-2}[A]^{-1}$	η'

10-2

Since we now know that this law must be valid for all choices of angle scales within the class similar to our Radian scale, we may write

$$T = C\eta'^{\alpha} l^{\beta} r^{\gamma} \theta'^{\delta},$$

where C is a constant which is neither system- nor scale-dependent. Now, making the dimensional analysis, we find:

$$[F][L] \equiv [F]^{\alpha}[L]^{-2\alpha}[A]^{-\alpha}[L]^{\beta}[L]^{\delta}[A]^{\delta}.$$

Whence, $\alpha = 1$, $\delta = 1$, and $\beta + \gamma = 3$, and the law of torsion must be of the form
$$T = \eta' l^{\beta} r^{\gamma} \theta' \qquad (10)$$
where $\beta + \gamma = 3$.

Comparison with (6) reveals that (10) is in complete agreement with the empirical formula; and comparison with (8) reveals that this new dimensional analysis has yielded considerably more information.

The moral to be drawn from this is that we can only get out of our dimensional formulae what we put into them. And, if we choose to express our laws with respect to particular scales, we shall inevitably impoverish our dimensional formulae. They will contain much less information, than they might otherwise do, concerning the forms of the laws, on which our derivative scales and scale-dependent constants are defined.

If this lesson applies, even in the field of mechanics, it applies with much greater force outside this field. For, it is only in the field of mechanics that the practice of expressing our laws with respect to classes of similar scales is widely followed. The attentive reader of scientific periodicals will find literally dozens of perplexed and confused articles concerning the dimensions of temperature and other 'non-mechanical' quantities. The reason is, simply, that the question makes no sense. Until the practice of expressing our temperature laws with respect to classes of similar temperature scales (for example the class of scales similar to the Absolute scale) is adopted, there are no dimensions of temperature involved in the expression of any of our temperature laws.

There are many different ways that we could approach the problem of assigning dimensional formulae to temperature and other quantities concerning heat. We could use the gas law of Gay-Lussac to define a dependent scale of temperature. Then we should have that
$$\frac{pV}{n} = T, \qquad (11)$$

where n is the number of gram-molecules in a given mass of gas, p is its pressure on any scale similar to our dyne/cm.² scale, and v is its volume on any scale similar to our cm.³ scale. Then, the dimensional formula for temperature must be $[M][L]^2[T]^{-2}$. This means that in the c.g.s. system, temperature would be measured in g. cm.²/sec.², that is temperature would be measured in the units of energy. But, to do this consistently, the universal scale-dependent constant R which occurs in the usual expression: $pV = nRT$, must be banished altogether from science.

Our Calorie scale of heat is generally used for the expression of laws involving heat; and a Calorie is usually said to be the quantity of heat required to raise 1 g. of water from 0 to 1° C. But obviously, if we wish dimensions of heat to be concerned in the expressions of laws involving this quantity, we must express our laws with respect to, say, the class of scales similar to our Calorie scale. Now such a class of scales is readily definable simply by taking the measure of the work that must be done to raise the temperature of a given object to a certain level as a measure of the heat that must be supplied to raise it to the same level. Thus we should have $W = Q$, and the heat supplied to an object would be measured in work units. We should, therefore, if we wish to express our heat laws in the required fashion, abolish that universal scale-dependent constant we call 'the mechanical equivalent of heat' and measure heat on a dependent scale which, like temperature, belongs to the dimension $[M][L]^2[T]^{-2}$.

Now, supposing that these conventions have been adopted, then specific heat must be assigned the dimensional formula $[M]^{-1}$. For specific heat is simply the name of a quantity defined via a scale- and system-dependent constant which occurs in the law: $Cm\Delta t = \Delta Q$, where Δt and ΔQ are the temperature and heat changes (now guaged in work units), and m is the mass of the substance on any scale similar to our gram scale.

Entropy, on the other hand, would now turn out to be a system-dependent, but not a scale-dependent constant, since the ratio $\Delta Q/T$ would be independent of our choices of scales for the measurement of work and energy (within the usual scale classes). Hence, if we wish to give information, in our dimensional formulae, concerning the way in which entropy enters into our numerical laws, we must express them with respect to the class of scales similar to our usual entropy scale. If we say that entropy is a 'dimensionless' quantity, like angle, then we shall frustrate the purposes of dimensional analysis; just as the practice of saying that angle is a 'dimensionless' quantity has rendered dimensional analysis powerless to tell us anything about the way in which angle is involved in numerical laws. Hence, entropy must be assigned a unique dimensional name of its own, say $[S]$.

Probability can now be brought into the picture; although this presents unusual problems. Probability as I shall argue later, is quantity; and like other quantities, it may be measured on a variety of different kinds of scale. In fact, however, no such variety of scales is in common use. But clearly, we could define a class of scales $[P]$ similar to, say, Boltzmann's scale of state probability. And since $S = k \ln p$ expresses a numerical law with respect to the *particular* scales of entropy and probability we use, where k is Boltzmann's constant, we may write: $\alpha S = k \ln \beta p$ as the expression of this law with respect to $[S]$ and $[P]$. However, this is an 'unorthodox' expression; that is it is not in standard form. If we wish to put it in standard form, we must use scales of entropy or probability dissimilar to our usual ones. The simplest alternatives are to use a 'logarithmic' scale of entropy, or an 'exponential' scale of probability. Of these, it is not clear which is to be preferred.

But whichever choice is made, we may obviously remove yet another universal constant from the statute books by defining a derivative scale of entropy (or probability) on the basis of Boltzmann's law. Entropy can then be measured in probability units, or probability in entropy units, whichever we please.

In the field of electricity, it is probably better to introduce new dimensional symbols at the outset, since, as far as we know, the laws pertaining to this field are not derivable from the laws of mechanics. We may, for example, define the class of scales similar to our Coulomb scale of electric charge, denote this class by a simple dimension name, say $[q]$, and in future, express all laws involving electric charge with respect to $[q]$. Electric current must then be assigned the dimension name $[q][T]^{-1}$. Potential difference may now be assigned a simple dimension name, say $[V]$, and then a derivative scale of electric resistance defined via Coulomb's law. Electric resistance must then be assigned the dimension name $[V][T][q]^{-1}$.

However, it is really beside the main point of this essay to continue this development further. My only concern, in making these suggestions, is to show how my concept of a dimension may have practical applications; and to illustrate the general principles which should govern the expression of numerical laws, given that we wish to obtain the maximum of information through dimensional analysis. These principles are:

(*a*) that we should always express our numerical laws with respect to classes of similar scales for the measurement of *all* quantities involved;

(*b*) that we should always use similarly defined scales for the measurement of the one quantity.

(*c*) that wherever a so-called 'dimensionless' scale appears in our system of measurement, we should invent a new dimension name for the class of scales similar to this scale, and express all numerical laws with respect to this class of scales.

(*d*) that 'unorthodox' numerical laws should be put in standard form by making suitable changes of scales, and then expressed with respect to the classes of scales similar to these resulting scales.

(*e*) that derivative scales should be defined on the basis of laws that we consider to be fundamental ones in our system of physics; so that, the dimensional formulae we assign to quantities measured derivatively should contain information about the forms of these laws;

(*f*) that we should have no hesitation in eliminating universal constants, if this is necessary to achieve a suitable system of derivative scales; for as we have seen, such constants have only a conventional existence.

CHAPTER X

THE PHYSICAL CONCEPT
OF NUMBER

In this and the next chapter I shall consider two special quantitative concepts, 'number' and 'probability'. I have left the discussion of them to the end, because they are unique among our quantitative concepts, and because, by doing so, I am better able to bring out the points of similarity and contrast.

In considering the concept of number I shall deal only with the physical concept, that is the concept of number which is employed in such expressions as 'Here are seven apples'. To deal with mathematical number concepts as well would be altogether too vast an undertaking, and in any case, not very relevant to the present discussion.

A

Is number a quantity?

The word 'number' is certainly used as a quantity name. We talk of groups being equal in number, or of one group being greater in number than another, just as we talk of objects being equal in length, or of one object being longer than another. Also, it is not difficult to specify ordering relationships, by which groups of things may be arranged in order of number. We can say:

(i) two groups A and B are equal in number, if and only if every member of group A can be paired with a member of group B, and vice versa;

(ii) a group A is greater in number than a group B, if and only if every member of group B can be paired with a member of group A, but not vice versa.

These definitions are not merely stipulative; they represent necessary conditions for the use of the terms 'equal in number' and 'greater in number' in ordinary discourse.

It may be thought that there is some circularity in these definitions. For must we not already have certain numerical concepts in order to understand them? Yes; at least we must have the concepts of 'one', 'none', and 'more than one'. The idea of 'none' is required for the understanding of 'every'. For, we can say that we have paired every member of a group A with a member of a group B, if and only if we have paired each member of a group A with a member of group B until none remains to be paired. The distinction between one, and more than one, is required for the understanding of singular and plural, and hence for the understanding of 'each'. If we could make no such distinction, we could never distinguish an apple from a group of apples, and we could make no sense of the instruction to pair the members of one group with those of another.

Hence the distinctions between 'one', 'none' and 'more than one' are a prerequisite for understanding the basic numerical ordering relationships. However, when we consider the matter, we can see that much the same could be said of length relationships. To understand the basic length ordering relationships, we need the concept of 'overlap'. For this we need concepts of spatial and temporal coincidence, and we need to understand what it is for one thing to be spatially between two others. That is, an understanding of the basic length ordering relationships requires an understanding of certain spatial and temporal relationships. These spatial relationships are already, in a sense, length relationships. For, to say that two points are in the same place is to say that they are separated by no distance, and to say that one point C lies between two others, A and B, is to imply that the distances AC and BC are each less than the distance AB. We may say, therefore, that to understand the basic length ordering relationships, we need to have some basic concepts of length. However, neither analysis involves circularity. For there is a hierarchy of both length and numerical relationships, some being logically prior to others. Here, I shall try to show how the more derivative numerical relationships depend on the more fundamental.

It is clear that we should say that number is a quantity. But on the other hand, it seems to make no sense to speak of measuring the number of things in a group. We can speak of counting, calculating, or guessing the number, perhaps, but not of measuring it. Moreover, there appears to be no such thing as a scale or unit of number. For these reasons, it may be somewhat misleading to say this. Of course, if 'counting' were only the name given to a special kind of measuring procedure that is appropriate to the quantity, number, then at least one of my prima facie objections to saying that number is a quantity must be dismissed. But in some respects counting is like measuring, and in others it is not.

The verb 'to count' can be used transitively or intransitively. Intransitive counting, that is the idle recitation of the numeral sequence, is admittedly not very like measuring. If we are measuring, then we must always be measuring something in some respect. We cannot simply be measuring. But transitive counting certainly has some of the essential characteristics of a measuring procedure. For it is an objective and determinative procedure for assigning numerals to groups—('objective' in the sense that anyone who follows the same procedure with sufficient care will be led to assign the same numerals to the same groups). Also, the numerals, thus assigned, will be the same, if and only if the groups are equal in number, and those groups higher in the order of number will be assigned numerals which occur later in the sequence of numerals.

On the other hand, we can say what it is for a group to contain a specific number of things without describing a counting procedure. Also, there are procedures for making numerical assignments that would qualify as procedures for measuring number (according to our criteria), but which would not qualify as counting procedures. The restrictions imposed upon counting procedures are more severe than those imposed upon measuring procedures.

With regard to the first of these points, we can say:

(i) a group B contains 2 things, if and only if it is greater in number than a group A containing one thing, and there is no conceivable group greater in number than A and less in number than B;

(ii) a group C contains 3 things, if and only if it is greater in number than a group B containing two things, and there is no conceivable group greater in number than B and less in number than C; and generally;

(iii) a group N contains n things if and only if it is greater in number than a group M containing $n-1$ things, and there is no conceivable group greater in number than M and less in number than N.

Thus, it seems possible to give criteria for saying how many things there are in a given group solely in terms of the basic ordering relationships for number. We do not need to be able to count (in the transitive sense).

Next, any counting procedure must lead to the correct assignment of numerals to groups. It is not enough that groups equal in number should be assigned the same numeral, or that the sequential order of the numerals assigned to groups should correspond to the numerical order of the groups (given by the numerical ordering relationships). Thus, Gasking's 'counting procedure'* is not a counting procedure. If I take an object from a given group of objects; count 'ONE'; place it separately; count 'TWO'; take a second object; count 'THREE'; place it separately, count 'FOUR'; and so on, until the group is exhausted, then whatever I have done, I have not counted the number of objects in the group. It is true that this procedure would lead to the same numerals being assigned to groups equal in number, and to higher numerals being assigned to groups greater in number. But the procedure must, nevertheless, be rejected as a counting procedure. If counting were like, say, length measuring, then it would have to be admitted as an alternative. But it must be rejected, because the sentence: 'This group contains four things of such and such a type' already has a precise meaning that is independent of counting operations. It does not state that if you follow a certain objective procedure with the things concerned you will finish with the numeral 4. It states that the given group has certain numerical relationships with other groups. Our counting procedures are admitted as counting procedures, if and only if they give correctly the numbers of things in groups.

Counting also seems to differ from, say, length measuring in that there is, apparently, nothing corresponding to a standard set. In all fundamental measurement, the thing to be measured is matched, in respect of the quantity concerned, by a series of operations with the members of a set of standards, or their equivalents. The standards are kept under special conditions, are made of special materials and so on. At first sight, it seems that there is nothing corresponding to this for the quantity, number. But when we consider the matter more carefully, we see that the numeral sequence itself plays a role in counting similar to that of a standard

* Gasking (1940), pp. 97–116.

set. For it is certainly true that in all counting, we pair members of the numeral sequence with those of the group being counted. Accordingly, we can say that we match numerically the group to be counted with a subset of the numeral sequence. The subset, 1, 2, 3, 4, therefore, serves as a standard group of four. And when we count a group of four things, we automatically show that it is equal in number to the subset of numerals 1 to 4.

It is conceivable that we should use groups of stones or marbles as numerical standards, and that they should be kept in special museums to protect them from destruction. All number determination would then be done by matching the group whose number is to be determined with one of the standards, or its equivalent in number. We can imagine, indeed, that we should all carry round little bags of marbles labelled 2, 3, 4, and so on, and that when we wish to find the number of things in a given group, we simply find the bag which contains the same number of marbles. This would be logically very similar to carrying around a set of feeler gauges. In fact, of course, this would be very cumbersome, and it is much easier to use subsets of the numerical sequence as numerical standards. The subset of numerals 1 to 12 is a far more convenient numerical standard than a bag of 12 marbles.

In all fundamental measurement, the standard set is built up from an initial standard by some sort of combination procedure. In the case of length, a second member of the standard set is usually obtained by placing two objects equal in length to the initial standard, end to end; a third member by placing one of the second members, thus formed, end to end with an initial standard; and so on. We can imagine a similar procedure being used to produce sets of stones standard in number. Here the combination procedure would be simply that of forming a composite group. A standard group of two stones would be formed by making a composite group out of two groups each containing one stone, a standard group of three, by combining a standard group of two with another of one, and so on.

In forming a scale of length, however, I may select any object, which bears stable length relationships to sufficiently many other objects as an initial standard, and assign the numeral 1 to it. Further, I may choose whatever combination procedure I like, provided that it enables me to form a standard set and subset.

156

Finally, I may assign numerals to the members of the standard set according to whatever rules I like, provided only that the sequential order of the numerals indicates the length order of the objects to which they are assigned. Depending on which choices I make, I may assign different numerals to the same objects as the measure of their length. I must, of course, indicate which of the above choices I have made, by specifying a unit. It is useless to say 'This has a length of 4'. I must, for example, say that it is 4 in., or metres, long.

But with the quantity, number, there are no such choices. The only area of choice lies in the way we regard a given group. For example, we may regard 2 men as a group of 4 legs, 4 arms, 2 bodies, and 2 heads, that is 12 bodily parts. We may regard a group of 2 men and 2 women as a group of 2 couples. The number of things in a group may therefore depend on how we regard it; and, in this respect, there is certainly a degree of freedom. Nevertheless, the words 'men', 'women', 'couples', 'heads', and so on, are not much like unit names such as 'inch' and 'foot'. The function of the latter words is, roughly, to indicate which of the above choices we have made in defining our length scales. But the use of the former is not to indicate any such or analogous choices.

Indeed, there are no such choices. I cannot arbitrarily select a group of, say, apples and assign to it the numeral 1, saying 'This group contains one apple'. For this statement is already true or false. Nor can I simply invent a word and say: 'This group contains one clong'. For until I know what a clong is, I can never find a group which I should say contains 2 clongs. Moreover, I can never give instructions for pairing. I cannot pair the members of a group A with those of a group B, unless I can recognize a member of group A and a member of group B when I see one. It follows that I cannot arbitrarily select a group as an initial standard for number in the way that I can arbitrarily select an object as an initial standard for length. Any object which bears stable length relationships to sufficiently many other objects will do as an initial standard for length. But only a group which contains one, as opposed to none and more than one, recognizable thing can be said truly to contain one X (where X is the name of the thing). With the selection of a unit of length, no question of truth or falsehood arises. If I say 'Let this be 1 minch long', what I say is neither true nor false. The 'let' signifies that I am giving a part definition in use for the word 'minch'. But I cannot say, analogously, 'Let this group contain one apple'. For, it contains no term whose use is not already fixed. The proposition 'This group contains one apple' is *already* true or false.* Nor can I say, significantly, 'Let this group contain one clong'. For if I do *not* know what a clong is, I cannot match the given group in number with any other group. And, if I *do* know what a clong is, then it is like saying 'Let this group contain one apple'.

It follows that there is nothing which can be described as a unit or scale of number. Accordingly, it is very misleading to speak about correlating numerals with groups. Such talk is only appropriate where there is arbitrariness and choice. To specify a group, we must always say what it is a group *of*—whether of physical objects, numerals, ideas, events, or what. Once the specification has been made, the number of the group is now entirely an empirical question—with one important exception.

This exception is the numeral sequence itself. It is not an empirical fact that the numeral sequence 1, 2, 3, 4, contains 4 numerals. For one way that we may establish that a group contains four things is simply to show that it is equal in number to this group of numerals. We cannot call into question the proposition that the group of numerals 1 to n contains n numerals without automatically calling into question our primary means of deciding the number of things in a group. It follows that the proposition 'The sequence of numerals 1 to n is n in number' is an analytic proposition.

But, it will be objected, surely there is more than one criterion for saying that a group contains a specific number of things. Haven't I already given another criterion in terms of numerical ordering relationships? Yes, a group contains 4 things, if and only if it contains one more than a group of 3. A group contains 3 things, if and only if it contains one more than a group of 2, and so on. And we can explain the concept of 'containing one more than' by saying that a group A contains one more than a group B, if and only if A is greater in number than B, and there is no

---

* We can, of course, say 'Let us *suppose* that this group contains one apple'. But this is a hypothesis, and obviously very different from 'Let this be 1 minch long'.

conceivable group greater in number than B and less in number than A. But when all this is said, it does not follow that the proposition: 'The sequence of numerals 1 to 4 contains 4 numerals' is a synthetic proposition. If our criteria for the number of things in a group diverged, then we should not know what to say.

It should be clear, then, that the concept of number occupies a very special position in the logic of measurement. We may say that number is a quantity on the grounds that the necessary ordering relationships exist. But then, it is peculiar in that it does not make much sense to speak of a scale for the measurement of this quantity. We can call counting a measuring procedure, if we wish. For it certainly has many of the essential characteristics of measuring procedures. But then, it lacks arbitrariness. There seems to be nothing which corresponds to a choice of unit. Once a group has been specified, the numeral that we must assign in order to indicate the number of things it contains is completely determined. Hence, if we must speak of counting as a measuring procedure, it is unique among all measuring procedures.

CHAPTER XI

THE CONCEPT OF PROBABILITY

Most philosophers nowadays distinguish at least three different senses of the term 'probability'—The 'relative frequency', the 'degree of confirmation' and the 'subjective probability' senses. These distinctions are made on various grounds, but perhaps the most usual is that we have at least three different kinds of procedures for determining probability relationships.

The procedures that relate to the 'relative frequency' and 'subjective probability' senses are clearly empirical: their outcomes depend on how the world is, not merely on how we talk about it. Accordingly, these concepts are called *empirical probability* concepts. Those procedures relating to the 'degree of confirmation' sense, however, are non-empirical: their outcomes do not depend on how the world is, but simply on the language we use to describe it and the principles of inductive reasoning that we have adopted. Accordingly, this kind of probability is called *logical probability*.

There is no doubt that our concept of logical probability is different from any of our empirical probability concepts. Nevertheless, the relationship between logical and empirical probability is a curious one. For, when we examine in detail the grounds for making the distinction, we see that precisely the same arguments apply to every other quantity concept. Hence, if the word 'probability' is ambiguous, sometimes designating a logical concept and sometimes an empirical one, then so is every other quantity name in our language. If there are two concepts of probability, one logical and the other empirical, then in precisely the same sense, and on precisely analogous grounds, there are two concepts of temperature, one logical and the other empirical; two concepts of mass, one logical and the other empirical; two concepts of length, one logical and the other empirical; and so for every other quantity.

In fact, no one speaks of logical mass, or logical temperature— partly because these concepts are relatively uninteresting, but mainly because, if anyone did discuss these concepts, he would not think he was doing so. He would quite naturally (and quite rightly) think he was discussing the logic of mass measurement, or the logic of temperature measurement. Similarly, I shall argue, the study of logical probability is really that of the logic of probability measurement. I do not deny the great importance of this study; nor that we *can* think of it as the study of some quantity other than probability, namely logical probability. Nevertheless, I believe that it is anomalous and confusing to regard logical probability as a separate quantity. Moreover, it leaves the relationship between logical and empirical probability rather obscure.

It will be argued here that if anyone wishes to think of probability as a single quantity, that is consider that there is a unique objective probability order, then he is free to do so. No attempt will be made to offer a theoretical interpretation of probability, however, and no claim is made that such an interpretation is even possible. To use Carnap's terminology, there will be no attempt at *explication*. For Carnap's claim that there are two distinct probability orders is not based upon the existence of different explications of probability. In his own words, the distinction is one between two different *explicanda*.*

The structure of the following argument is:

(*a*) There is a crude order of probability which, in many respects, is like the pre-thermometric temperature order. Its existence depends upon the fact that different people tend to draw, or can be trained to draw, the same conclusions from the same evidence. That is, the existence of a crude probability order depends upon there being a certain consistency (artificially created or otherwise) among the rational activities of different human beings. In a similar way, the existence of a crude atmospheric temperature order depends upon there being a certain consistency among the biological reactions of different human beings. This analogy suggests that we may regard probability as a quantity, that is assume that there is an objective probability order, and consider it the function of probability theory to devise a suitable scale for its measurement.

(*b*) The first problem of probability theory concerns the proper subject of probability statements. It is argued that if probability

* Carnap (1950), § 9.

is a quantity, then it is a quantity possessed by propositions. It is shown, however, that the concept of proposition must be taken to include some assertions which would not be regarded as propositions within the traditional framework of the Propositional Calculus of Russell and Whitehead. A suitable concept of proposition is developed and explained.

(c) The second problem of probability theory is to devise objective procedures for ordering propositions in respect of probability. There are various kinds of such procedures—some purely inductive, others depending on theoretical considerations and considerations of symmetry. It is then shown that where different kinds of procedures may be used to decide the probability of a given proposition, these procedures are regarded as complementary. That is, where the different kinds of procedures yield different probability judgements, at least one of them is regarded as being inaccurate. It is not insisted that both are accurate, but in different senses of 'probability'.

(d) A purely inductive procedure is understood to be any which consists simply in applying inductive rules. The concept of an inductive rule is examined, and it is shown that inductive rules are strictly limited in their range of applicability. This limitation in the range of applicability of inductive rules implies that the probability of many propositions cannot be determined inductively.

(e) The third problem of probability theory is to devise a suitable scale for the measurement of probability. It is usually required that such a scale should meet certain specifications. In particular, the probability numbers that are assigned to various propositions on such a scale must satisfy the axioms of the probability calculus (under a certain interpretation). It is then shown that if these specifications are met, and if there is an objective probability order, then such a scale must be a ratio scale with two fixed points, that is it must be unique. Hence, if it is required that all probability measurements be made on this scale (the normal scale), then probability numbers are unambiguous. However, there are various inductive procedures for *estimating* normal probability, and the problem of choosing between them remains unsolved. This problem is then seen to be entirely analogous to the problem of choice of mathematical averaging function.

(f) The concept of logical probability, that is Carnap's 'degree of confirmation', is then examined, and the chief arguments for considering this to be a quantity distinct from probability are considered. It is shown that if these arguments are sound, we must likewise distinguish between two concepts of temperature—one logical and the other empirical. Indeed, we must consider every quantity name to be ambiguous. Moreover, it is shown that the concept of logical probability is superfluous—to define a procedure for determining logical probability is just to describe a procedure for estimating probability.

(g) It is concluded that if anyone wishes to believe that there is a single objective probability order, there is no reason at all why he should not do so. Logical probability is not a genuine quantity, and its study is simply that of the logic of probability measurement. There is no denying the importance of this study, however, for it embraces the whole field of inductive logic.

A

The crude order of probability

There is no doubt that a crude probability order can be agreed upon by people whose background knowledge is relatively fixed. We can all agree that a coin is more likely to land heads or tails than it is to land, say, heads; that this in turn is more likely than that we should throw a six first go with a standard die; that the throwing of a six is more likely than that I should die before the end of the week and that this again is more likely than a revival of the phlogiston theory.

Of course, there will be disagreements—often marked ones where our background knowledge differs. If you know, and I don't know, that I have just drunk a cup of cyanide, you may think it very likely that I will die before the end of the week and I may think it very unlikely. Even where our background knowledge is the same, our probability estimations may differ. Consider, for example, how various people, badly tutored in probability theory, would judge whether a straight or a flush is more likely in a game of poker. As a matter of fact, then, our probability judgements depend on our background knowledge, our intellectual capacity, and our intellectual training.

Nevertheless, there is sufficient consistency among the judgements of probability made by different people to make objective probability talk intelligible. That is, there is enough objectivity in the order of probability to make the expressions 'is as probable as' and 'is more probable than' meaningful ones. If our background knowledge were too various or our estimations of the strength of evidence too diverse, the use of such expressions could never be taught, learned, or understood. We have the concept of probability that we have, just because there is no such diversity.

We may compare this crude concept of objective probability with the crude pre-thermometric concept of temperature. Here the judgements that we make depend less on our background knowledge and intellectual training (although they are not independent of such factors), and more upon heat sensation. And this in turn depends on our previous conditioning. But, nevertheless, there is a good deal of consistency in our judgements of temperature order. If this were not so, we could form no objective concept of temperature without instrumental aids. In other words, our temperature judgements have to be reasonably consistent with one another, or else it must be impossible to make any direct temperature judgements at all.

Imagine a world in which people reacted very differently to changes in the weather. Suppose that on any day of the year, rain or shine, you could find some people dressed up as for a polar expedition, others in suits, and yet others in shorts and open-necked shirts. Suppose further that there was no consistency in people's behaviour. When the weather changed you could find some people pulling on heavy sweaters, and others taking them off. Now, in such a world, we could form no crude concept of day temperature. We might find instruments which would enable us to arrange the days of the year in a unique and objective order. But the order would correspond to no primitive concept. Temperature talk could not get going until some instrument (which we would call a themometer) was discovered or invented.

Now, our crude probability concept is similarly dependent upon a certain consistency in human behaviour. It depends on the fact, for example, that when different people are presented with the same facts they can draw, or be trained to draw, the same conclusion. Not that all people always draw the same conclusions from the same facts, but that this happens fairly often. It also depends upon the fact that people have, or can be trained to have, more or less the same degree of confidence in these conclusions. And this comes out in the fact that people take similar precautions, similar risks, accept similar bets and so forth.

This analogy with temperature suggests that the problem of probability theory is to take this crude semi-objective probability order, to replace it by an objective and more refined one, and to devise a suitable scale for its measurement. The new probability order must come to 'replace' our various subjective probability orders in the sense that it becomes the standard against which our subjective probability judgements may be assessed. In other words, where there are discrepancies between our subjective and objective probability judgements it is essential that we should be prepared to regard our subjective judgements as inaccurate or mistaken. We should be prepared to say, for example, that while such and such *seems* improbable, it is *really* very probable. If this condition is not fulfilled, then, whatever other interest it may have, the new linear order we have constructed will not be considered to be a probability order.

B

Probability as an attribute of propositions

We must accept that there is a crude probability order; but what sorts of things can be put into it? We may talk of the probability of events, of states of affairs, of theories, of conclusions, of propositions, and so on; but we can hardly suppose that things of such very different categories can all occur in the one order and be connected by objective probability relationships. If there is only one order, then at least some of these ways of speaking must be elliptical; and so our first problem is to decide what sorts of things possess probability.

Various suggestions have been made, but most writers seem to agree that the choice, if there is one, lies between kinds or classes, on the one hand, and propositions on the other. But they would deny that there is really any question of choice. Following Carnap, they would say that kinds or classes (usually of events or states of affairs) form the proper subject-matter of empirical or statistical probability statements, while propositions form the proper subject-matter of logical probability statements.

However, until we are forced to decide otherwise, we should, in accordance with our approach to quantities generally, proceed on the assumption that there is only one objective probability order. Hence, we must ask whether probability statements expressed as propositions about kinds or classes, for example 'There is a probability p that an A is a B', can also be expressed as propositions about propositions, or vice versa. If such a reduction cannot be achieved, in either direction, then we shall be forced to conclude that there are two logically distinct probability orders, and hence, two logically distinct quantities.

There is, as far as I can see, no way at all of expressing many probability statements (which appear to attribute probability to propositions) so that they appear to attribute probability to classes. How, for example, could one express the proposition 'It is highly probable that there is intelligent life elsewhere in the universe' in the form 'It is highly probable that an A is a B'. For reasons too well-known to bear repeating, I would not accept the translation 'It is highly probable that an intelligent being elsewhere in the universe is *existent*', as one of the required form. Nor would I accept 'It is highly probable that an intelligent being is a being elsewhere in the universe', since that is not equivalent to the original proposition. Nor would I accept 'It is highly probable that a region of space elsewhere in the universe is a container of intelligent beings', since that is not what is being asserted either.

The same point can be made with many different kinds of probability statements. Thus, the assertion that it is highly probable that Japan would have won the war, had she developed atomic weapons before the United States, does not appear to be expressible in the form 'It is highly probable that an A is a B'. Again, how could one possibly translate 'The existence of a luminiferous ether is extremely improbable'?

There is no need for me to multiply examples, however, for the point is not likely to be strongly contested. Relative frequency theorists have dismissed such examples as involving loose, secondary or derivative uses of the term 'probability', but no one, to my knowledge, has attempted to assimilate such propositions to a frequency theory (or to any other theory which attributes probability to classes or kinds). Consequently, we may reasonably assume that the only possibility of reduction lies in the direction from kinds to propositions.

Consider first a statement of the form 'It is probable that an A is a B'. If this statement ascribes probability to a proposition, then what is this proposition? If we say it is the proposition that an A is a B, then what is the logical form of this proposition? Suppose I say that an A is a B (for example 'A triangle is a three-sided figure', or 'A whale is a mammal'). Then, usually, I imply that: $(x)[Ax \supset Bx]$. But when I say that it is probable that an A is a B (I will use the operator 'P' for 'it is probable that'), then clearly I do not mean to assert or to imply that $P(x)[Ax \supset Bx]$. To make this assertion, I must say 'It is probable that *all* A's are B's'.

To make the distinction between

(*a*) it is probable that *all* A's are B's, and

(*b*) it is probable that *an* A is a B;

we might try symbolizing (*a*) by the expression

(*a'*) $P(x)[Ax \supset Bx]$,

and (*b*) by the expression

(*b'*) $(x)P[Ax \supset Bx]$.

But then, clearly, we shall still need to distinguish between two kinds of P-operators. For the operator, P, in the expression (*a'*) operates upon a proposition, while the operator, P, in the expression (*b'*) operates upon a propositional function. Hence, this manœuvre brings us no nearer to making the required assimilation.

However, the cause is not yet lost. For the two-valued logic within which this analysis has been attempted, makes it impossible to speak of a significant proposition which is neither true nor false. But, as we shall see, this is a somewhat arbitrary restriction. For there are many assertions (I cannot call them 'propositions') which are neither true nor false, but which we may describe as probable or improbable. Consider, for example, the counter-factual assertion:

(*c*) if I had thrown this coin on to the table an hour ago, it would have landed heads.

Clearly this assertion might be true. The coin might be double-headed. There might have been some special device under the table which would have affected the coin mechanically so that it would have landed heads. Again, it might be false. It might be a double-tailed penny, for example. But then again, it might be neither true nor false. If the coin in question is a fair one, and there are no special mechanical devices, then perhaps the only true statement we can make about the assertion (c) is that it has a probability of $\frac{1}{2}$.

It should be noted that this is not to say that the assertion (c) has a probability of $\frac{1}{2}$ of being true. For, we know that the assertion (c) is not true. The assertion (c) is neither true nor false, but is significant, and has a probability of $\frac{1}{2}$.

Now, in raising the objection that an assertion of the form 'An A is a B' (which we have supposed is the assertion said to be probable when we make a statement of the form 'It is probable that an A is a B'), cannot be a proposition in the sense of the two-valued propositional calculus of Russell and Whitehead, a somewhat narrow concept of proposition has tacitly been adopted. Accordingly, we seem to be forced to say that in the context of the probability statement (b) '...an A is a B' is not a proposition at all, although it is, perhaps, a propositional function. However, this is to achieve victory by brute force. If the question of whether it is a proposition that is said to be probable, (when we say it is probable that an A is a B), is to be settled by any other than Procrustean methods, the opportunity must be given, to anyone who wishes to do so, to develop a more general concept of proposition.

To this end, we may note that the concept of proposition may be widened sufficiently for our purposes, if we are prepared to adopt a new attitude to quantifiers, and to distinguish between what I shall call *propositional functions* and *indefinite propositions*.

A propositional function is expressed by a sentence, which might otherwise be used to express a proposition, except that some or all of its referring terms are replaced by variables. By a *referring term* I mean any term which might be used to refer to an individual or group of individuals (for example names, definite descriptions). By a *variable*, I mean any one of a set of terms, 'x', 'y', 'z', ..., which indicate the places in the expression of a propositional function which must be filled by referring terms if it is to be converted into the expression of a proposition—it being understood that the same variable must always be replaced by the same referring term, and that different variables may, but need not be replaced by different referring terms. It is important to note, however, that according to these definitions, 'x', 'y', 'z', ..., are not terms whose meaning is ambiguous or variable (Lewis and Langford) and they do not refer indifferently or indefinitely to any of those things which lie within their ranges. It should be quite clear that their sole purpose is to indicate places for referring expressions. Propositional functions will be symbolized in the usual way by such expressions as $F(x)$, $G(x, y)$, $H(x, y, z)$, ...

In contrast with propositional functions, indefinite propositions do contain indefinite references. Consider, for example, the proposition: 'All men are mortal'. The usual way of expressing such a proposition in symbolic terms is to write

$$(x)\{(x \text{ is a man}) \supset (x \text{ is mortal})\}. \tag{1}$$

But clearly, the x in this expression is not a variable in the sense just explained. It is not a place for a referring expression; for if we substitute such an expression, for example 'John Jones' (which we shall abbreviate to 'J.J.'), we get the nonsense sentence

$$(\text{J.J.}) \{(\text{J.J. is a man}) \supset (\text{J.J. is mortal})\}.$$

To make sense of this, we might think of '(J.J.)' as meaning 'For anything that is *called* "J.J."'. But then we should write

$$(x) \{[(x \text{ is called 'J.J.'}) (x \text{ is a man})] \supset (x \text{ is mortal})\}$$

if we wish to express this proposition in the symbolism of the predicate calculus. Hence, it is impossible to regard the various occurrences of 'x' in the expression (1) as having the role of a variable in a propositional function.

The significance of this point seems generally to have escaped notice. If the various occurrences of the term x in the expression (1) do not serve to indicate places for referring expressions, then what purpose do they serve? What, in particular, is the role of the universal quantifier (x)? If x is understood to be a place for an individual referring expression (that is if x is a variable), then we cannot read (x) as 'For any x' or 'For all x', because these expressions make no sense.

The answer that I would give is that a universal quantifier has the logical role of changing the status of the variable over which it quantifies—so that it becomes an *indefinite referring expression*. '$(x) \{x...\}$' means roughly 'Anything at all you care to choose...', (which is what I call an indefinite referring expression). Consequently, we may regard universal quantification as the process of substituting indefinite referring expressions for variables. Therefore, it is neater, and far less misleading to introduce a system of indefinite referring expressions into our logical symbolism and to abolish universal quantifiers which would then be redundant. Here, we shall use the term $\overset{\circ}{x}$ as an indefinite referring expression, and to express the sentence (1) in the new symbolism, we shall write

$$(U\overset{\circ}{x}); \quad [(\overset{\circ}{x} \text{ is a man}) \supset (\overset{\circ}{x} \text{ is mortal})]. \tag{2}$$

The indefinite referring expression $\overset{\circ}{x}$ in (2) ranges over the whole universe and the symbol $(U\overset{\circ}{x})$; indicates this fact.

The indefinite referring expressions that occur commonly in ordinary discourse, however, are somewhat more restricted. They do not refer to anything at all in the universe, but to anything that belongs to a certain class, or meets certain specifications. Accordingly, we need some device for specifying the range of an indefinite referring expression. We shall simply state the range of $\overset{\circ}{x}$ first, and then, after a semi-colon, state the proposition. Thus, to express the proposition that any *man* you care to name is mortal, we shall write

$$(\overset{\circ}{x} \text{ is a man}); \quad (\overset{\circ}{x} \text{ is mortal}), \tag{3}$$

which we may read, quite simply, as 'A man is mortal'.

Now, it will be noticed that the expressions (2) and (3) are not equivalent. For, the falsity of (3) is compatible with the strong probability of (2). Thus, even though all men may be immortal, it is yet extremely probable that anything you care to choose will *not* be a man, and hence it is extremely probable that anything you care to choose will either not be a man, or else be mortal.

It will also be noticed that propositions containing indefinite referring terms are characteristically propositions which may be neither true nor false. The examples (2) and (3) happen to be true. But the proposition

$$(\overset{\circ}{x} \text{ is a man of thirty}); \quad (\overset{\circ}{x} \text{ is married}), \tag{4}$$

is neither true nor false. To say that it is true is to imply that all men of thirty are married. To say that it is false is to imply that no men of thirty are married. The only thing we can say is that it is probable that a man of thirty is married. We shall call any proposition that contains indefinite referring terms an *indefinite proposition*.

Let us now return to the original objection. If probability may be attributed to propositions, then what proposition is said to be probable when we assert that it is probable that an *A* is a *B*? My answer is that it is the indefinite proposition

$$(\mathring{x} \text{ is an } A); \quad (\mathring{x} \text{ is a } B).$$

Let *T* be the predicate 'It is true that' and *P* the predicate 'It is probable that'. If now we wish to assert that is probable that an *A* is a *B*, we must write

$$P\{(\mathring{x} \text{ is an } A); \quad (\mathring{x} \text{ is a } B)\}.$$

If we wish to assert that it is probable that all *A*'s are *B*'s, then we must write

$$P[T\{(\mathring{x} \text{ is an } A); \quad (\mathring{x} \text{ is a } B)\}].$$

The distinction between these two propositions is thus retained in our symbolism, while at the same time, we have sufficiently broadened our concept of proposition to enable us to assert that every probability statement may be regarded as a statement about propositions.

Summary. The propositional function '*x* is mortal' may be evaluated in either of two distinct ways:

(i) by replacing *x* by some *uniquely* referring expression such as a proper name or definite description;

(ii) by replacing *x* by an *indefinite* referring expression, and indicating its range.

Whichever procedure we follow we obtain a proposition. If now we wish to assert that all men are mortal, then we may write

$$T\{(\mathring{x} \text{ is a man}); \quad (\mathring{x} \text{ is mortal})\}. \tag{5}$$

If we wish to say that it is probable that *a man* is mortal, then we must write

$$P\{(\mathring{x} \text{ is a man}); \quad (\mathring{x} \text{ is mortal})\}. \tag{6}$$

If we wish to say that it is probable that *all* men are mortal, then we must write

$$PT\{(\mathring{x} \text{ is a man}); \quad (\mathring{x} \text{ is mortal})\}. \tag{7}$$

Thus, probability and truth are both seen as attributes of propositions. And, those probability statements which seemed hardest to regard as statements about propositions now fall neatly into place.

There is no danger that this extension of the symbolism of the predicate calculus and of the concept of proposition will create any special difficulties. For the formulae (5) and

$$(x)\{(x \text{ is a man}) \supset (x \text{ is mortal})\} \qquad (8)$$

are logically equivalent, while (6) and (7) are not expressible anyway except as p or q. On the contrary, it should enable us to unify the probability and predicate caculi into a single calculus. For, in place of the operator P, we may write $P(p)$, where p ranges from 0 to 1, and where $P(p)$ may be read: 'There is a probability of p that'.

C

Towards an objective probability order

Having decided that probability relationships are relationships between propositions, the next step is to find an objective procedure for placing propositions in a probability order. It must be an objective procedure in the sense that whatever the intellectual backgrounds of those who follow it accurately may be, the same probability order must be generated. It must be a probability order in the sense that it is highly correlated with our various subjective probability judgements, and that it comes to act as a standard against which these judgements are gauged as accurate or inaccurate. This, at least, is the problem analogous to that of finding a thermometric property, which, as we have seen, was the first step towards devising a temperature scale.

The comparison between probability and temperature may be illuminating in other ways. The first thermometers were useful mainly for comparing atmospheric temperatures. The air thermometers of the seventeenth century, for example, were not adaptable for comparing or measuring the temperatures of small solid objects. Consequently, in the early history of thermometry, there were many things which possessed temperature which could not be fitted into an objective temperature order. Similarly, then, we should not necessarily expect to find any single objective procedure capable of ordering all propositions in respect of probability, even if we assume that all propositions possess probability. Rather, we should expect there to be certain kinds of propositions that are much easier to fit into an objective probability order than others (for example indefinite propositions).

We may even find that some propositions cannot be fitted into an objective probability order at all. Thus, to take an example from psychology, we are all inclined to say that porpoises are very intelligent creatures. But it is by no means obvious that there is *any* procedure for fitting them into an objective intelligence order (in which men also occur). It is at least possible that the intelligences of men and porpoises are simply incomparable.

But, whatever is the case with intelligence or temperature, if we find that there are certain kinds of propositions which we cannot fit into an objective probability order, or that there are propositions which can be fitted into such an order, but only in a very crude way, we must not conclude that there are different kinds of probability. To show that there are different kinds of probability we must show that there are significant inversions in the probability orders generated by two or more logically independent procedures—significant in the sense that, where such discrepancies occur, we are not prepared to say that at least one of the procedures has given us inaccurate probability comparisons, but maintain that both are accurate—although in different senses of 'probability'.

Now, in fact, there are several different kinds of procedures which lead to objective probability judgements. Some of these involve quite complex theoretical considerations, for example from statistical and quantum mechanics. Others involve our concept of physical symmetry; and our probability judgements are seen to depend on symmetry determinations. Yet others depend on our use of inductive rules—an inductive rule being, roughly, any rule for making probability estimates or comparisons solely on the basis of known facts about particulars. Procedures which consist simply in the application of inductive rules will be called *inductive procedures*, and will be discussed in more detail in the following sections.

Where procedures of different kinds are available for estimating the probability of a given proposition, they do not always lead to the same results. And, where this happens, we find that the various procedures are complementary. That is, we insist that at least one of our estimates is inaccurate. Hence, the existence of such a variety of probability estimating procedures does nothing at all to show the existence of different kinds of probability.

Consider, for example, the interplay between the use of

'straight' inductive rules* and symmetry considerations in the following case: suppose we take a regular dodecahedron, mark its faces 1, 2, ..., 12, and test it for geometrical symmetry and physical homogeneity. Then, if all our tests are positive, we may conclude without further experiment that there is a probability of $\frac{1}{12}$ that if the object were thrown on to a horizontal table, the face marked '6' would come to rest downwards.

However, suppose we now try the experiment of rolling the dodecahedron 1000 times on to the table, and find that the face marked '6' never came to rest face downwards. Should we not re-examine the object for geometrical and physical symmetry in the belief that there must be a relevant asymmetry somewhere? And, if all our attempts failed to reveal what we had thought to be a relevant asymmetry, should we not either:

(i) speak of an extraordinary run of chance occurrences (that is dismiss the relative frequency evidence as inconclusive),

(ii) maintain that there must be a relevant asymmetry which had not yet been discovered (that is dismiss the symmetry evidence as inconclusive), or

(iii) come to regard some known asymmetry (for example the facial markings) as a *relevant* asymmetry (that is change our concept of physical symmetry)?

But one thing we should not do, is accept both sets of results at face value. We should not accept (*a*) that there is a probability (in, say, a relative frequency sense) of *zero* that if the dodecahedron is thrown on to a table a '6' will come to rest face downwards; and (*b*) that there is a probability (in some other sense) of $\frac{1}{12}$ that a '6' will come to rest face downwards.

Therefore, although the procedures for obtaining these results are logically very different from one another, and certainly logically independent, we do not regard them as procedures for ordering things in respect of different quantities. For, where symmetry considerations, and inductive considerations lead to different probability estimations, we insist that these estimations are incompatible with each other. If we accept one of them as accurate, we must reject the other as inaccurate.

* The 'straight' inductive rule is: 'if the observed relative frequency with which A's are B's is p, then estimate the probability of an A being a B as p.'

D

The scope of inductive procedures

We have seen that the probability judgements we make depend on our background knowledge, our intellectual training, and our intellectual capacity (see Section A above). By background knowledge, I include not only present observations, memories and records of past observations, but also knowledge of physical laws and theories, and the vast penumbra of more or less firmly held beliefs about nature, however vague they may be, which influence us in making predictions about the unknown. I include, for example, such vague and indeterminate principles as those of symmetry, simplicity and essential connectivity. In short, by a person's background knowledge I mean everything he knows or believes.

That part of a person's background knowledge which consists of knowledge of particulars, and which influences him to make a particular probability judgement, is usually termed the 'evidence' upon which his probability judgement is based. By 'knowledge of particulars' I include any facts about individuals or groups of individuals which can be stated without the use of indefinite referring expressions. Laws and theories, although they un-doubtedly have an indispensable and decisive role in the making of such judgements, are generally not regarded as items of evidence. Hence in reasonable accord with ordinary usage, I will use the term 'evidence' to refer to known facts about particulars.

One reason why laws and theories are not included as items of evidence may be that our laws and theories are themselves supposed to arise out of the consideration of evidence. Hence, it is argued, if laws and theories play any part in determining what probability judgements we make, then their role is in principle dispensable. Thus, in the opinion of some writers on probability, if we are justified in making certain probability judgements, then it must be possible to justify these judgements entirely by reference to inductive rules and the evidence upon which the judgements were ultimately based—that is without any reference at all to the theoretical superstructure of science. Thus, until recently at any rate, the problem of vindicating induction was usually seen as that of justifying the use of certain rules for deciding what probability judgements should be made on the basis of what evidence, that is as the problem of choosing and vindicating a particular inductive rule. The idea that theoretical considerations might have some essential role in the formation of probability judgements seems not to have been taken seriously.

However, while it is undoubtedly true that theories arise out of the consideration of evidence, no serious philosopher of science nowadays contends that there is any rule for deciding what theory should be constructed on the basis of what evidence. Yet, if there is no such rule, and if theoretical considerations do have a legitimate role in determining what probability judgements we should make, then how is it possible, even in principle, to circumvent these considerations? It seems that no inductive rule could possibly be powerful enough to justify all legitimate probability judgements.

An inductive rule, as I understand it, is any rule for making probability judgements *solely* on the basis of evidence. Consequently, any legitimate probability judgements, in which theoretical considerations are also involved, cannot possibly be justified by reference to an inductive rule. Consequently, the scope of inductive rules is severely limited. A vindication of induction, such as Salmon's,* which at best succeeds only in justifying the use of a certain inductive rule in circumstances in which there are no relevant theoretical considerations, falls a long way short of the ultimate goal of vindicating scientific procedures for predicting the unknown.

Now, this limitation in the scope of inductive rules is a limitation on their usefulness for making probability estimations, and there must be many propositions, for example theoretical statements and theoretical predictions, whose probability cannot reliably be estimated inductively. Thus we find many philosophers who distinguish between inductive and other kinds of probability on these grounds. But this, as we have seen, is a mistake. One might as well distinguish between visual and non-visual intelligence, on the grounds that some I.Q. tests depend on the visual recognition of patterns of arrangement or succession, and with colour-blind people, these tests are not very reliable.

However, the main point to note here is that there are infinitely many inductive rules,† and hence an infinite variety of inductive

---

* Salmon (1961), pp. 245–56.
† See, for example, Carnap (1952), or Burks (1953).

procedures. And, for a given basis of evidence, and a given language with which to describe it, each different inductive procedure yields a different set of probability judgements. Consequently, there arises the problem of choice of inductive procedure. No attempt will be made here to solve this problem. But in the following section, I shall attempt to say something about its nature.

E

The normal probability scale, and the problem of choice of inductive procedure

A probability scale is any scale on which the order of our numerical assignments is highly correlated with our crude subjective probability orders, and which we are prepared to regard as a standard against which our subjective ordinal probability judgements are to be assessed for accuracy or inaccuracy.

Of the possible probability scales, those in practical use are based upon the application of certain classes of arithmetical formulae, and may be called *normal* probability scales. Thus, if we make the following abbreviations:

$(A; B)$ for $(\mathring{x}$ is an $A)$; $(\mathring{x}$ is a $B)$

$(A; B \vee C)$ for $(\mathring{x}$ is an $A)$; $(\mathring{x}$ is a $B) \vee (\mathring{x}$ is a $C)$

$(A; B.C)$ for $(\mathring{x}$ is an $A)$; $(\mathring{x}$ is a $B).(\mathring{x}$ is a $C)$

$(A.B; C)$ for $(\mathring{x}$ is an A and a $B)$; $(\mathring{x}$ is a $C)$

$P(p)$ for There is a probability of measure p.

Then, on any normal probability scale, it is required that $p = 0$ for any contradiction and $p = 1$ for any analytic proposition.

It is also required that

$$[P(p) (A; B \vee C).P(q) (A;B).P(r) (A; C).P(s) (A; B.C)]$$
$$\equiv (p = q+r-s), \quad (9)$$

$$[P(p) (A; B).P(q) \sim (A; B)] \equiv (p+q = 1), \quad (10)$$

$$[P(p) (A; B.C).P(q) (A; B).P(r) (A.B; C)] \equiv (p = q.r). \quad (11)$$

These are the disjunction, negation and conjunction theorems of the probability calculus.

From (9) and (11) it follows that a normal probability scale is a ratio scale. But it is a ratio scale with two fixed points (1 and 0). Hence, a normal probability scale is not subject to scale-transformation, and provided that there is an objective probability order, the normal inductive probability scale is unique.

We cannot, therefore, speak of a variety of different normal probability scales. Hence, there is no need to use unit names in connection with probability so long as it is understood that only normal scales may be used. However, we can speak of a variety of different ways of *estimating* normal probability; and the choice of inductive rule is really the choice of an estimation procedure. Thus, if we use different inductive rules we may make different estimates of the probability of a given indefinite proposition. But we cannot consider ourselves to be measuring this proposition on different normal probability scales.

The argument that the normal probability scale is unique is undeniable, *if* one accepts that there is an objective probability order. But our judgements of probability order, and hence our estimates of probability on the normal inductive probability scale, depend at least partly on our choice of inductive rule. The theoretical uniqueness of the normal inductive probability scale does not by itself guarantee that any inductive rule for assigning probability numbers to propositions defines a procedure for measuring on that scale. Hence, we still have the problem of choice of inductive rule.

The problem that is analogous to the choice of inductive rule in other forms of measurement is that of choice of mathematical averaging procedure. Here, from a number of individual results, we must attempt to estimate what we may regard as the true measure of the quantity concerned. We do this by taking a certain mathematical averaging function, which meets certain requirements depending on the kind of scale that we are using, and determining the appropriate average or mean in order to estimate the true measure of the quantity we are dealing with.

In view of the fact that we generally prefer an estimate based on a longer sequence of results to one based on a shorter sequence, the concept of *true measure* might be defined thus: let $x_1, x_2, ..., x_n$ be any sequence of results of measurements of some particular thing P on a scale X, and let the mathematical averaging function $A_n(x_1, x_2, ..., x_n)$ be deemed to be appropriate for assessing these results. Then, the true measure $\bar{x}$ of P on X might be defined as:

$$\bar{x} = \lim_{n\to\infty} (\bar{x}_n) = \lim_{n\to\infty} A_n(x_1, x_2, ..., x_n). \tag{12}$$

Of course, we have no guarantee that such a limit exists. But this situation is also analogous to that in probability measurement where we have no guarantee that any sequence of probability estimations (on any given inductive rule) tends to a limit.

It is outside the scope of this work to investigate the problem of choice of inductive rule. This is one of the long-standing problems of the philosophy of science. The only point that I wish to make here is that the problem is analogous to that of choice of mathematical averaging function. It is, of course, a much more acute problem than the latter one, since probability estimations made on the basis of the same evidence, but using different inductive rules, may differ widely. Moreover, it may be argued that the solution of this problem is a matter of the most fundamental importance, since it concerns the whole field of human knowledge. But essentially, it is a problem of the same kind. Consequently, the fact that there is a variety of inductive rules no more shows the existence of different kinds of probability than the fact that there is a variety of mathematical averaging functions, suitable for handling temperature measurements, demonstrates the existence of different kinds of temperature.

F

Probability₁ and probability₂

We are now in a position to examine the two fundamental reasons why philosophers have distinguished between different kinds of probability.

(*a*) Consider any statement of the form:

(i) 'On the evidence that *e*, there is a probability *p* that *h*.' According to Carnap, and most other philosophers who have considered the concept of probability in the past fifteen years, any statement of the form (i) is either *L*-true or *L*-false. That is to say, the only sorts of considerations that are relevant to its truth or falsity are linguistic or conventional (*L*-considerations). Our decision on (i) may depend upon what inductive rules we have chosen to use, or what language or concepts we have chosen to employ to describe observed events. But, all of these considerations are of the linguistic-conventional kind.

Whether or not Carnap is right in maintaining that (i) is either L-true or L-false depends on how the phrase, 'On the evidence that $e\ldots$' is taken. If it is taken to imply the truth of e, then (i) is clearly not, in general, either L-true or L-false. (It would, in fact, often be taken to imply the truth of e—for example, when a doctor says to his patient: 'On the evidence that your heart-beat is very irregular, it is probable that you do not have more than a week to live'.) If the phrase 'On the evidence that $e\ldots$' is uttered against a commonly accepted background of physical theory, then again the statement (i) is, in general, neither L-true nor L-false. (Consider, for example, the statement 'On the evidence that the cylinder contains a mixture of hydrogen and oxygen, it is probable that if a naked flame is put into the cylinder an explosion will occur'.) In fact, if Carnap's contention is to be maintained, then the evidence e must be understood to consist of a set of premisses, and the statement (i) must be taken as asserting that the proposition 'There is a probability of p that L' follows from e *alone* (on the basis of whatever inductive and/or deductive rules we have adopted). Carnap himself is quite clear that this is the way in which the phrase 'On the evidence that $e\ldots$' is to be understood; but it is important for the argument that follows that this point be clearly understood.

Next, consider any statement of the form:

(ii) 'There is a *probability* p of an A being a B.' Now, provided that it is neither logically necessary nor logically impossible that an A is a B, any statement of the form (ii) is empirical. Various kinds of considerations may be relevant to its truth or falsity, including those which we have described as linguistic or conventional, but they cannot consist *entirely* of considerations of these kinds. Usually, some investigations into the characteristics of A's would have to be made in order to decide whether (ii) is true or false. Of course, a statement of the form (ii) might be derived from a theory (for example statistical mechanics). But then, our acceptance of this theory must in turn depend upon our making some empirical investigations. In this sense, then, statements of the form (ii) are empirical.

To mark this distinction, Carnap uses the terms 'probability$_1$' and 'probability$_2$'. Probability$_1$ is used for the kind of probability concept that occurs in the statement (i) and probability$_2$ for that which occurs in the statement (ii). Accordingly probability$_1$ is another name for what we initially called *logical probability*, and probability$_2$ refers to our *empirical probability* concept.

(*b*) The distinction between probability$_1$ and probability$_2$ is further highlighted by the fact that they appear to be characteristic of different kinds of entities. Probability$_1$-relationships seem to be relationships between propositions, while probability$_2$-relationships are apparently between kinds or classes of things (usually of events, or states of affairs). This is the second fundamental reason why philosophers, almost universally, have accepted the distinction between probability$_1$ and probability$_2$, and regarded these as being two distinct, although somehow closely related quantities.

I shall now show, using precisely the same arguments, that there are two senses of 'temperature'—one logical, and the other empirical.

(*c*) Let T_i be the statement 'The well-calibrated thermometer M has been immersed in the liquid L and the temperature reading $t_i°$ C. has been obtained' ($i = 1, 2, ..., n$). Now, consider the following statement:

(iii) 'On the evidence that $T_1, T_2, ..., T_n$, the temperature of L is $\bar{t}_n°$ C.' How should we decide whether or not this proposition is true? Clearly, there is no point in examining or checking the evidence, if 'evidence' is understood in the way that Carnap understands it. For, in his sense of 'evidence', there is no need for statements of evidence to be true. Indeed, it is perfectly clear that if the assertion (i) were taken to imply the truth of the evidence e, it would be an empirical statement. Consequently, any investigation into the truth of $T_1, T_2, ..., T_n$ must be regarded as irrelevant to the truth of (iii). What would be relevant is an investigation of whether $\bar{t}_n$ is the appropriate mean of the various readings $t_1, t_2, ..., t_n$. Now, we have already seen that choosing a mathematical averaging procedure is a problem entirely analogous to choosing an inductive rule. If one can be regarded as an L-consideration (linguistic or conventional), then so can the other. Therefore, we are forced to conclude that if (iii) is true, then it is L-true, and if it is false, then it is L-false.

Obviously, the statement:

(iv) 'The temperature of L is $t°$ C.'

is an empirical statement. We have to measure to find out whether or not it is true.

Therefore, if Carnap's argument is sound, and there are two senses of 'probability', then in precisely the same sense, there are two senses of 'temperature'—one logical and the other empirical.

(*d*) The second basic reason why philosophers have distinguished between two senses of 'probability' has already been dealt with at length. We have shown that if a sufficiently broad, but not question-begging concept of proposition is adopted, then all probability statements may be regarded as attributing probability to propositions. But there is no need to repeat these arguments here.

However, it should be noted that if temperature, in the sense of proposition (iii) is called 'temperature$_1$' and temperature in the sense of proposition (iv) is called 'temperature$_2$'; then temperature$_1$ appears to express a relationship between propositions, while temperature$_2$ expresses a relationship between physical objects. Hence, if the parallel argument reinforces the distinction between probability$_1$ and probability$_2$, then this argument also reinforces the distinction between temperature$_1$ and temperature$_2$.

*   *   *

It is clear that similar arguments may be constructed for every quantity name in our language. Therefore, if 'probability' is ambiguous in view of (*a*) and (*b*) above, then so is every other quantity name. I conclude, therefore, that Carnap has failed to show that there is any ambiguity at all in our use of the word 'probability'.

Of course, I do not deny that Carnap's concept of logical probability (or 'degree of confirmation', as he prefers to call it) is extremely important. For, to devise a procedure for determining logical probability is to describe an inductive rule, that is a rule for making probability estimations. But there is no reason whatever for regarding 'logical probability' as the name of a quantity distinct from probability. The study of logical probability is simply that of the logic of probability measurement.

APPENDIX I

CRITIQUE OF THE CONCEPT
OF TEMPERATURE

Translation of E. Mach, *Die Principien der Wärmelehre* (Leipzig, 1896), pp. 39–57.*

1. It appears that the volume of a body can serve as a criterion or sign of its heat-state, and so change of volume is to be looked upon as a sign of the change of heat-state. It is clear that only those volume changes come into consideration here which are not brought about by pressure changes, alteration of electrical force, and other circumstances, which independently, according to our experience, influence the volume in known ways. Together with the sensation of warmth that a body produces in us other properties also change, for example, resistance, dielectric constant, thermo-electromotive force, refractive index, etc. All of these properties could be used as criteria of heat-state, and have in fact been used as such from time to time. Even although this is accompanied by fairly obvious practical reasons, there lies in the preference for the volume of a body as criterion of its heat-state an *arbitrariness*; and in the adoption of this alternative, an *agreement*.†

2. In the first place, a body which we imagine arranged as a thermometer shows only its own heat-state. But crude observation teaches us that two bodies, *A* and *B*, which produce different heat sensations in us, excite our sense organs equally after a longer mutual contact, so that these bodies equalize their differences of heat-state. If this experience is transferred by analogy to the use of volume as a criterion, then we assume that a body used as a thermometer reveals not only its own state but also that of any other body which has been in sufficiently long contact with it. This transference is not permissible without further examination. For the heat sensation and the volume are two different elements of observation. Experience has taught us that they generally go together; how, and how far they do, again only experience can teach us.

3. It is easy now to see that volume and the sensation of heat are criteria of very different sensitivity and of a completely different kind. We are enabled to notice changes of state with the help of volume which

---

* Translated by M. J. Scott-Taggart and myself in collaboration.
† Mach's terms are 'willkürlich' and 'Übereinkunft'.

would entirely escape the heat sensations. Further, the thermometer and the sense organs can occasionally give very different, or even contradictory results, because of their differing properties. A sufficient illustration of this has already been given on page 30.* But the results also turn out differently in relation to equality of state. After long contact two pieces of iron give the same heat sensations. A piece of wood and a piece of iron give the same reading on a thermometer after a sufficiently long contact. However long the contact has lasted, if, when we touch them, both bodies feel warm, then the iron always feels warmer, and if both bodies feel cold, the iron is always colder than the wood. As is well known, the reason for this is that the iron is a better conductor and so transmits its heat-state to the hand more quickly.

As, now, volume is a much more sensitive criterion of heat-state than sensations of heat, so it is both more advantageous and more rational to derive our results from observations of volume, and to base all our definitions upon it. Observation of heat sensations may indeed guide us, but after what has been said a simple and uncritical use of them is quite impermissible. With this insight we adopt quite a new standpoint, which is essentially different from that of the first founders of thermometry. The imperfect separation of the two standpoints, which was unavoidable because of the gradual transition from the old to the new, has, as will become apparent, led to various confusions in heat theory.

It is indubitable that a thermometer will show a volume increase on a distinguishably warmer body, and a decrease on a distinguishably colder one. But our heat sensation cannot tell us that this carries through to complete equality of the heat-states. On the other hand, corresponding to the new standpoint, we can lay down dogmatically: *different bodies shall be said to be in the same heat-state if* (apart from pressure, electrical force, etc.) *they do not occasion any volume change in one another.* This definition can be immediately applied to the thermometer. This will indicate the state of the body touching it as soon as no further mutual change of volume is caused through the contact.

If two bodies are, in the usual sense (and therefore in relation to heat sensations), just as warm as a third body, C, then they are also as warm as one another. This is a logical necessity, and we are not in a position to think otherwise. The denial of this would entail that we held two sensations to be at once both similar and different. But according to the above definition we cannot simply accept that if A does not produce a volume change in C, nor B in C, then A will not produce a volume change in B. This is an experience upon which we must wait and which is not already given in the two other experiences. This is simply a consequence of the above mentioned standpoint.

Now experience teaches us on the one hand that if there is a row of

---

* That is p. 30 of the original German.

bodies $ABCD\ldots$, such that each is in sufficiently long contact with the one after it, then the thermometer will give the same reading on each body. And on the other hand we should be led to extraordinary contradictions with our everyday experiences of heat if we were to accept that the equality of state of A and C was not (physically) determined by the equality of state of both A and B, and B and C (determined by the above definition). Transposing the order of bodies which produce no further change of volume in one another ought now to have further changes as a consequence. As far as our thermometric experience reaches, this is never the case.

So far as I know Maxwell was the first to draw attention to this. It is perhaps not beside the point to remark that Maxwell's observations are quite analogous to those which I have made concerning the concept of mass.* It is imperative to notice that whenever we apply a definition to nature we must wait to see if it will correspond to it. With the exception of pure mathematics we can create our concepts at will, even in geometry and still more in physics, but we must always investigate whether and how reality corresponds to these concepts.

The consistent interpretation of known experiences therefore demands that we accept that two bodies, A and B, which, according to the above definition, are in an equal heat-state to a third, C, are in the same heat-state as one another.

4. Stronger sensations of heat correspond to greater volumes of the thermometric substance. We shall therefore again state dogmatically (according to the analogy): *higher heat-states are those in which the bodies produce a greater volume reading on the thermometer*. By analogy with the heat transactions observable through the senses, we must expect that of two bodies, A and B, that which gives the greater thermometer reading will, in contact with the other, produce an increase in its volume, and a reduction of its own. The analogy works in general, but can lead to error in special cases. An example here is water. Two masses of water at 3 and 5° C. both diminish in volume when in contact. Two masses of water at 10 and 15° C. represent the normal case, but two masses of water at 1 and 3° C. behave in a way exactly opposite to the analogy.

It follows from this that water used as a thermometric substance can, in some circumstances, give the same reading for two heat-states which by other thermometers are shown as different. The use of water as a thermometric substance is therefore to be avoided, at least in the regions of heat-states to which we have drawn attention.

* Maxwell, *Theory of Heat* (London, 1888). I suspect that the remark was already contained in the edition of 1871, but I cannot confirm this as I can now only obtain the *Auerbach* translation of the fourth edition (1877). My treatment of mass was first given in the fourth volume of Carl's Repositorium, subsequently in my paper on the 'Conservation of Energy', and in 1883 in 'The Development of Mechanics'. [Mach's footnote.]

5. The heat sensations, as well as the thermometric volumes, form a simple sequence, a simple continuous manifold, but it does not follow immediately from this that the heat-states also form such a sequence. The properties of the system of signs do not by themselves determine those of what is signified. If, for example, we should have chosen the attraction which is imposed upon an iron ball on a balance by an underlying body K as a sign of the state of this body, then these attractions, whose totality also represents a simple manifold, would be caused by electrical, magnetic, and gravitational properties of K, and so by a triple manifold. Investigation must first of all teach us whether the system of signs has been happily chosen.

Let $ABCDE$ be a row of bodies of which each in turn represents a higher heat-state. So far as experience goes, we can change a body from the state of A to that of E in only one way, that is through the

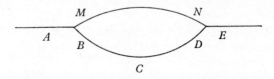

states of BCD, so that all the intermediate states have also been passed through. There is no experience at all which would necessitate the view that this could also happen through the states MN which lie outside this sequence. The acceptance of a simple continuous manifold of heat-states is sufficient.

6. We remarked above that there is an arbitrary agreement in the choice of volume as thermometric indicator. There is a further convention in the choice of the thermometric substance. Should one such choice, however, become generally accepted, then the thermometer concerned could do in the main everything that was required of it. We should expose the thermometer to as large a number of heat-states as possible, which would be unchanging reference points during the standardization, and then indicate these settings by marks and names: the freezing point of mercury, the melting point of ice, the freezing point of linseed oil, of aniseed oil, the melting point of butter, blood heat, the boiling point of water, or mercury, etc. These marks would enable us not only to recognize a recurring heat-state again, but also to reproduce a known heat-state. In this lies the essential job of the thermometer.

7. The defect of such a system, one which did in fact persist for a long time, would soon show itself. The finer the investigations became, the more such fixed points would become necessary, and finally there would be no more to be found. Moreover, the number of the marking names would increase unpleasantly, and it could not be seen

from the names in what order the heat-states concerned should follow upon one another. This order has to be particularly noticed.

There is a system of names which is at the same time a system of ordered signs, which can be increased or diminished without limit: these are the numbers. By co-ordinating numbers as names of the thermometric criteria we remove all of the above-mentioned difficulties. Numbers can be continued indefinitely without any effort, new numbers can be inserted as will between any two in accordance with an existing system, and for any number we can see immediately between which others it lies. This could not escape the notice of the inventors of the thermometer, but the observation was used only to varying extents and with varying appropriateness.

8. In order to bring the advantageous system into use a new agreement is necessary, an agreement on the principle of correlation of the numbers and thermometric signs. In this, however, new difficulties arise. One method that has been suggested is that of marking on the fine tube of the thermometer two fixed points (the melting point of ice, the boiling point of water). The apparent volume increase of the thermometric substance (and thus without regard to the expansion of the vessel) is divided into a hundred parts (degrees), and this division is extrapolated beyond the boiling and freezing points. By means of the two fixed points and the principle of correlation there now seems to be a physically determinate heat-state connected unequivocally to each number.

9. This connection is immediately destroyed, however, by the choice of another thermometric substance or another material for the vessel. If we plot the volumes of a substance as abscissae, and those of another substance with the same heat-states as ordinates, then connecting of the ordinates à la Dulong and Petit does not produce a straight line but a curve that is *different* for each pair of substances. The following figure makes this clear:

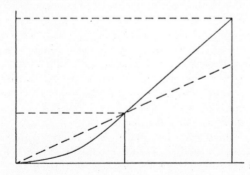

The substances do not expand proportionately to one another with equal changes of heat-state, as this in fact demonstrates. For each thermometric substance noticeably different numbers are not applicable, therefore, according to the one principle of correlation to the same heat-state.

But if we stick to mercury as the thermometric substance, then the ineliminable expansion of the glass vessel against the expansion of the mercury has an effect upon the course of the apparent expansion which follows an individual law for each kind of glass. In spite of the similar principles of correlation the correspondence between number and heat-state is, taken precisely, peculiar to each thermometer.

10. As attention became directed to the similar behaviour of gases under equal changes of heat-state, so, because of this property, the choice of a gas as a thermometric substance appeared to be less conventional, to be more grounded in nature. This view is clearly in error, but there are other reasons for this choice, and so it was a happy one, although nobody could know this at the time at which it happened.

One of the greatest advantages which a gas offers is its large expansion, and the resultantly great sensitivity of the thermometer. Also, because of this great expansion, the disturbing influence of the varying material of the vessel passes into the background. Mercury expands only about seven times as much as glass. The expansion of the glass and its variability are revealed markedly in the expansion of the mercury. But gas expands 146 times as much as glass.* The expansion of the glass has therefore only a small influence upon the apparent expansion of the gas, and its change with different sorts [of glass] is of negligible influence. With given fixed points and a determinate principle of correlation the numbers are therefore connected more exactly with the heat-states for a gas thermometer than for any other kind. The choice of material for the vessel, that is the individuality of the thermometer, can only disturb this relation insignificantly: thermometers become comparable to a high degree. This is the basis of the view of Dulong and Petit. In what follows we shall base our remarks upon air thermometers.

11. The number which is given by any principle of correlation with the volume reading of the thermometer, and which consequently is correlated unequivocally with a heat-state, we shall call temperature, and in what is to follow we shall generally denote this by t. A very different temperature number from that which was dependent upon the principle of correlation $t = f(v)$, where v denotes the thermometric volume, will then belong to the one heat-state.

12. It is instructive to note that in fact different principles of correlation have been proposed, even if essentially only one has acquired any practical scientific importance, and has remained in use. We can call this one principle that of Galileo. This makes the temperature numbers

---

* Cf. Pfaundler, *Lehrbuch der Physik*, vol. II, p. 2.

proportional to the real or apparent growth in volume from a determinate original volume v_0, which corresponds to a determinate heat-state.

To the volumes $$v_0, v_0(1+\alpha), v_0(1+2\alpha), \ldots v_0(1+t\alpha),$$
these temperatures correspond $\quad$ 0, $\quad$ 1, $\quad$ 2, $\quad \ldots \quad$ t.

Here we elect for $\alpha = 1/273$, that is the one-hundredth part of the volume-growth coefficient from the freezing to the boiling point of water, to which latter the temperature number of 100 is therefore assigned. This principle will also admit temperatures above the boiling point of water and below the freezing point—the latter temperature numbers naturally being negative.

Another quite different principle of correlation is that of Dalton. This consists in the following:

to the volumes $$\frac{v_0}{(1 \cdot 0179)^2}, \quad \frac{v_0}{1 \cdot 0179}, \quad v_0, \quad v_0 \times 1 \cdot 0179, \quad v_0 \times (1 \cdot 0179)^2,$$

these temperatures correspond $\quad -20, \quad -10, \quad 0, \quad 10, \quad 20\ldots$

If one chooses, as did Amontons and Lambert, the pressure of a gas at constant volume as providing thermometric readings, and puts the temperature number proportional to the gas pressure, then strictly speaking this provides another principle. The extended validity of the Mariotte–Gay-Lussac law, the small deviation of the pressure coefficient from the expansion coefficient—circumstances which were only incompletely known at the time of the proposal of the scale—have since shown that the properties of Amonton's scale are not noticeably different from those of Galileo's.

Let p be the pressure of a mass of gas at constant volume, p_0 its pressure at the freezing point of water, and k a constant; then Amonton's principle of correlation is given by the equation

$$t = \frac{kp}{p_0}.$$

A second fundamental point is here unnecessary. Since p_0 and p are dependent on the heat-states in the same way as v_0 and v, so the new scale has properties which are already familiar. For $p = 0$, $t = 0$. If one puts $k = 273$, then the degrees have their normal size: $t = 273$ falls at the freezing point of water, and $t = 373$ falls at the boiling point. The scale corresponds exactly to the common one if the freezing point of water is placed at zero, and the temperature numbers below it are counted as negative.

13. The use of air thermometers, whether volume or pressure is used as thermometric indicator, includes a definition of temperature.

From the equations $p = p_0(1 + \alpha t)$ or $v = v_0(1 + \alpha t)$ we state arbitrarily that the temperature shall be given through the equation:

$$t = \frac{p - p_0}{\alpha p_0} \quad \text{or} \quad t = \frac{v - v_0}{\alpha v_0} .$$

The Amontons temperature, which we distinguish by the name Absolute temperature and denote by T, and which stands to the previous definition in the relation that I have stated, is defined by the following equation

$$T = \frac{273p}{p_0} .$$

14. It is remarkable how long it was before the insight forced its way through that the denoting of the heat-state by a number rested on an agreement. There are heat-states in nature, but the concept of temperature is created by an arbitrary definition, which could have been made otherwise. Until contemporary times, however, workers in this field seem more or less unconsciously to have sought for a natural measure of temperature, a real temperature, a kind of Platonic Idea of temperature, of which the temperature read from thermometers is only an incomplete and imperfect expression.

Before Black and Lambert the concepts of temperature and heat-quantity were not generally distinguished from one another, as, for example, for Richmann, who simply spoke of 'calor' in both of these cases. We cannot therefore expect clarity here. But the uncertainty extends farther than we might suspect. Let us convince ourselves by looking at some cases.

Lambert described the state of opinion among his contemporaries very well in the words: 'One hesitates as to whether the actual degrees of heat are really proportional to the degrees of the expansion. And even if this is the case, the question still remains as to which degree we should start counting from.'[*] He then discusses Renaldini's proposal for graduating the thermometer by mixtures of water, and it seems that he believes such a scale to be a natural one.

In Dalton we find the following statement: 'If we make experiment with fluids, then we find that they do not expand uniformly. All of them expand more at high than at low temperatures.... Mercury seems to show the least variation of all, or to approach more nearly to a uniform expansion.'[†]

Gay-Lussac says: 'The thermometer as it is today cannot serve to indicate the exact proportion of heat, as we do not yet know what relation there is between the degrees of the thermometer and the

* Lambert, *Pyrometrie*, p. 52.
† Dalton, *New System of the Chemical Part of the Natural Sciences*, Wolf Trans. (Berlin, 1812), p. 12.

quantity of heat which it is supposed to indicate. We generally believe, it is true, that equal divisions of the tube represent equal quantities of the caloric, but this opinion is not founded on anything positive.'* Clearly Gay-Lussac is on the way to resolving the confusion of his contemporaries upon the question, but he has not yet succeeded in doing so.

It is extremely strange that such exact researchers as Dulong and Petit, who first achieved clarity on this subject, time and again fall back into the old errors, at least verbally. We read at one point: 'One sees by the variation which there is at 300° how much the increase in volume of the glass departs from uniformity.'† We ask in astonishment, how ought we to judge or measure this 'uniformity' or 'disuniformity'? The following place is also typical: '...we should say, meanwhile, that the uniformity which is well known in the principal physical properties of gases, and above all the perfect identity of their laws of expansion, makes it very probable that in this class of bodies the causes of the discrepancies have no longer the same influence as on solids and liquids, and that in consequence the changes of volume produced by the action of heat are here more directly dependent on the force which produces them.'‡

This oscillation between a physical and a metaphysical view-point has not quite disappeared even today. In a modern textbook, written by one of the most prominent investigators of heat, we read: 'The data of air thermometers is therefore similar in all cases. This, however, does not yet prove that the air thermometer really is a measure of what we understand by temperature: it has not, namely, been proved that the pressure increase of the gas is proportional to its temperature rise, for we have until now simply assumed this.'

No less a man that Clausius expresses himself in the following way: 'One can conclude from certain properties of gases that the mutual attraction and average size of their molecules is extremely small, and thus they provide very little resistance to the expansion of gases, so that the resistance which the walls of the vessel exerts must maintain the equilibrium against almost the whole effect of the heat. Therefore the externally perceptible pressure of a gas forms an approximate measure of the reciprocal force of the heat contained in it, and consequently, according to the above law, the absolute temperature must be approximately proportional to the pressure. The correctness of this result has, in fact, so much to be said for it that many physicists since Gay-Lussac and Dalton have supposed this proportionality to exist without anything further, and have used absolute temperature as a justification (!).'§

In an admirable paper on the pyrometer we find the following: 'After

---

* *Ann. de Chim.* XLIII (1802), 139.   † *Ibid.* VII (1817), 139.
‡ *Ibid.* VII (1817), 153.
§ Clausius, *Mechanische Wärmetheorie* (1864), I, 248.

Gay-Lussac, had in 1802, discovered that all gases expand by the same amount for equal increases in temperature, the hypothesis is well justified that the expansion is uniform for all degrees of temperature, because it is more probable that the expansion is uniform than that all gases should show the same variability.'*

It is to be emphasized, however, that W. Thomson, in proposing his absolute thermodynamic temperature scale in 1848 saw through this fallacy with full critical clarity. This will be explained more fully in a later chapter.

It seems, after these examples, that the above exposition was not superfluous, however obvious it may seem to many individual physicists. Let it be repeated that we can never be concerned with more than a sure and precisely reproducible, generally comparable, temperature scale; never with a 'true' or 'natural' one.

15. It could easily be proved through analogous examples drawn from other branches of physics that men generally have a tendency to hypostatize their abstract concepts—to ascribe to them a reality beyond the mind. Plato made a somewhat free use of this tendency in his theory of Ideas. Even such researchers as Newton were not always sufficiently careful, despite their basic principles. It is therefore well worth while to take the trouble to investigate what this tendency might depend on in this particular case. We begin from our observation of heat sensation, but later we come to see the necessity of replacing this criterion of the condition of a body by other criteria. These criteria, however, varying with circumstances, do not take exactly parallel courses. Because of this the original heat sensation, which was to have been replaced by one of these other criteria which do not precisely correlate one with another, remains secretly and unconsciously the nucleus of our concepts. Even if it becomes theoretically clear to us that this heat sensation is nothing more than a sign of the total condition of a body, which we know already and are to learn more about,† still we find it conceptually necessary to hold all these together in one unity and to denote them by one symbol: heat-state. If we examine ourselves closely then we again discover as the shadowy nucleus of the symbols the heat-sensation, which we take to be the primary and most natural representative of the whole group of concepts. It appears to us that we must ascribe reality to this symbol, which is not entirely our own free creation. And so there resulted the impression of a 'real temperature' of which the actual temperature measurements were only a more or less inexact expression.

Newton's conception of an 'absolute time', an 'absolute space', etc., which I have criticized elsewhere, arises in an analogous way.‡ The

* Bolz, *Die Pyrometer* (Berlin, 1888), p. 38.
† Mach, *Analysis of Sensations*, p. 155.
‡ Mach, *The Development of Mechanics* (1883), p. 209.

sensation of duration plays to the different lengths of time the same role for the concept of time that heat sensation plays in the above case.* Much the same holds for space.

16. If we have once understood clearly that with the introduction of a new arbitrarily defined and more sensitive criterion of heat-state a quite new standpoint has been adopted, and that henceforth only the new criterion is the basis of our enquiries, then the whole illusion disappears. This new criterion is the temperature number, or, shortly, the temperature, which by arbitrary agreement depends on:

  (i)   the choice of the volume as a sign,
  (ii) the thermometric substance,
  (iii) the correlation principle of number to volume.

17. An illusion of a different kind lies in a typical sort of conclusion which is almost universally drawn, of which we shall now speak. If we take the temperature number to be proportional to the pressure of a mass of gas at constant volume, then we see that the pressures and the temperatures can indeed climb as high as we like, but the pressure and temperature cannot sink below zero. The equation

$$p = p_0(1 + \alpha t)$$

says that for each degree temperature rise the pressure will increase by $1/273$ of the pressure at the freezing point of water, or, conversely, that for each $1/273$ pressure rise we shall count a temperature of $1°$ higher. For temperatures below the freezing point of water we should have

$$p = p_0(1 - \alpha t)$$

and we see that if one has decreased 273 times $1/273$ of the pressure at p_0, and arrives at $-273°$ C., then the pressure is zero. One likes to imagine that a gas which has been cooled this far will contain no more 'heat' at all, and that, therefore, it would not be possible to cool it below this temperature; or, in other words, that the sequence of heat-states has no *upper* limit, but that it reaches a lower limit at $-273°$ C.

Dalton's principle of correlation has indeed not remained in use, but there is in itself nothing at all to count against its admissability. If we multiply, according to this principle, the gas pressure by $1·0179$, then we must count the temperature as being $10°$ (Daltonian) higher. If the pressure is reduced by a factor of $1·0179$ then the temperature falls by $10°$ [D]. This operation we can perform as often as we like without reaching zero gas pressure. By use of the Daltonian scale we should never be obliged to conceive of a heat-state corresponding to zero gas pressure being achieved, or that the sequence of heat-states is bounded below. Certainly, this would not change the possibility of a zero gas pressure, as Dalton does not reach it simply because he approaches it

---

* Mach, *Analysis of Sensations*, pp. 101 ff.

with steps of decreasing size, as in the notorious paradox of Achilles and the Tortoise. It should be remarked here only how dubious it is to believe without more ado that the properties of a sign system are the properties of the things signified.

18. When formulating his scale Amontons proceeded in the belief that the gas pressure was produced by heat. His absolute zero, however, is not the only one which has been put forward, and still less the only one which could be put forward on grounds of quite as legitimate interpretation. If we proceeded with the expansion coefficient of mercury, just as we are accustomed to for air, then we would obtain an absolute zero of $-5000°$ C. With mercury, just as with air or any other body, we can use the pressure coefficient instead of the expansion coefficient in order to avoid the awkward conception of a volumeless body at absolute zero temperature.*

Dalton† suggested that a body contained a certain amount of heat-material. An increase in this raises the temperature, while the complete absence of it brings a body to absolute zero. This concept of a material was due to Black, although he was no friend of such conjectures, as we shall explain. If ice at $0°$ C. is transformed into water at $0°$ C., and in the process absorbs 80 kg. calories per kilogram, then it is to be considered, according to Gadolin and Dalton, that due to the doubling of the heat capacity by the melting of the ice, the whole loss of the heat-material from absolute zero to $0°$ C. is covered by those 80 heat units. From which it follows that absolute zero lies 2 times $80 = 160°$ C. below the freezing point of water. The same zero could be maintained for a whole range of bodies by the same argument. For mercury, however, which has a small latent heat, and shows a small difference in specific heat between solid and liquid states, absolute zero is given as $2021°$ C. below freezing point.

If one mixes two bodies, A and B, with equal temperatures, and the mixture exhibits a temperature change, then in an analogous way, by the determination of the specific heats of A, B, and $A + B$, we can derive absolute zero from the change. By mixing water and sulphuric acid Gadolin found absolute zero to be between 830 and $1720°$ C. below the freezing point of water. Other mixtures, or chemical combinations, have been interpreted similarly, and have again yielded other results.

19. We therefore have quite a number of different 'absolute zeros'. Today only Amontons' continues to be used, which, corresponding to dynamical gas theory, is now brought into relation with the cessation of motion of the gas molecules. All deductions, however, depend in similar ways on hypotheses over the processes by which we think of the heat appearances as being brought about. Whatever the value we put on

---

* mit dem absoluten Wärmeverlust.
† Dalton, *New System of Chemistry*, etc.

these hypothetical concepts, we must allow that they are both unproven and unprovable, and that we cannot decide in advance about reality, which can be arrived at only through observation.

20. We return now to a point which has already been touched on. Gas pressures are signs of heat-states. If the pressures were to disappear, then the chosen signs would be lacking and gas useless as a thermometer, so that we should have to look around for another. It does not follow that the thing signified also disappears. If, for example, a thermoelectric force should disappear on approaching a certain high temperature, or rather became nothing, then it would be found a very bold supposition that the temperature concerned formed an upper limit to the heat-states.

The temperature numbers are signs of signs. From the limitation of the sign system which we happen to have chosen nothing follows about the limits of what is signified. I can denote sensations of tone by frequency numbers. These, as positive real numbers, have a lower limit but no upper boundary. I can signify the sensations of tone by the logarithm of the frequency numbers, which gives a much better picture of the tone interval. Then the sign system is unbounded both above $(+\infty)$, and below $(-\infty)$. The system of tone sensations naturally pays no regard: it is bounded above and below. If in my sign system I can define an infinitely high or an infinitely deep note, it still does not follow that such a note exists.

All conclusions of this type remind one vividly of the so-called ontological proof for the existence of God. It is eminently scholastic. A concept is defined to whose characteristics existence belongs, and from this we conclude the existence of what we defined. One will concede that an analogous logical nonchalance has no place in present day physics.

We can therefore say: if the gas pressures can be brought to zero through mere cooling, then it is only the uselessness of gases as thermometers from then on that would come to light. About the lower boundedness or unboundedness of the sequence of heat-states nothing at all would follow.

The limitation of the sequence of heat-states above, or rather, that the sequence of temperature numbers has no upper limit, follows just as little from the fact that we can think of gas pressure as increasing so much as we like. A body melts and boils at a definite temperature. It is doubtful whether a gas can reach any stipulated high temperature without changing its properties significantly.

21. Whether the range of heat-states has an upper or a lower limit can only be decided through experience. The existence of a limit is only provided if, having a body with a definite heat-state, we cannot find one which is either hotter or colder.

This view does not exclude one's passing off the Amontonian zero as a fiction, or giving the above simple expression to the Mariotte–Gay-Lussac law, through which many of the remarks made later will be essentially simplified.

22. Temperature, as we can easily see after what has been said, is nothing but a characterization, or identification,* of the heat-states by a number. This temperature number has the property merely of an index number, by which we can recognize the same heat-state again, and, if necessary, locate and reproduce it. At the same time, this number allows us to recognize the order in which the signified heat-states follow upon one another, and between which other states a given state lies. In the following investigations it will indeed be shown that temperature numbers can be made to serve further and very important services. For this, however, we do not have the astuteness of the physicists to thank—which has given us the system of temperature numbers—it is more the result of fortunate circumstances that nobody could foresee, and over which nobody could have had command.

23. The concept of temperature is a concept of level, like the weight of a heavy body or the speed of a moving one, the electrical or magnetic potential, or the chemical difference. Thermal influence occurs between bodies of different temperature in a similar way to that in which electrical influence occurs between bodies of different potential. While, however, the concept of potential has been formed with advantage through a constant awareness of the goal, this has only turned out beneficially for the concept of temperature accidentally and approximately.

In most areas of physics it is only difference of level that plays a role in providing a measure. Temperature seems to have in common with the levels of chemistry that the level itself provides a measure. The fixed melting points, boiling points, critical temperatures, combustion temperatures, and dissociation temperatures are fairly obvious examples of this.

* Kennzeichnung.

APPENDIX II

It is required to find a function f which satisfies the following conditions:

(i) $f(a) \gtreqless f(b)$ according as $a \gtreqless b,$ and

(ii) $|f(a)-f(b)| \gtreqless |f(c)-f(d)|$ according as $|a-b| \gtreqless |c-d|.$

From condition (i) it follows that

$$f \text{ is a single valued,} \tag{1}$$

and, $\qquad\qquad f$ is strictly monotonic increasing. $\qquad\qquad$ (2)

Assume $|f(a)-f(b)| = |f(c)-f(d)|$ when $|a-b| = |c-d|$. Call the equation on the left-hand side, the equation (3), and that on the right-hand side, (4).

Now, put $\qquad\qquad a = x+h, \quad b = x,$

$$c = y+h, \quad d = y,$$

(3) then becomes

$$|f(x+h)-f(x)| = |f(y+h)-f(y)|.$$

And, from (2)

$$f(x+h)-f(x) = f(y+h)-f(y),$$

that is $\qquad\quad f(x+h)-f(y+h) = f(x)-f(y).$

Put $\qquad\qquad\quad f(x)-f(y) = \phi(x, y).$

Then $\qquad\qquad \phi(x+h, y+h) = \phi(x, y).$

For $h = -y$, we get:

$$\phi(x-y, 0) = \phi(x, y) =_{Df} \Phi(x-y),$$

$$\therefore \quad f(x)-f(y) = \Phi(x-y). \tag{5}$$

In particular, $\qquad f(x)-f(0) = \Phi(x),$

that is $\qquad\qquad\quad f(x) = \Phi(x)+n. \tag{6}$

And, substituting in (5),

$$\Phi(x)-\Phi(y) = \Phi(x-y). \tag{7}$$

Now, with this condition, we can easily solve for the function Φ.

Putting $y = x$ in (7), we have

$$\Phi(0) = 0. \tag{7a}$$

Putting $x = 0$, and substituting x for y, we have

$$\Phi(-x) = -\Phi(x). \tag{7b}$$

Putting $y = \overline{n+1}x$, we have

$$\Phi(x) = \Phi(\overline{n+1}x) - \Phi(nx). \tag{7c}$$

Lemma 1. For n an integer, $n\Phi(x) = \Phi(nx)$

Proof. (i) For $n \geqq 0$: (i*a*) $0\Phi(x) = \Phi(0x)$ by (7*a*).

$\quad$ (i*b*) If $n\Phi(x) = \Phi(nx)$,

$\quad$ then $\Phi(\overline{n+1}x) = \Phi(x) + \Phi(nx)$

$$\text{by } (7c),$$
$$= \Phi(x) + n\Phi(x),$$
$$= \overline{n+1}\,\Phi(x).$$

Hence, by mathematical induction,

$$n\Phi(x) = \Phi(nx) \quad \text{for} \quad n \geqq 0.$$

(ii) for $n < 0$, $\quad \Phi(nx) = -\Phi(-nx)$ by (7*b*),

$$= n\Phi(x) \quad \text{by (i}a).$$

Hence Lemma 1.

Lemma 2. For k rational, $k\Phi(x) = \Phi(kx)$

Proof. (i) For $k = 1/n$, $n \neq 0$.

From Lemma 1,

$$n\Phi\left(\frac{x}{n}\right) = \Phi\left(\frac{nx}{n}\right) = \Phi(x),$$

$$\therefore \quad \frac{1}{n}\Phi(x) = \Phi\left(\frac{x}{n}\right).$$

(ii) For $k = m/n$,

From (i)

$$\frac{m}{n}\Phi(x) = \Phi\left(\frac{mx}{n}\right).$$

Hence Lemma 2.

Lemma 3. For k real, $k\Phi(x) = \Phi(kx)$

Proof. For any real k, there exists a sequence $\{k_n\}$ such that k_n is rational for all n, and $\lim_{n\to\infty} k_n = k$. From Lemma 2,

$$k_n \Phi(x) = \Phi(k_n x)$$

and hence $\quad \lim_{n\to\infty} k_n \Phi(x) = \lim_{n\to\infty} \Phi(k_n x).$

But,
$$\lim_{n \to \infty} \Phi(k_n x) = \lim_{k_n \to k} \Phi(k_n x)$$
$$= \Phi(kx).$$

Hence
$$k\Phi(x) = \Phi(kx).$$

Lemma 4. Φ *is continuous*

Proof. $|\Phi(x+h) - \Phi(x)| \leqslant |\Phi(x+h_1) - \Phi(x)|,$

for
$$(x+h) \leqslant (x+h_1) \leqslant (x+2h) \quad \text{by (2)}$$
$$\therefore \quad |\Phi(x+h) - \Phi(x)| \leqslant |\Phi(h_1)|,$$

since
$$\Phi(x) - \Phi(y) = \Phi(x-y).$$

But
$$\Phi(h) = h\Phi(1)$$
$$\therefore \quad |\Phi(x+h) - \Phi(x)| \to 0 \quad \text{as} \quad h \to 0.$$

Hence continuity.

We are now in a position to solve for Φ

$$\Phi(x-y) = \Phi(x) - \Phi(y).$$

Put $y = x$, then from Lemmas

$$\Phi(x) = x\Phi(1)$$
$$= cx.$$

And now, substituting in (6), we get

$$f(x) = cx + n.$$

Q.E.D.

Note. The inequality conditions in (ii), above, are not used in this proof. Hence, both nominal-interval and ordinal-interval scales must be classed simply as linear interval scales in Stevens' classification.

APPENDIX III

Given that $f_{(2)}$ is a single-valued function of two variables which satisfies the following conditions for all values of these variables within some specified domain:

(a') $f_{(2)}(x_1, x_2)$ is strictly monotonic increasing in each argument.

(b') $f_{(2)}(x_1, x_2) = f_{(2)}(x_2, x_1)$.

(c') $f_{(2)}[x_1, f_{(2)}(x_2, x_3)] = f_{(2)}[f_{(2)}(x_1, x_2), x_3] =_{df} f_{(3)}(x_1, x_2, x_3)$.

(d') If $f_{(n)}(x_1, x_2, \ldots x_n) =_{df} f_{(2)}[f_{(n-1)}(x_1, x_2, \ldots x_{n-1}), x_n]$ then there is a unique $\bar{x}_{(n)}$ such that

$$f_{(n)}(\bar{x}, \bar{x}, \ldots, \bar{x}) = f_{(n)}(x_1, x_2, \ldots, x_n).$$

Then it is required to prove that if

$$A_{(n)}(x_1, x_2, \ldots, x_n) =_{df} \bar{x}_{(n)},$$

$A_{(n)}$ must satisfy the following conditions for all values of the variables within the specified domain:

(a) If x_i and x_j are the extreme values of the set $x_1, x_2, \ldots, x_n$, and $x_i \leqq x_j$, then
$$x_i \leqq A_{(n)}(x_1, x_2, \ldots, x_n) \leqq x_j.$$

(b) $A_n(x_1, x_2, \ldots, x_n)$ is strictly monotonic increasing in each argument.

(c) $A_n(x_1, x_2, \ldots, x_n)$ is commutative with respect to each pair of arguments.

(d) $x_{n+1} \gtreqless \bar{x}_{(n+1)} \gtreqless \bar{x}_{(n)}$ according as $x_{n+1} \gtreqless \bar{x}_{(n)}$.

Proof. (i) From (b') and (c'), it follows quickly that $A_{(n)}$ must be commutative for each pair of arguments. Hence condition (c) is satisfied.

(ii) From (a') and (c'), it follows that $f_{(n)}$ must be strictly monotonic increasing in each argument. Hence, if for any set of values $x_1, x_2, \ldots, x_i, \ldots, x_n$, we replace x_i by $x_i' > x_i$, it follows that $f_{(n)}(x_1, x_2, \ldots, x_i', \ldots, x_n) > f_{(n)}(x_1, x_2, \ldots, x_i, \ldots, x_n)$. Let $\bar{x}'$ be such that
$$f_{(n)}(\bar{x}', \bar{x}', \ldots, \bar{x}') = f_{(n)}(x_1, x_2, \ldots, x_i', \ldots, x_n).$$
And let $\bar{x}$ be such that
$$f_{(n)}(\bar{x}, \bar{x}, \ldots, \bar{x}) = f_{(n)}(x_1, x_2, \ldots, x_i, \ldots, x_n).$$

Then
$$f_{(n)}(\bar{x}', \bar{x}', ..., \bar{x}') > f_{(n)}(\bar{x}, \bar{x}, ..., \bar{x}).$$

But $f_{(n)}$ is strictly monotonic increasing in each argument,
$$\therefore \quad \bar{x}' > \bar{x}.$$

Hence, $A_{(n)}$ is also strictly monotonic increasing in each argument. Hence condition (b) is satisfied.

(iii) Let the sequence of arguments $x_1, x_2, ..., x_n$ be arranged in increasing order, and change the nomenclature, so that x_1 designates the lowest reading, and x_n the highest. Now suppose that
$$A_{(n)}(x_1, x_2, ..., x_n) > x_n.$$

Then
$$A_{(n)}(x_n, x_n, ..., x_n) > x_n \quad \text{(from } (b)),$$
$$\therefore \quad f_{(n)}(x_n, x_n, ..., x_n) > f_{(n)}(x_n, x_n, ..., x_n).$$

But this is impossible. Hence $A_{(n)}(x_1, x_2, ..., x_n) \leqq x_n$.

Similarly,
$$A_{(n)}(x_1, x_2, ..., x_n) \geqq x_1.$$

Hence
$$x_1 \leqq A_{(n)}(x_1, x_2, ..., x_n) \leqq x_n.$$

Hence, condition (a) is satisfied.

(iv) Let
$$\bar{x}_{(n)} = A_{(n)}(x_1, x_2, ..., x_n),$$
and
$$\bar{x}_{(n+1)} = A_{(n+1)}(x_1, x_2, ..., x_n, x_{n+1}).$$

Now, it is required to prove that
$$\bar{x}_{(n)} \lesseqgtr \bar{x}_{(n+1)} \lesseqgtr x_{n+1} \quad \text{according as} \quad \bar{x}_{(n)} \lesseqgtr x_{n+1}.$$

(a) Suppose that $\bar{x}_{(n)} = x_{n+1}$.

Then
$$\bar{x}_{(n+1)} = A_{(n+1)}(\bar{x}_{(n)}, \bar{x}_{(n)}, ..., \bar{x}_{(n)}) = \bar{x}_{(n)} = x_{n+1}.$$

(b) Suppose that $\bar{x}_{(n)} < x_{n+1}$. Then
$$\bar{x}_{(n+1)} > A_{(n+1)}(\bar{x}_{(n)}, \bar{x}_{(n)}, ..., \bar{x}_{(n)}) = \bar{x}_{(n)},$$
and
$$\bar{x}_{(n+1)} < A_{(n+1)}(x_{(n+1)}, x_{(n+1)}, ..., x_{n+1}) = x_{n+1}.$$

(c) Suppose that $\bar{x}_{(n)} > x_{n+1}$. Then
$$\bar{x}_{(n+1)} < A_{(n+1)}(\bar{x}_{(n)}, \bar{x}_{(n)}, ..., \bar{x}_{(n)}) = \bar{x}_{(n)},$$
and
$$\bar{x}_{(n+1)} > A_{(n+1)}(x_{n+1}, x_{n+1}, ..., x_{n+1}) = x_{n+1}.$$

Hence, condition (d) is also satisfied.

APPENDIX IV

It is required to prove:

Theorem 1. That if S_i and S_j are any two members of an extended system of standards such that $S_i <_p S_j$, then there exists another member S_k such that $S_i <_p S_k <_p S_j$; that the system is everywhere dense with respect to the relationships $>_p$ and $<_p$.

Theorem 2. That if $O(S_i, S_j, S_k, ..., S_r)$ and $O(S_x, S_y, S_z, ..., S_w)$ are any two members of an extended system of standards, designated by A and B respectively, then

$$A \gtreqless_p B \quad \text{according as} \quad (i+j+k+...+r) \gtreqless (x+y+z+...+w).$$

Proof. (i) Suppose that $i, j, k, ..., r$ and $x, y, z, ..., w$ are all integers. Then S_i may be expanded to $O_{(i)}(S_1, S_1, ..., S_1)$, where the latter expansion signifies the result of combining i systems equal in p to S_1 successively by the operation O. Similarly, $S_j, S_k, ..., S_r$ and $S_x, S_y, S_z, ..., S_w$ may be expanded; S_j becoming $O_{(j)}(S_1, S_1, ..., S_1)$, S_k becoming $O_{(k)}(S_1, S_1, ..., S_1)$, and so on. Hence, if $(i+j+k+...r) = a$, and $(x+y+z+...w) = b$, it follows that

$$\left. \begin{aligned} A &=_p O_{(a)}(S_1, S_1, ..., S_1), \\ \text{and} \qquad B &=_p O_{(b)}(S_1, S_1, ..., S_1). \end{aligned} \right\} \tag{ia}$$

Hence it follows immediately that

$$A \gtreqless_p B \quad \text{according as} \quad a \gtreqless b. \tag{ib}$$

(ii) Since $S_i, S_j, S_k, ..., S_r$ and $S_x, S_y, S_z, ..., S_w$ are all members of a system of standards, it follows that the subscripts are all of the form n, or $1/n$, where n is an integer. Let

$$S_{m/n} =_{df} O_{(m)}(S_{1/n}, S_{1/n}, ..., S_{1/n}). \tag{ii$a$}$$

And suppose that $n = mp$.

Then from the definition of a standard sub-set, and condition (iii) on p. 75, it follows that

$$S_{m/n} =_p S_{1/p}. \tag{ii$b$}$$

Next, let c be the lowest common denominator of $i, j, k, ..., r$ and

$x, y, z, \ldots, w$, and in place of S_1, choose $S_{1/c}$ as initial standard, and designate it by S'_1. Then, from (ii$b$) we have:

$$\left. \begin{aligned} A &=_p O(S'_{ci}, S'_{cj}, S'_{ck}, \ldots, S'_{cr}), \\ \text{and} \quad B &=_p O(S'_{cx}, S'_{cy}, S'_{cz}, \ldots, S'_{cw}), \end{aligned} \right\} \tag{ii$c$}$$

where $ci, cj, ck, \ldots, cr$ and $cx, cy, cz, \ldots, cw$ are all integers. And theorem 2 follows immediately from (ib).

(iii) Given theorem 2, the proof of theorem 1 is obvious. It follows at once from the density of the sequence of rational numbers.

APPENDIX V

(i) Assume that
$$f(x, y, z, ...) = \text{const.}$$
is a numerical law expressed with respect to the classes of similar scales $[X], [Y], [Z], ...$ We want to find the permissible forms of the function f.

Let $X_1, Y_1, Z_1, ...$ and $X_2, Y_2, Z_2, ...$ be two sets of scales belonging to the classes $[X], [Y], [Z], ...$ Then if $x_1, y_1, z_1, ...$ are the results of any measurements on the scales $X_1, Y_1, Z_1, ...$ respectively, and $x_2, y_2, z_2, ...$ are the results of the measurements on the same particulars under the same conditions on the scales $X_2, Y_2, Z_2, ...$ respectively, then

$$x_1 = \alpha x_2,$$
$$y_1 = \beta y_2,$$
$$z_1 = \gamma z_2,$$

where α is the conversion factor from X_1 to X_2,

β is the conversion factor from Y_1 to Y_2,

γ is the conversion factor from Z_1 to Z_2,

$\vdots$

and so on.

Hence if $\qquad f(x, y, z, ...) = \text{const.}$
is a numerical law holding for all sets of scales within the classes $[X], [Y], [Z], ...,$ then

$$f(x_1, y_1, z_1, ...) = K_1,$$
and $\qquad f(x_2, y_2, z_2, ...) = K_2.$

Consequently, the function f must be such that

$$f(\alpha x_2, \beta y_2, \gamma z_2, ...) = \phi(\alpha, \beta, \gamma, ...) f(x_2, y_2, z_2, ...)$$
for all $\alpha > 0, \beta > 0, \gamma > 0, ...$

(ii) Given that

$$f(\alpha x, \beta y, \gamma z, ...) = \phi(\alpha, \beta, \gamma, ...) f(x, y, z, ...)$$
it is required to find the function f.

Assume that f is partially differentiable with respect to $x, y, z, \ldots$. Then, holding $y, z, \ldots$ constant, we may expand $f(x, y, z, \ldots)$ in a Taylor Series. Thus,

$$f(x, y, z, \ldots) = a_0 + a_1 x + a_2 x^2 + \ldots + a_m x^m + \ldots, \qquad (\text{1})$$

where
$$a_m = \frac{1}{m!} \frac{\partial^m}{\partial x^m} (f(0, y, z, \ldots)).$$

Put $\beta = \gamma = \ldots = 1$, and signify $\phi(\alpha, 1, 1, 1 \ldots)$ by ϕ_a. Then multiplying (1) by ϕ_a we get

$$\phi_a f(x, y, z, \ldots) = a_0 \phi_a + a_1 \phi_a x + a_2 \phi_a x^2 + \ldots + a_m \phi_a x^m + \ldots. \qquad (\text{2})$$

But $\quad \phi_a f(x, y, z, \ldots) = f(\alpha x, y, z, \ldots)$
$$= a_0 + a_1 \alpha x + a_2 \alpha^2 x^2 + \ldots + a_m \alpha^m x^m + \ldots. (\text{3})$$

Hence, identifying (2) and (3),

either
$$\phi_a = 1 \quad \text{or} \quad a_0 = 0,$$
$$\phi_a = \alpha \quad \text{or} \quad a_1 = 0,$$
$$\phi_a = \alpha^2 \quad \text{or} \quad a_2 = 0,$$
$$\vdots$$
$$\phi_a = \alpha^m \quad \text{or} \quad a_m = 0.$$

But if $\phi_a = \alpha^i$ then $\phi_a \neq \alpha^j$ where $j \neq i$. For assuming that $\phi_a = \alpha^i$ and $\phi_a = \alpha^j$, $j \neq i$, it follows that $\alpha = 1$, which is contrary to the original assumption that

$$f(\alpha x, y, z, \ldots) = \phi(\alpha, 1, 1, \ldots) f(x, y, z, \ldots)$$

for all $\alpha > 0$.

Hence

$$\phi(\alpha, 1, 1, \ldots) = \alpha^m, \quad \text{and} \quad \begin{cases} a_m = \dfrac{1}{m!} \dfrac{\partial^m}{\partial x^m} f(0, y, z, \ldots), \\ a_n = 0, \quad m \neq n. \end{cases}$$

And so, $\quad f(x, y, z, \ldots) = a_m x^m \quad$ (from (1)),

where a_m is a function of $y, z, w, \ldots$ only. Similarly

$$f(x, y, z, \ldots) = b_n y^n,$$

where b is a function of $x, z, w, \ldots$ only. And generally,

$$f(x, y, z, \ldots) = C x^m y^n z^o \ldots.$$

(iii) Consequently, if

$$f(x, y, z, \ldots) = \text{const.}$$

is a numerical law expressed with respect to the classes of similar scales $[X]$, $[Y]$, $[Z]$, ..., it must be of the form

$$x^m y^n z^o \ldots = \text{const.}$$

Q.E.D.

Note. A somewhat neater proof of this proposition appears to have been offered by Bridgman (1931), p. 21, but I confess that I am unable to follow it. I have included this proof on the grounds that it may be more perspicuous.

BIBLIOGRAPHY

ADAMS, E. W. (1964). Remarks on inexact additive measurement. Unpublished paper, University of California.

ADAMS, E. W., FAGOT, R. & ROBINSON, R. (1964). Invariance, meaningfulness and appropriate statistics. Unpublished paper, University of California.

ANDERSON, N. H. (1961). Scales and statistics: parametric and nonparametric. *Psychol. Bull.* **58**, 305–16.

BARNETT, M. K. (1956). The development of the thermometer and the temperature concept. *Osiris*, **12**, 269–431.

BARTLETT, R. J. (1940). Measurement in psychology. Address to Section J, Psychology. *Rep. Brit. Ass.* **1**, 422–41.

BEHAN, E. L. & BEHAN, R. A. (1954). Football numbers (continued). *Amer. Psychol.* **9**, 262–3.

BENACERRAF, P. & PUTNAM, H. (ed.) (1964). *Philosophy of Mathematics*, New Jersey: Prentice-Hall, parts I and III.

BERGMANN, G. (1951). The logic of psychological concepts. *Phil. Sci.* **18**, 93–110.

BERGMANN, G. & SPENCE, K. W. (1944). The logic of psychophysical measurement. *Psychol. Rev.* **51**, 1–24.

BETH, E. W. (1959). *The Foundations of Mathematics*. Amsterdam: North-Holland.

BLACK, M. (1933). *The Nature of Mathematics*. New York: Harcourt.

BORING, E. G. (1929). *A History of Experimental Psychology*. New York: Appleton.

BORING, E. G. (1920). The logic of the nomal law of error in mental measurement. *Amer. J. Psychol.* **31**, 1–33.

BRAITHWAITE, R. B. (1953). *Scientific Explanation*. Cambridge University Press.

BRIDGMAN, P. W. (1927). *The Logic of Modern Physics*. London: Macmillan.

BRIDGMAN, P. W. (1931). *Dimensional Analysis*. New Haven: Yale University Press.

BRIDGMAN, P. W. (1936). *The Nature of Physical Theory*. Princeton University Press.

BRODBECK, M. & FEIGL, H. (1953). *Readings in the Philosophy of Science*. New York: Appleton.

BROUWER, L. E. J. (1913). Intuitionism and formalism. *Bull. Amer. Math. Soc.* **20**, (Reprinted in P. Benacerraf and H. Putnam (ed.) (1964). *Philosophy of Mathematics*. New Jersey: Prentice Hall.)

BROWN, G. B. (1942). A note on W. Wilson's 'Dimensions of physical quantities'. *Phil. Mag.* **33**, no. 220, 367–8.

BUCHDAHL, H. A. (1949). On the principle of caretheodory. *Amer. J. Phys.* **17**, no. 1, 41–3.

BURKE, C. J. (1953). Additive scales and statistics. *Psychol. Rev.* **60**, 73–5.

BURKS, A. W. (1953). The presupposition theory of induction. *Phil. Sci.* **20**, 177–97.

CAMPBELL, N. R. (1920). *Physics, the Elements.* Cambridge University Press. (Republished as *Foundations of Science*, New York: Dover, 1957.)

CAMPBELL, N. R. (1921). *What is Science.* (Reprinted New York: Dover, 1952.)

CAMPBELL, N. R. (1928). *An Account of the Principles of Measurement and Calculations.* London: Longmans, Green.

CAMPBELL, N. R. (1938). Measurement and its importance for philosophy. *Arist. Soc. Supp.* **17**, 121–42.

CAMPBELL, N. R. (1942*a*). Dimensions. *Phil. Mag.* **33**, no. 220, 398.

CAMPBELL, N. R. (1942*b*). Dimensions and the facts of measurement. *Phil. Mag.* **33**, no. 225, 761–71.

CARNAP, R. (1945). Two concepts of probability. *Philosophy and Phenomenological Research*, **5**. (Reprinted with slight modifications in Feigl, H. and Brodbeck, M. (ed.) (1953). *Readings in the Philosophy of Science.* New York: Appleton, pp. 438–55.)

CARNAP, R. (1950). *Logical Foundations of Probability.* Chicago: University of Chicago Press.

CARNAP, R. (1952). *The Continuum of Inductive Methods.* University of Chicago Press.

CARNAP, R. (1953). Formal and factual science. In *Readings in the Philosophy of Science.* Ed. H. Feigl and M. Brodbeck. New York: Appleton.

CARNAP, R. (1955). Foundations of logic and measurement. *International Encyclopedia of Unified Science*, vol. 1. Chicago: University of Chicago Press.

CASTANEDA, H. N. (1964). Arithmetic and reality. *The Australasian Journal of Philosophy*, **37**, no. 2, 92–107. (Reprinted in P. Benacerraf and H. Putnam. (ed.) (1964). *Philosophy of Mathematics.* New Jersey: Prentice Hall.)

CAWS, P. (1959). Definition and measurement in physics. In *Measurement: Definition and Theories.* Ed. C. W. Churchman and P. Ratoosh. New York: Wiley.

CHURCHMAN, C. W. (1959). Why measure? In *Measurement: Definition and Theories.* Ed. C. W. Churchman and P. Ratoosh. New York: Wiley.

CHURCHMAN, C. W. & RATOOSH, P. (ed.) (1959). *Measurement: Definitions and Theories.* New York: Wiley.

COBB, P. W. (1932). Weber's law and the Fechnerian muddle. *Psychol. Rev.* **39**, 533–51.

COHEN, M. R. & NAGEL, E. (1934). *An Introduction to Logic and Scientific Method.* New York: Harcourt.

COMREY, A. L. (1950*a*). An operational approach to some problems in psychological measurement. *Psychol. Rev.* **57**, 217–28.

COMREY, A. L. (1950*b*). A proposed method for absolute ratio scaling. *Psychometrika*, **15**, 317–25.

COMREY, A. L. (1951). Mental testing and the logic of measurement. *Educ. Psychol. Meas.* **11**, 323–34.

COOMBS, C. H. (1950). Psychological scaling without a unit of measurement. *Psychol. Rev.* **57**, 145–58.

COOMBS, C. H. (1952*a*). A theory of psychological scaling. *Bull. Engng. Res.* no. 34. Ann Arbor: University of Michigan Press.

COOMBS, C. H. (1952*b*). The theory and methods of social measurement. In *Research Methods in the Behavioural Sciences.* Ed. L. Festinger and D. Katz. New York: Dryden Press.

COOMBS, C. H., RAIFFA, H. & THRALL, R. M. (1954). Some views on mathematical models and measurement theory. *Psychol. Rev.* **61**, 132–44.

CROMBIE, A. C. (1961). Quantification in medieval physics. *Quantification.* Ed. H. Woolf. Indianapolis–New York: Bobbs-Merrill, pp. 13–30.

CULLER, E. A. (1926). Studies in psychometric theory. *Psychol. Monogr.* **35**, no. 163, 56–137.

CURRY, H. B. (1951). *Outlines of a Formalist Philosophy of Mathematics.* Amsterdam: North Holland.

DAVIDSON, D., SUPPES, P. & SIEGEL, S. (1957). *Decision Making.* Stanford University Press.

DAVIES, J. T. (1956). On extrapolation, with special reference to the 'Age of the Universe'. *Brit. J. Phil. Sci.* **7**, no. 26, 129–38.

DINGLE, H. (1942*a*). On the dimensions of physical magnitudes. *Phil. Mag.* **33**, no. 220, 321–44.

DINGLE, H. (1942*b*). On the dimensions of physical magnitudes (second paper). *Phil. Mag.* **33**, no. 224, 692–7.

DINGLE, H. (1943). On the dimensions of physical magnitudes (third paper). *Phil. Mag.* **34**, no. 236, 588–99.

DINGLE, H. (1944*a*). On the dimensions of physical magnitudes (fourth paper). *Phil. Mag.* **35**, no. 244, 296–9.

DINGLE, H. (1944*b*). On the dimensions of physical magnitudes (fifth paper). *Phil. Mag.* **35**, no. 248, 616–18.

DINGLE, H. (1946). On the dimensions of physical magnitudes (sixth paper). *Phil. Mag.* **37**, no. 264, 64–6.

DINGLE, H. (1949). On the dimensions of physical magnitudes (seventh paper). *Phil. Mag.* **40**, no. 300, 94–9.

DINGLE, H. (1950). A theory of measurement. *Brit. J. Phil. Sci.* **1**, no. 1, 5–26.

DOBBS, H. A. C. (1951). The relation between the time of psychology and the time of physics. *Brit. J. Phil. Sci.* **2**, no. 6, 122–41.

DUHEM, P. (1954). *The Aim and Structure of Physical Theory.* Princeton; Princeton University Press.

DUNCAN, W. J. (1953). *Physical Similarity and Dimensional Analysis.* London: Edward Arnold.

DURAND III, L. (1960). On the theory of measurement in quantum mechanical systems. *Phil. Sci.* **27**, 115–33.

EDDINGTON, A. S. (1935). *New Pathways in Science.* Cambridge University Press.

ELLIS, B. D. (1955). Has the Universe a beginning in time? *Aust. J. Phil.* **33**, 33–37.

ELLIS, B. D. (1960). Some fundamental problems of direct measurement. *Aust. J. Phil.* **38**, 37–47.

ELLIS, B. D. (1961). Some fundamental problems of indirect measurement. *Aust. J. Phil.* **39**, 13–29.

ELLIS, B. D. (1963). Derived measurement, universal constants, and the expression of numerical laws. In *Philosophy of Science: the Delaware Seminar.* vol. II. Ed. W. L. Reese and B. Baumrim. New York: Wiley, pp. 371–92.

ELLIS, B. D. (1964). On the nature of dimensions. *Phil. Sci.* **31**, 357–80.

FEIGL, H. & BRODBECK, M. (ed.) (1953). *Readings in the Philosophy of Science.* New York: Appleton.

FEYERABEND, P. K. (1957). On the quantum-theory of measurement. In *Observation and Interpretation in the Philosophy of Physics*, pp. 121–30. Ed. S. Körner. New York: Dover.

FOCKEN, C. M. (1953). *Dimensional Methods and their Applications.* London: Arnold.

FREGE, G. (1950). *The Foundations of Arithmetic.* Trans. J. L. Austin. Oxford: Blackwell.

FREGE, G. (1952). *Translations from the Philosophical Writings.* Ed. P. Geach and M. Black. Oxford: Blackwell.

GASKING, D. A. T. (1940). Mathematics and the World. *Aust. J. Psych. Phil.* **18**, (Reprinted in Benacerraf, P. and Putnam, H. (ed.) (1964). *Philosophy of Mathematics.* New Jersey: Prentice-Hall.)

GASKING, D. A. T. (1960). Clusters. *Aust. J. Phil.* **38**, no. 1, 1–36.

GOODSTEIN, R. L. (1962). The foundations of mathematics. *Arist. Soc. Supp.* **36**.

GRÜNBAUM, A. (1963). *Philosophical Problems of Space and Time.* New York: Knopf.

GUGGENHEIM, E. A. (1942). Units and dimensions. *Phil. Mag.* **33**, no. 222, 479–95.

GUILFORD, J. P. (1936). *Psychometric Methods.* New York: McGraw Hill. (2nd ed., 1954. New York: McGraw Hill.)

GULLIKSEN, H. (1946). Paired comparisons and the logic of measurement. *Psychol. Rev.* **53**, 199–213.

HANSON, N. R. (1963). *The Concept of the Positron.* Cambridge University Press.

HELMHOLTZ, H. V. (1887). Zählen und Messen erkenntnis — theoretisch betrachtet. In *Philosophische Aufsätze Eduard Zeller gewidmet.* Leipzig. (Reprinted in *Gesammelte Abhandlungen,* **3** (1895), 356–91.)

HEMPEL, C. G. (1945). On the nature of mathematical truth. *Amer. Math. Monthly,* **52**, (Reprinted in P. Benacerraf and H. Putnam (ed.) (1964). *Philosophy of Mathematics.* New Jersey: Prentice-Hall.)

HEMPEL, C. G. (1952). Fundamentals of concept formation in empirical science. *International Encyclopaedia of Unified Science,* **2**, no. 7, Chicago: University of Chicago Press.

HENMÜLLER, F. & MENGER, K. (1961). What is length? *Phil. Sci.* **28**, 172–7.

HEYTING, A. (1956). *Intuitionism: an Introduction.* Amsterdam: North-Holland.

HÖELDER, O. (1901). Die Axiome der Quantität und die Lehre vom Mass. *Berichte Uber die Verhandlungen der königlich Sächsischen Gesellschaft der Wissenschaften zu Leipzig* (*Math.-Phys. Klasse*), **53**, 1–64.

IPSEN, D. C. (1960). *Units, Dimensions and Dimensionless Numbers.* New York: McGraw Hill.

JAUNCEY, G. E. M. & LANGSDORF, A. S. (1940). *M.K.S. Units and Dimensions and a Proposed M.K.O.S. System.* New York: Macmillan.

JEFFREYS, H. (1938). Measurement and its importance for philosophy. *Artist. Soc. Supp.* **17**, 143–51.

JEFFREYS, H. (1943). Units and dimensions. *Phil. Mag.* **34**, no. 239.

KÖRNER, S. (ed.) (1957). *Observation and Interpretation in the Philosophy of Physics.* New York: Dover.

KÖRNER, S. (ed.) (1960). *The Philosophy of Mathematics.* London: Hutchinson University Library.

KUHN, T. S. (1961). The function of measurement in modern physical science. *Quantification,* pp. 13–30. Ed. H. Woolf. Indianapolis–New York: Bobbs-Merrill.

LAKATOS, I. (1962). The foundations of Mathematics. *Arist. Soc. Supp.* **36**.

LANCHESTER, F. W. (1936). *The Theory of Dimensions and Its Applications for Engineers.* London: Crosby Lockwood.

LANGHAAR, H. L. (1951). *Dimensional Analysis and Theory of Models.* New York: Wiley.

LAZARSFELD, P. F. (ed.) (1954). *Mathematical Thinking in the Social Sciences.* Glencoe, Illinois: The Free Press.

LENZEN, V. F. (1936–7). The interaction between subject and object in observation. *Erkenntnis,* **6**, 326–35.

LENZEN, V. F. (1938). Procedures of empirical science. *International Encyclopedia of Unified Science*, **1**, no. 5. Chicago: University of Chicago Press.

LERNER, D. (ed.). (1961). *Quantity and Quality*. Glencoe, Illinois: The Free Press.

LORD, F. M. (1953). On the statistical treatment of football numbers. *Amer. Psychol.* **8**, 750–1.

LUCE, R. D. (1959). On the possible psychophysical laws. *Psychol. Rev.* **66**, no. 2, 81–95.

MACH, E. (1960). *Science of Mechanics*. Trans. T. J. McCormack. La Salle, Illinois: Open Court.

MACH, E. (1900). *Die Principien der Wärmelehre*, 2nd ed. Leipzig.

MARGENAU, H. (1950). *The Nature of Physical Reality*. New York: McGraw Hill.

MARGENAU, H. (1959). Philosophical problems concerning the meaning of measurement in physics. In *Measurement: Definition and Theories*. Ed. C. W. Churchman and P. Ratoosh. New York: Wiley.

McGREGOR, D. (1935). Scientific measurement and psychology. *Psychol. Rev.* **42**, 246–66.

McKINSEY, J. C. C. & SUPPES, P. (1955). On the notion of invariance in classical mechanics. *Brit. J. Phil. Sci.* **5**, 290–302.

McKNIGHT, J. L. (1957). The quantum theoretical concept of measurement. *Phil. Sci.* **24**, 321–30.

MENGER, K. (1953). The idea of variable and function. *Proc. Nat. Acad. Sci., Wash.*, **39**, 956–61.

MENGER, K. (1954). On variables in mathematics and natural sciences. *Brit. J. Phil. Sci*, **5**, no. 18, 134–42.

MENGER, K. (1959). Mensuration and other mathematical connections of observable material. In *Measurement: Definition and Theories*. Ed. C. W. Churchman and P. Ratoosh. New York: Wiley.

MENGER, K. (1961). 'Variables, constants, fluents' with comments by E. W. Adams. In *Current Issues in the Philosophy of Science*. Ed. H. Feigl and G. Maxwell. New York: Holt, Reinhart and Winston, pp. 304–18.

MILL, J. S. (1875). *A System of Logic*, Book II. London: Longman's, Green.

NAGEL, E. (1931). Measurement. *Erkenntnis*, **2**. 313–33.

NAGEL, E. & COHEN, M. R. (1934). *An Introduction to Logic and Scientific Method*. New York: Harcourt.

NELSON, T. M. & BARTLEY, S. H. (1961). Numerosity, number, arithmetization, measurement and psychology. *Phil. Sci.* **28**, 178–203.

PAP, A. (1959). Are physical magnitudes operationally definable? In *Measurement: Definition and Theories*. Ed. C. W. Churchman and P. Ratoosh. New York: Wiley.

POPPER, K. R. (1959). *The Logic of Scientific Discovery*. London: Hutchinson.

PRATT, C. C. (1939). *The Logic of Modern Psychology*. New York: Macmillan.

RAMSEY, F. P. (1931). *The Foundations of Mathematics*. New York: Harcourt.

REICHENBACH, H. (1944). *Philosophic Foundations of Quantum Theory*. Berkeley: University of California Press.

RESCHER, N. (1960). A problem in the theory of numerical estimation. *Synthese*, **12**, no. 1, 34–9.

ROBINSON, R. E. (1963). A set-theoretical approach to empirical meaningfulness of measurement statements. *Technical Report*, no. 55. Institute for Mathematical Studies in the Social Sciences, Stanford University.

RUSSELL, B. (1937). *The Principles of Mathematics*, 2nd ed. New York: Norton.

SALMON, W. (1961). Vindication of induction. In *Current Issues in the Philosophy of Science*. Ed. H. Feigl and G. Maxwell. New York: Holt, Reinhart and Winston.

SAVAGE, L. J. (1951). *Foundations of Statistics*. New York: Wiley.

SCOTT, D. & SUPPES, P. (1958). Foundational aspects of theories of measurement. *Journal of Symbolic Logic*, **23**, no. 2, 113–28.

SCRIVEN, M. (1954). The age of the universe. *Brit. J. Phil. Sci.* **5**, no. 19, 181–90.

SENDERS, V. L. (1953). A comment on Burke's additive scales and statistics. *Psychol. Rev.* **60**, 423–4.

SHWAYDER, D. S. (1961). *Modes of Referring and the Problem of Universals*. Berkeley: University of California Press. (Vol. 35 of University of California Publications in Philosophy.)

SIEGEL, S. (1956a). *Nonparametric Statistics*. New York: McGraw Hill.

SIEGEL, S. (1956b). A method for obtaining an ordered metric scale. *Psychometrika*, **21**, 207–16.

SMART, J. J. C. (1959). Measurement. *Aust. J. Phil.* **37**, 1–13.

SMITH, B. O. (1938). *Logical Aspects of Educational Measurement*. New York: Columbia University Press.

SPIKER, C. C. & McCANDLESS, B. R. (1954). The concept of intelligence and the philosophy of science. *Psychol. Rev.* **61**, no. 4, 255–66.

STEVENS, S. S. (1935). The operational definition of psychological concepts. *Psychol. Rev.* **42**, 517–27.

STEVENS, S. S. (1939a). On the problem of scales for the measurement of psychological magnitudes. *J. Unif. Sci.* **9**, 94–9.

STEVENS, S. S. (1939b). Psychology and the science of science. *Psychol. Bull.* **36**, 221–63. (Reprinted in M. H. Marz (ed.) (1951). *Psychological Theory, Contemporary Readings*. New York: Macmillan, pp. 21–54; P. P. Wiener (ed.) (1953). *Readings in Philosophy of Science*. New York: Scribner's, pp. 158–84.)

STEVENS, S. S. (1946). On the theory of scales of measurement. *Science*, **103**, 677–80.

STEVENS, S. S. (ed.) (1951*a*). *Handbook of Experimental Psychology*. New York: Wiley.

STEVENS, S. S. (1951*b*). Mathematics, measurement and psychophysics. In *Handbook of Experimental Psychology*. Ed. S. S. Stevens. New York: Wiley.

STEVENS, S. S. (1957). On the psychophysical law. *Psychol. Rev.* **64**, 153–81.

STEVENS, S. S. (1959). Measurement, psychophysics, and utility. In *Measurement: Definition and Theories*. Ed. C. W. Churchman and P. Ratoosh. New York: Wiley.

STEVENS, S. S. & GALANTER, E. H. (1957). Ratio scales and category scales for a dozen continua. *J. Exp. Psychol.* **54**, 377–411.

STOUFFER, S. A. *et al.* (1950). *Measurement and Prediction*. Princeton University Press.

SUCHMAN, E. A. (1950). The logic of scale construction. *Educ. Psychol. Meas.* **10**, 79–93.

SUPPES, P. (1951). A set of independent axioms for extensive quantities. *Portugaliae Mathematica*, **10**, 163–72.

SUPPES, P. (1959). Measurement, empirical meaningfulness, and three-valued logic. In *Measurement: Definition and Theories*. Ed. C. W. Churchman and P. Ratoosh. New York: Wiley.

SUPPES, P. & ZINNES, J. L. (1963). Basic measurement theory. In *Handbook of Mathematical Psychology*, vol. 1. Ed. R. D. Luce, R. R. Bush and E. Galanter. New York: Wiley.

SÜSSMANN, G. (1957). An analysis of measurement. In *Observation and Interpretation in the Philosophy of Physics*. Ed. S. Körner. New York: Dover, pp. 131–6.

THORNDIKE, E. L. *et al.* (1927). *The Measurement of Intelligence*. New York: Columbia University Teachers College Bureau of Publications.

THURSTONE, L. L. (1927*a*). A law of comparative judgment. *Psychol. Rev.* **34**, 273–86.

THURSTONE, L. L. (1927*b*). A mental unit of measurement. *Psychol. Rev.* **34**, 415–23.

THURSTONE, L. L. (1927*c*). Three psychophysical laws. *Psychol. Rev.* **34**, 424–32.

THURSTONE, L. L. & CHAVE, E. J. (1929). *The Measurement of Attitude*. Chicago: University of Chicago Press.

TORGERSON, W. S. (1952). Multidimensional scaling. I. Theory and method. *Psychometrika*, **17**, 401–19.

TORGERSON, W. S. (1958). *Theory and Methods of Scaling*. New York: Wiley.

BIBLIOGRAPHY

URMSON, J. O. (1947). Two of the senses of 'probable.' *Analysis*, **8**, no. 1. (Reproduced in M. Macdonald (ed.), *Philosophy and Analysis*, (1954) Oxford.)

VON NEUMANN, J. (1958). *Mathematical Foundations of Quantum Mechanics*. Princeton University Press.

VON NEUMANN, J. & MORGENSTERN, O. (1947). *Theory of Games and Economic Behaviour*, 2nd ed. Princeton University Press.

WAISMANN, F. (1951). *Introduction to Mathematical Thinking*. Trans. J. Benac. New York: Ungar.

WEYL, H. (1949). *Philosophy of Mathematics and Natural Science*. Princeton University Press.

WHYTE, L. L. (1951). Fundamental physical theory. *Brit. J. Phil. Sci.* **1**, no. 4, 303–27.

WHYTE, L. L. (1954). A dimensionless physics? *Brit. J. Phil. Sci.* **5**, no. 17, 1–17.

WIENER, N. (1920). A new theory of measurement: a study in the logic of mathematics. *Proc. Lond. Math. Soc.* ser. 2, **19**, 181–205.

WILKS, S. S. (1961). Some aspects of quantification in science. *Quantification*. Ed. H. Woolf. Indianapolis–New York: Bobbs-Merrill, pp. 5–12.

WILSON, W. (1942). Dimensions of physical quantities. *Phil. Mag.* **33**, no. 216, 26–33.

WILSON, W. (1944). Dimensions. *Phil. Mag.* **35**, no. 245, 420–5.

WITTGENSTEIN, L. (1956). *Remarks on the Foundations of Mathematics*. Ed. G. H. von Wright, R. Rhees and G. E. M. Anscombe; trans. G. E. M. Anscombe. Oxford: Blackwell. (Excerpts reprinted in P. Benacerraf and H. Putnam (ed.) (1964). *Philosophy of Mathematics*. New Jersey: Prentice Hall.)

WOOLF, H. (ed.) (1961). *Quantification*. Indianapolis–New York: Bobbs-Merrill.

INDEX